Voting Amid Violence

VOTING AMID VIOLENCE

Electoral Democracy in Colombia

Steven L. Taylor

Northeastern University Press
Boston

Published by
University Press of New England
Hanover and London

Northeastern University Press
Published by University Press of New England,
One Court Street, Lebanon, NH 03766
www.upne.com

Printed in the United States of America
5 4 3 2 1

Library of Congress Cataloging-in-Publication Data

Taylor, Steven L. (Steven Lynn), 1968–
  Voting amid violence: electoral democracy in Colombia / Steven L. Taylor.
    p.   cm. — (Northeastern series on democratization and political development)
  Includes bibliographical references and index.
  ISBN 978-1-55553-698-5 (cloth: alk. paper)
  1. Elections—Colombia. 2. Voting—Colombia.
  3. Political violence—Colombia. 4. Political parties—Colombia.
  5. Colombia—Politics and government—1974– I. Title.
  JL2892.T39 2009
  324.09861—dc22   2008055187

 University Press of New England is a member of the Green Press Initiative.
The paper used in this book meets their minimum requirement for recycled paper.

For Alexander, Garrett, and Austin

May you all grow up fascinated by the world and with a love for books.

CONTENTS

TABLES, FIGURES, AND BOXES

Tables

Figures

Boxes

PREFACE AND ACKNOWLEDGMENTS

I have often been asked, why Colombia? (which is often a polite way of wondering what kind of crazy person would study, let alone visit, a country so known for violence). Depending on the person inquiring and time available, I may give the short answer, which focuses on the wide variety of social and political forms present in Latin America in general and specifically on Colombia as a dramatic case that is rife with serious and interesting questions that beg answering.

The longer answer is that, like many undergraduates studying politics in the 1980s, I was drawn to the Cold War conflict between the Soviets and the United States. One of the key battlegrounds in those days was Central America. A seminar on the subject taught by Caeser Sereseres at the University of California, Irvine, turned a latent interest in Latin America into a major focus, and specifically merged with my existing interest in revolutionary political violence. The synergy of interest in the region and political change via violence (or the failure thereof) was further reinforced by two classes taught by Matthew Shugart (whose influence on my work has been immense).

Essentially, an initial question that arose regarding Colombia was why, with its unrelenting political violence, did the state persist? This led to an interest in institutions and their role in perpetuating the state. I started graduate school at the University of Texas at Austin with the intention of studying revolutionary violence, but Colombia ended up more fully grabbing my attention, and the sage advice of Peter Cleaves, then director of the Institute of Latin American Studies at Texas, led to a trip to Bogotá in the spring of 1992. This led, eventually, to a Fulbright grant and a roughly yearlong sojourn in Colombia in 1994–1995.

I have not stopped studying Colombia since that time.

This book, therefore, is the culmination closing in on two decades of considering this case, and is specifically about how institutions have shaped the current democracy of Colombia. Ultimately (and I suppose, like all authors, to one degree or another) I have written the book that I have long wanted to read—in this case, one on Colombian politics that deals with the basic questions of overall democratic development, with a focus on constitutional evolution, political parties, and especially elections. Further, now is a good time to reexamine Colombia. There is no doubt that Colombia is a key focus of U.S. foreign policy, and yet despite the money spent there, public and scholarly attention has been scant.

Certainly if one judged by press coverage in the United States, one would never guess that Colombia is the fifth-largest recipient of direct U.S. aid. As such, it is a case that needs more scholarly attention than it receives. I hope very much that this book makes some contribution in that direction.

There are many to thank in regard to this project.

First and foremost is my wife, Sherry, who journeyed with me to Colombia, coming to love the country along with me, and who has patiently tolerated me as I wrote this book whilst we wrangled our three boys and dealt with the exigencies of daily life. I cherish her love and support.

Second, I owe special debts of gratitude to Matthew Shugart. As a newly minted Ph.D. at the University of California, Irvine, Matthew was first a professor and quickly became a dear friend. His two classes at UCI were the first to introduce me to the study of institutions and governance in Latin America. Later, early in my graduate school career, it was Matthew who first piqued my interest in Colombia. His comments on an early draft of this book were most thorough, quite helpful, and very much appreciated.

I wish to also thank Jan Cooper for proofreading and data entry help as well as Lauren McMahan (then Peters), who, as an undergraduate Leadership Scholar worked with me from 2001 to 2002 and helped with data entry that would lay the foundation for what would become important portions of this book. Brian Crisp, Marci Ribetti, and Felipe Botero were all of help at various times as I sought specific electoral data. Going back to my days as a Ph.D. student at the University of Texas, I wish to thank the aforementioned Peter Cleaves as well as the cochairs of my dissertation committee, Henry Dietz and Larry Graham, whose mentoring helped me come to this point in my career.

I need to thank Bill Crotty for first inviting me to contribute to his book *Democratic Development and Political Terrorism: The Global Perspective* and then giving me the opportunity to contribute this book to the Northeastern Series on Democratization and Political Development. Along those same lines, I would like to thank the staff at the University Press of New England, specifically Ellen Wicklum and Ann Brash, and Will Hively.

Lastly, I would also like to thank my colleagues in the Department of Political Science at Troy University for their support and their collegiality.

ABBREVIATIONS

Colombian Politics

AD	Democratic Alternative (Alternativa Democrática)
AD/M-19	Democratic Alliance/Movement of the 19th of April (Alianza Democrática/Movimiento del 19 de Abril)
AEC	The Wing Movement/Team Colombia (Movimiento Alas-Equipo Colombia)
AFRO	Afrounincca
AICO	Indigenous Authorities Movement of Colombia (Movimiento Autoridades Indigenas de Colombia)
AL	Liberal Opening Movement (Movimiento Apertura Liberal)
ANAPO	National Popular Alliance (Alianza Nacional Popular)
ASA	Afro-Colombian Social Alliance (Alianza Social Afrocolombiana)
ASI	Social Indigenous Alliance (Alianza Social Indígena)
AUC	United Self-Defense Forces of Colombia (Autodefensas Unidas de Colombia)
CC	Citizens' Convergence Party (Partido Convergencia Ciudadana)
CM	Citizens' Movement (Movimiento Ciudadano)
CNE	National Electoral Council (Consejo Nacional Electoral)
CR	Radical Change (Cambio Radical)
CRS	Current of Socialist Renovation (Corriente de Renovación Socialista)
CV	Colombia Lives (Colombia Viva)
DAS	Administrative Department of Security (Departamento Administrativo de Seguridad)
ELN	National Liberation Army (Ejército Nacional de Liberación)
EPL	Popular Liberation Army (Ejército Popular de Liberación); also, Hope, Peace and Liberty (Esperanza, Paz y Libertad)
ERG	Guevarist Revolutionary Army (Ejército Revolucionario Guevarista)
ERP	People's Revolutionary Army (Ejército Revolucionario del Pueblo)
FARC	The Revolutionary Armed Forces of Colombia (Las Fuerzas Armadas Revolucionario del Colombia)
FI	Independent Force (Fuerza Independiente)
FP	Progressive Force (Fuerza Progresista)
FUP	People's United Front (Frente Unido del Pueblo)
HNL	New Huila and Liberalism (Huila Nuevo y Liberalismo)
La U	Party of National Social Unity (Partido Social de Unidad Nacional)
M-19	Movement of the 19th of April (Movimiento del 19 de Abril)
MAS	Death to Kidnappers (Muerte a Secuestradores)
MCCC	Communal and Community Movement of Colombia (Movimiento Comunal y Comunitario de Colombia)
MIL	Movement of the Liberal Left (Movimiento de Izquierda Liberal)
MIPOL	Movement for Popular Integration (Movimiento Integración Popular)
MIRA	Independent Movement for Absolute Renovation (Movimiento Independiente de Renovación Absoluta)
MN	National Movement (Movimiento Nacional)
MNC	National Conservative Movement (Movimiento Nacional Conservador)
MNP	National Progressive Movement (Movimiento Nacional Progresista)
MNR	National Reconciliation Movement (Movimiento de Reconciliación Nacional)

MOIR   Independent and Revolutionary Worker's Movement (Movimiento Obrero Independiente y Revolucionario)
MORAL   Liberal Action Renovator Movement (Movimiento Renovador de Acción Liberal)
MPCC   Popular Civic Convergence Movement (Movimiento Político Comunal y Comunitario)
MPP   Popular Participation Movement (Movimiento de Participación Popular)
MQL   Quintín Lame Movement (Movimiento Quintín Lame)
MRDN   Movement for Democratic Reconstruction (Movimiento de Reconstrucción Democrático)
MRL   The Liberal Revolutionary Movement (Movimiento Revolucionario Liberal)
MSN   National Salvation Movement (Movimiento de Salvación Nacional)
NCA   National Constituent Assembly (Asamblea National Constituyente)
NF   The National Front (Frente Nacional)
NFD   New Democratic Force (Nueva Fuerza Democrática)
NL   New Liberalism (Nuevo Liberalismo)
PAS   Social Action Party (Partido de Acción Social)
PC   Conservative Party (Partido Conservador)
PCD   Democratic Colombia Party (Partido Colombia Democrática)
PDA   Alternative Democratic Pole (Polo Democrático Alternativo)
PDI   Independent Democratic Pole (Polo Democrático Independiente)
PEPES   People Persecuted by Pablo Escobar (Perseguidos por Pablo Escobar)
PL   Liberal Party (Partido Liberal)
PNC   National Christian Party (Partido Nacional Cristiano)
POC   Center Option Party (Partido Opción Centro)
PPQS   For the Country We Dream of (Por el País que Soñamos)
PRT   Revolutionary Workers' Party (Partido Revolucionario de los Trabajadores)
PSC   Social Conservative Party (Partido Conservador Social)
UC   Christian Union (Unión Cristiana)
UNIR   Revolutionary Leftist National Union (Union Naciónal Izquierdista Revolucionaria)
UNO   National Opposition Union (Unión Nacional de Oposición)
UP   Patriotic Union (Unión Patriótica)

Electoral Studies Terms
HDS   Home district sufficient
LR   Largest remainder
LRS   Largest remainder seat(s)
M   District magnitude
NH   Needed help
N_S Effective number of parliamentary parties
PR   Proportional representation
q   Quota
QS   Quota seat(s)
SNTV   Single nontransferable vote
V   Votes

Voting Amid Violence

CHAPTER 1

An Introduction to Colombia

May you live in interesting times!
    —Ancient Chinese curse (apocryphal)

COLOMBIA MATTERS, and Colombia is fascinating. Certainly, to one degree or another everywhere matters and everywhere is fascinating, but Colombia can make some special claims in these areas. Colombia is a significant political and economic actor in the Western Hemisphere and is
specifically of great interest in terms of U.S. foreign policy. Further, Colombia is rife with politics. If one is interested in elections or in guerrilla
violence, institutional development or the narcotics trade, there is much to
study and to understand in Colombia (hence the fascinating part). Indeed,
given all this, the relative lack of interest that has been shown in the country in the last half century is rather surprising.[1]

When Colombia is mentioned by the U.S. press, it is invariably described as being locked in a "decades-long civil war" or in some similar
way. It is a sad commentary on the recent history of this land that the
words most likely to come to mind when someone sees or hears the
country's name are "cocaine" or "drug lords." Maybe "coffee" springs to
mind, but only secondarily. If a movie is set in Colombia, it is about kidnapping or drug cartels. And despite Colombia's potential to be a fantastic
vacation destination, with the exception of passengers on cruise ships that
visit Cartagena, only the bravest (or perhaps most foolish) take pleasure
trips there.

Beyond its more colorful recent experiences, there is little doubt that
Colombia has a long, puzzling history. On the one hand it has been a nation whose history deviates from the region insofar as it has avoided the
cycle of military governance that has plagued essentially the rest of Latin
America. Further, it is has had a far better economic record that most of
the region. It also has a record of constitutionalism and elections. Yet on
the other hand its history has been marred by unrelenting political violence. It is more difficult to find extended periods of peace in Colombia's
history than it is to find times of protracted fighting. The juxtaposition
between success and stability, violence and chaos makes Colombia a cipher
that is difficult, perhaps impossible, to wholly decode.

The purpose of this book is to examine in detail Colombia's democratic development. Yes, Colombia's democracy is incomplete, but it is also true that within the fabric of the country's almost two centuries of independence there are important threads of democracy and institution building woven together with threads of violence and bloodshed.

Key Themes

On one level this work simply seeks to make Colombia more understandable to a broader audience, whether such readers are interested in foreign policy questions or in more detailed explanations of the internal workings of Colombian politics. The Colombian experience illustrates empirically that alteration of the rules of the game can alter the behavior of political actors in the system. On another level this book is a work specifically focused on elections and the rules that influence all involved in them. To engage the work on either level, of course, requires a general understanding of the context of Colombian politics.

Here's the conundrum: there is so much of relevance to the question of political development in Colombia that one is tempted to launch forth in multiple directions all at once, leading to intellectual paralysis. Still, while it is impossible to address everything that one might want to (or even should) know about Colombian politics, there is a need to highlight key themes before the book embarks on its specific analysis of Colombian political development. These include the general history of violent politics alongside nonviolent politics in Colombia's past, Colombia's current place in global politics, and the degree to which Colombia represents a good case for the study of institutions.

Violence (and Voting)

Colombia is, indisputably, a violent country. If we look at the 1995–2005 period we find an annual average of 24,228 murders, 2,142 kidnappings, and 272,443 persons displaced from their homes because of violence. Add to that 1.6 million Colombians who fled their native homeland from 1996 to mid-2003—half of whom left during the height of the violence between 1999 and 2001. Overall, the picture is not a pretty one.[2]

Yet, despite the violence (and political violence in Colombia is no new phenomenon, but rather one that seems part of its very DNA), the country can be said to be one of the longest-functioning electoral democracies in Latin America and has had a record of political and economic stability that is remarkable for the region.

Table 1.1

Postauthoritarian Elections (Selected Major Cases with Notes)

Argentina	1983	From late December 2001 to early January 2002, Argentina had five presidents in two weeks.
Brazil	1990	Civilian transitions began in 1985, first presidential elections in 1990.
Chile	1990	Praetorian elements of the Chilean constitution finally excised in 2005.
Colombia	1958	Likely electoral fraud in the 1970 presidential election.
Mexico	2000	It could be argued that given the presence of international observers, 1994 was the first competitive presidential election in Mexican history.
Peru	1980/2001	In 1980 the military retreated from politics, and there was electoral democracy until the *fujigolpe* (coup) in 1992. Fujimori was removed in 2000, leading to the resumption of electoral democracy in 2001.
Venezuela	1958	In 1992 there were two coup attempts, one led by Hugo Chávez and another by his followers while he was in jail. By 1995 the party system, which had been a hallmark of Venezuelan democracy, had collapsed. Chávez was elected president in 1998. A coup attempt failed to remove him in 2002. The democratic nature of the regime is questionable.

For example, table 1.1 details the transition dates for major Latin American democracies. Of those on the list, Venezuela shares 1958 with Colombia. However, as the text in the table indicates, Venezuela's status as a democracy is currently questionable. In regard to the rest of the cases, the oldest uninterrupted democracy is Argentina (transition in 1983), with the rest transitioning in 1990 or later.

Table 1.2 details some macroeconomic indicators that further demonstrate, in a comparative sense, remarkable economic success by Colombia. Looking at the 1970–2005 period, we can see that Colombia avoided the roller coaster that most of the major regional economies experienced in the 1980s and into the 1990s. Colombia's lone year of economic contraction (1999) was linked to its own internal security problems. And in terms of the Lost Decade of the 1980s, Colombia wholly avoided the radical inflation woes experienced in Argentina, Brazil, Chile, and Peru. While the Colombian economy has been far from perfect, it has clearly been healthier and far more stable than that of its neighbors.

Table 1.2

Indicators of Macroeconomic Performance of Selected Latin American Countries, 1970–2005

	Years of GDP growth <1%	Years of negative GDP growth	Years of triple-digit increases in CPI	Years of quadruple-digit increases in CPI
Argentina	0	14	14	2
Brazil[a]	5	4	10	4
Chile	1	6	4	0
Colombia	1	1	0	0
Mexico	1	4	3	0
Peru	4	7	4	2
Venezuela	2	9	0	0

Source: IMF International Financial Statistics database, *http://www.imfstatistics.org/*
[a] The inflation statistics for Brazil are from 1981 to 2005 only.

The paradox of violence alongside stability should be enough to intrigue any student of politics. Colombia is the manifestation, in one country, of all that is appealing about the study of Latin America. It contains within its borders and history what Charles Anderson (1982, 316) called a "living museum" of politics. There exists, or has existed, a panoply of political phenomena within Colombia, whether one studies the long-term struggle to establish a viable state or whether one looks at the ongoing conflict of power contenders that has yet to be resolved.

Consider, for example, the internal wars of the nineteenth century and the contest among elites to hammer out acceptable rules of the political game. In the twentieth century there is the issue of how Colombia avoided its neighbors' experience with substantial military rule and the effects on its political development of the National Front power-sharing agreement between the Liberals and Conservatives.

Indeed, for anyone interested in the roles of institutions in politics, Colombia is a treasure trove. Not only were the wars of the nineteenth century fought over rules; the twentieth century had both the National Front and the 1991 Constitution as examples of how rules affect politics. The start of the twenty-first furthers the issue by a set of electoral reforms that clearly demonstrate that yes, institutions do matter.

Beyond the niceties of rules and their effects is the other side of the Colombian coin: political violence. As has already been noted, Colombia's early political history was marked by internal warfare, and it is quite clear to anyone with even a passing knowledge of the country that it continues to be wracked by violence even today. One of the most significant events in the first half of the twentieth century was called simply *La Violencia*—a partisan civil war that killed hundreds of thousands and demonstrated the odd and tragic synergy that exists in Colombia between civil and uncivil politics.

The scion of that violence evolved into the guerrilla war that started in the 1960s and continues to this day. A parallel violence emerged—and then merged with that guerrilla war—in the guise of paramilitaries and drug traffickers. Voting and violence have coexisted in Colombia before the country was even fully formed.

Importance in Global Affairs

Beyond being interesting or a worthwhile object of the study of political institutions, Colombia is undeniably important to the United States. For one, Colombia is a significant trading partner with the United States. In 2005, combined imports and exports between Colombia and the United States were (U.S.$)14.261 billion, putting Colombia fourth in Latin American in terms of U.S. trade.[3] Further, the United States and Colombia recently negotiated and signed a free trade agreement that will likely increase those numbers.[4]

And, of course, a major issue of importance to U.S. foreign policy, as well as to any understanding of Colombian politics, is that of illicit drugs. Colombia has long been the managerial nexus of the illicit drug trade in the Western Hemisphere, as well as a major host country for marijuana, cocaine, and heroin.

While Mexican cartels have come to share the job of shepherding the flow of drugs into the United States (Bachelet 2005), Colombia has become, since the late 1990s, the main supplier state for both the raw materials needed to create cocaine and the finished product. As crop eradication programs in Bolivia and Peru succeeded in the early to mid-1990s, coca production increased in Colombia. By 1997 Colombia had more hectares of coca bushes under cultivation than any other source country and also produced the most metric tonnage of potential manufactured cocaine. By 1998 it also produced the most metric tonnage of dry coca leaf (UNODC 2005, 61–62).

Colombia has also jockeyed with Mexico over the last decade and a half as the main producer in the Western Hemisphere of the opium poppies needed to produce heroin (UNODC 2005, 41). Of course, neither comes close to Afghanistan or Myanmar in this regard. Colombia's marijuana, on the other hand, is currently not a major concern. While Colombia does produce and export this product, North American production (in the United States, Mexico, and Canada) dwarfs the Colombian market's contribution.

The very presence of these drugs in Colombia is an issue in the United States and, more to the point, these drugs have been a major focus of U.S. foreign policy efforts in recent decades. Billions have been spent on the "War on Drugs" and especially on Colombia. Prior to the Afghanistan and Iraq invasions of the early 2000s, Colombia was the third-largest recipient of U.S. aid after Israel and Egypt. It is now the fifth (GAO 2004, 1).

The drug issue has taken on a greater saliency to U.S. foreign policy since the terrorist attacks on the United States in 2001, insofar as the U.S. administration has increasingly dubbed the violence in Colombia as a manifestation of global terrorism (Taylor 2005a and 2005b). Not only has this altered an already complex foreign policy relationship with the United States, but Colombia has recast its own internal struggle in the language of the war on terror. The case of Colombia thus becomes potentially more interesting to a broader audience because the decades-long drug war is being used as a policy model for Afghanistan, another state where illicit cultivation and trafficking has the potential to fund violence. In fact, Afghan police visited Colombia to receive counternarcotics training in early 2007, and the United States' ambassador to Colombia from 2003 to 2007, William B. Wood, was named ambassador to Afghanistan in April 2007.

The presence of armed groups in Colombia has contributed to further complexity in its relationship with the United States in the wake of the attacks on the United States of September 11, 2001. Those attacks led to policy moves by the Bush administration that were of consequence for Colombia. Specifically, they prompted the reformulation of U.S. policy toward violence in Colombia away from a two-track view (guerrillas on the one hand, narcotraffickers on the other, with only the latter being a focus of U.S. policy) to a unified view that saw all nonstate belligerents as part of the War on Drugs as well as a side front in the Global War on Terror.[5]

This shift is starkly illustrated by comparing statements of two recent ambassadors to Colombia. The first is from Myles Frechette (1994–1997), who stated in a cable to Washington: "There will be no U.S. government assistance for fighting the guerrillas." This was the U.S. policy at the time: provide aid in the drug war while leaving counterinsurgency to Colombians. While it could be argued that this view of separate wars was a false dichotomy at the time, it is still noteworthy that such was Washington's official policy stance. However, post-9/11, Ambassador Anne Patterson (2000–2003) stated that "the U.S. strategy is to give the Colombian government the tools to combat terrorism and narcotrafficking, two struggles that have become one. To fight against narcotrafficking and terrorism, it is necessary to attack all links of the chain simultaneously."[6] The shift is quite stark.

Additionally, there are other intersections between Colombia's experiences and key issues in contemporary politics. For example, there is the clear issue of the general intermingling of democratic and violent politics. While Hezbollah and Hamas deal with the duality of being political parties and militias, Colombia has seen one experiment in bridging that gap fail (the tragic experience of the Patriotic Union), and it has also seen the transition of armed groups to participants in civil society (most notably the Movement of the 19th of April and the Army of Popular Liberation). It is possible that a deeper understanding of the Colombian experience with violence and voting can be of use as we seek to deal with such issues elsewhere in the world.

Institution Building

Along those same lines of broader current relevance, the question arises as to what has made it possible for Colombia's democracy, imperfect as it may be, to persist over time. The answers to be offered herein have to do with the institutions that have been built (and fought over) during the country's political history. A main theme of this work is that Colombia's struggle has been, and continues to be, one that revolves around the rules of the game. Of course, the glaring caveat is that the violence, especially in more recent decades, has gone beyond questions of institutional structures and has taken on some of the worst elements of organized crime. As such, the notion that a final settlement on the institutions of the state will solve all the ills of Colombia is flawed.

Still, not all that there is to know about Colombian politics is about drugs, guerrillas, and paramilitaries. There is a rich history of institutional struggle and electoral democracy. While it is impossible to discuss Colombia without touching on its ugly side, there is much to be said and understood about its more pleasant face as well.

Approach of the Book

The overarching issue here is the tracing of Colombian political development, especially in terms of its democracy, by looking at institutions, parties, and elections. As such, the book is very much concerned with questions of the evolution of constitutionalism in Colombia, and with how that has, in turn, influenced the development and behavior of its political parties. In addition to this discussion of institutional evolution, it is directly necessary to address those forces that are antithetical to Colombia's democratic development—guerrillas, paramilitaries, and drug traffickers—and their ongoing armed behavior.

This book operates on two levels. On the one hand it should be of interest to those wanting simply to learn more about Colombia. Along those lines it provides a general overview of Colombian political development to the current period by looking through the lens of institutional development, with a focus on constitutional evolution. The book also is a case study of the effects of specific sets of electoral rules and reforms on a specific party system over a long period of time. As such, it also should be of interest to those whose primary concern is not necessarily Colombia but, rather, the more general study of electoral and party systems.

The party system is the focus because not only are parties generically important foci of study when looking at democracies, but political parties have long been essential actors in Colombia. As will be thoroughly discussed, Colombia's traditional parties are among the oldest in the hemisphere (indeed, in the world) and have been central to the basic evolution of the Colombian political system since the middle nineteenth century. Further, a major measure of determining change in Colombian politics is the behavior of the parties, both traditional and nontraditional.

The central thesis of this book is that Colombia well demonstrates the notion that institutions matter and specifically that constitutions and electoral systems are key shapers of the political arena. However, Colombia additionally demonstrates that a substantial number of power-seeking actors have to be willing to buy into the rules and to abide by them. Hence, Colombia also demonstrates that acceptance of the rules is essential.

The Literature on Colombia

In terms of the literature on Colombia, where does this book fit? At its most general level it will fill a gap in the literature that currently exists. Indeed, there has been no comprehensive book-length study of Colombian parties and democracy in English since Jonathan Hartlyn's 1988 tome, *The Politics of Coalitional Rule in Colombia*. Perhaps the closest would be Harvey Kline's 1999 work, *State Building and Conflict Resolution in Colombia, 1986–1994*, which looks at the Virgilio Barco and Cesar Gaviria administrations and their dealings with the politics of violence. However, that book's focus is limited and does not deal with the specific questions of parties, elections, and democratic reform.

Given the important changes to the Colombian state since the late 1980s/early 1990s, such a study is long overdue—especially since the country's long-standing two-party system is undergoing an important evolution toward a multiparty system. As such, the book fits into the tradition started by Dix (1967 and 1987) and furthered by Hartlyn (1988) and Kline (1983 and 1995).

On a more specific level, the investigation addresses how changes in the rules (such as the 1991 Constitution and the reform process surrounding it) have affected Colombian democracy. Aside from being of interest to scholars studying Colombia, the book will appeal to those studying regional political parties and to those interested in cases of democratic institutions functioning amid protracted political violence.

For a variety of reasons, Colombia has been understudied. This is not to say that it has not been studied, but it is not difficult to see, if one looks at the extant literature on Latin American politics, that Colombia has been given less consideration than other countries in the region. One reason for this marginalization is that Colombia has never fit neatly into the prevailing literature on the region. If we consider the major themes of the last several decades, we can see how Colombia was left out of the conversation. In the 1970s, a major question was the breakdown of democratic regimes, given the military coups in Argentina, Brazil, Chile, and Peru during the 1960s and 1970s. Colombia remained democratic during that period.[7] Then, in the 1980s, when those military authoritarian states were returning to democracy, Colombia was again left out of many conversations. In terms of political economy, Colombia was not as laden with debt, nor plagued by hyperinflation as were many of its neighbors. Hence, Colombia was also left out of much of the discussion of the Lost Decade and structural adjustment programs.

As an observer of such trends, Robert Dix made a statement almost two decades ago that continues to be true: "considering both its size and its other attributes, Colombia may be the least attended to, by scholars and media in the United States, of all the countries of Latin America (with the possible exception of the recent negative attention paid to the drug traffic)" (1987, 1). Jonathan Hartlyn, a year later, made an almost identical observation (1988, 1).

We can see this relative neglect by looking not just thematically, as noted above, but by considering the major general works on Latin American and their treatment of Colombia. Both Dix and Hartlyn noted that the two key texts on the region, those by Skidmore and Smith and by Wynia, both ignored Colombia. Even into the late 1990s and early 2000s this problem persisted. Skimore and Smith's text did not include a chapter on Colombia until its seventh (2006) edition. Another, more recent major introductory text on Latin American politics (Vanden and Prevost's *Politics of Latin America: The Power Game*) did not include Colombia in its first (2002) edition but did for its second (2006) edition. Jan Knippers Black's text on Latin America included a chapter combining Colombia with Ecuador and Venezuela in its 1998 (third) edition but did not grant Colombia its own chapter until the fourth edition in 2005 (*Latin America: Its Problems and Its Promise*).

There have been a number of books that focus either on the general problem of Colombian violence or on the drug question. For example, Bergquist, Peñaranda, and Sánchez (2001) provide a collection of essays that offers an excellent overview of the multifaceted political violence in Colombia. Livingstone (2004) provides a handbook-like description that is of use especially to those unfamiliar with the complexities of the conflict. Additionally, journalistic works such as Dudley (2004) and Kirk (2004) reveal the ugly side of Colombia politics. Further, one of the best recent books on the influence of the drug war on Colombian relations with the United States is Crandall (2002), which also examines the politics of the late 1990s and early 2000s. Welna and Gallón's (2007) edited volume, *Peace, Democracy and Human Rights in Colombia*, is also worthy of note.

None of this is intended to suggest that there has been no good work on Colombian parties and elections, just that it has primarily manifested in terms of journal articles and book chapters. Some examples along those lines include Dugas (2000 and 2001), Shugart, Moreno, and Fajardo (2007), and Crisp and Ingall (2002).

Theoretical and Conceptual Considerations

The main theoretical assumptions made herein are drawn from the generic notion that institutions matter and to the more specific idea that electoral rules and the basic design of democratic mechanisms affect the behavior of both power seekers and citizens. Specifically, much of this work falls into the basic tradition of the electoral studies literature (i.e., Duverger [1959] to Rae [1971] to Taagepera and Shugart [1989] to Lijphart [1994], and so forth).

Fundamentally it is assumed that within any polity there are numerous actors seeking power, and that the institutional parameters that exist within that polity will provide a series of incentives and disincentives influencing how those actors pursue their quest for power. The actors' perceptions of how those structures might provide access to their goals will, therefore, determine whether they are willing to play by established rules or whether they will seek to alter those rules (and such alterations can occur either via established routes or via extra-institutional routes, such as violence).

The concept of "power" here is to be understood in its most general sense and is not to be construed to imply specific motives on the part of the actors in question. Actors seek access to the government for any number of reasons, from the altruistic to the base. They may be seeking to forward a specific program or to pursue some localized, particularistic material desires. On a theoretical level, therefore, the reasons that motivate actors to pursue power are not directly relevant to the question of how the rules establish the basic incentive structure of the system. It is enough to understand that these actors seek power and that they will therefore respond to the institutional parameters to fulfill that quest. Now, the specific motivations can very much matter as given actors seek to strategize their way through a specific set of rules. If a party, for example, is programmatically oriented, its members are likely to seek strategies that lead to cohesion of the membership. Parties interested in more particularistic goals are likely less interested in cohesion, as the individual members of the parties are seeking to increase their own specific access to state resources.

The focus on elections means that the general approach to democracy herein is concerned primarily with procedural questions. The intellectual tradition is one that runs from Dahl (1971) to Huntington (1991) to Diamond (1999) to Freedom House (2005). It should be noted that the goal is not to look solely at elections themselves but rather to examine the quality of those processes, especially as they pertain to the ability of citizens to truly influence who governs as well as the general state of their rights and privileges as citizens.

In regard to political parties as essential actors in the process, the definition used herein is quite straightforward: political parties are organized groups of individuals who band together under a common label to compete for votes.[8] One further assumes that the goal is to win office for the purpose of influencing public policy, although whether the goals are particularistic or programmatic are not part of the definition. As simplistic as such a definition may seem, the issue of precisely how to define and understand a political party is of key significance in Colombia, where for historical and sometimes structural reasons there is some confusion over the classification of specific electoral actors. The specifics of this classification problem, and its relevance to analyzing Colombian politics, will be dealt with in detail later.

Plan of the Book

To accomplish these tasks, this book proceeds in the following fashion. Chapter 2 examines the issue of evaluating the nature of Colombian democracy. That discussion sets the overall foundation for the text: the notion that Colombia is an electoral democracy seeking to be a liberal one. Further the chapter notes that, alongside the well-established institutions within the Colombian state that allow for electoral democracy, violence is the primary disfiguring force that stops Colombian democracy from further development.

Chapter 3 examines the constitutional development of Colombia and sets the stage for a discussion of parties and elections. The chapter illustrates the duality within Colombian politics: the impulses for both formal rules and political violence. The chapter outlines the early constitutionalism of the Colombian state but focuses primarily on the key constitutional developments of the latter half of the twentieth century: the National Front, its dismantlement, and the advent of the 1991 Constitution.

Chapter 4 addresses the traditional parties, the Conservatives and the Liberals, from their origins to their long-term place in Colombian political development. The goal of the chapter is not only to address the current state of the party system, which has been going through a process of change that was accelerated by the new electoral rules, but also to argue that the existing conventional wisdom concerning the effects of the National Front rules on the Colombian party system ought to be rethought. Given that the baseline used for judging change in the party system is the status of the two traditional parties, it is important to understand them before heading into the discussion of reform.

Chapter 5 examines the electoral rules in Colombia over time and addresses the response of the party system to rules changes. The historical discussion ranges back to the nineteenth century, but the major focus is from the post–National Front period (i.e., starting in 1974) onward. The chapter contains a detailed account of the electoral rules, any changes made, and the responses by the parties. Here we investigate the distinct eras of the dismantlement of the Front (1974–1990), the advent of a new constitution in 1991, and the passage of key electoral reforms in 2003. The chapter also deals with the issue of party label in the Colombian context.

Chapter 6 examines the specific strategic choices made by the parties as they have pursued access to the Colombian Congress. The chapter examines the effects of the usage in Colombia of the simple Hare quota with largest remainders and no electoral threshold on the strategic choices made by power seekers. This chapter demonstrates how this system led to serious fragmentation within the parties and eventually in the entire party system. The important effects of the new rules on party formation and behavior implemented for the Congress in 2006 are also examined. This chapter specifically tracks the aforementioned evolution of the Colombian party system from a seemingly endless two-party system (with one party, the PL, in a dominant position) to a truly multiparty system. The focus of the chapter is skewed toward the Senate, as the most dramatic rules changes can be seen in that case.

Chapter 7 provides an overview of the numerous facets of the violence. The chapter seeks to place the current violence in its proper historical context as well as providing a primer on the panoply of actors involved. The chapter discusses the guerrillas, drug traffickers, and paramilitary groups. The main focus is the specific ways in which the violence has influenced Colombia's democratic development.

Chapter 8 brings these various threads together and highlights the key conclusions of the text. The specific issue of exactly how new the new parties are under the new rules is also addressed, as are Colombia's prospects in terms of its quest to move from electoral to liberal democracy.

CHAPTER 2

Colombian Democracy

*[I]n Colombia we see the combination of an impressive stability of
institutional macroforms and an almost permanent state of internal
war with violations of rights.*
— Gutiérrez and Stoller 2001, 59

COLOMBIA IS SOMETHING of a paradox. It has some of the longest-
standing democratic institutions in the hemisphere, and one of the
region's best records in terms of authoritarian rule. Yet it also has perhaps
the most violent history in the hemisphere. Colombian political history is
built on the twin pillars of elections and violence.

This chapter addresses the question of how to think about democracy in
Colombia, flaws and all. Specifically it details the degree to which Colombia can be deemed a full democracy (or a "liberal" one in the terminology
of Diamond [1999], as detailed below) or if it is in fact something less than
that. Indeed, as the discussion will demonstrate, Colombia has the basic
requisites needed to classify it as a functioning electoral democracy, but the
ongoing violence, and the state's incapacity to stop it, has made it impossible for Colombia's democratic goals to be fully realized. In fact, the bur-
geoning violence in the 1980s and 1990s has degraded the quality of democratic governance in Colombia—owing to state incapacity and state
participation in the violence.

Colombian Democracy in Perspective

There was a time when Colombia, if it was mentioned at all in texts on
Latin America, was cited in what might be called the "counterexample
three" along with Costa Rica and Venezuela. The usage was something like:
"Latin America has no democratic states save for Colombia, Venezuela, or
Costa Rica." This formulation was quite typical from around 1973 until the
early to mid-1980s, when the Third Wave of democratization firmly took
hold in Latin America.

At the start of the twenty-first century, all of Latin America, save for
Cuba, can now claim at least anemic democracy, although of the "counterexample three" only Costa Rica retains any claim to being an exemplar of
democratic governance for the region.

It is certainly the case, as will be described in detail below, that Colombia is a democratic state, but the continuing violence that tasks the state and bedevils its citizenry has tainted Colombia's claim to full democracy. When a country is known more for its kidnappings, murders, and displacements (not to mention drugs and guerrillas) than for its political parties and history of elections, there are reasons to approach the subject of its democratic health with some pause.

This overall picture can lead to conflicting responses and assessments of Colombian democracy. On the one hand, one can marvel that the country has survived its endless political turmoil holding onto anything resembling democratic governance. On the other, one can clearly see the injustices and lost opportunities that have robbed millions from fully partaking in the promises of democratic governance.

This chapter focuses first on how this book understands and applies the concept of democracy to the comparative study of politics, and therefore to Colombia. After the definitional discussion there is a section on the overall history and evolution of Colombian democracy, which leads into a lengthier discussion of the state of democracy in the current period.

Democracy with Adjectives

While many claim to know it when they see it, democracy is not as easily defined as we may wish it to be. Simple formulations, such as "government of, by, and for the people" may be poetic, but they are not adequate from the point of view of social scientific inquiry. Indeed, the problem of defining democracy has generated the problem that Collier and Levitsky (1996 and 1997) have termed "democracy with adjectives"—that is, the need to modify the term *democracy* to create a better fit for a given case or set of cases (e.g., O'Donnell's notion of "delegative" democracy or Remmer's [1986] "exclusionary" democracy). Collier and Levitsky's study identified 550 examples of such permutations (1996, 1).

Colombia could have its own subsection in such a study, given the number and variety of modifiers that have been attached to "democracy" in an attempt to come up with an adequate classification of this vexing case.[1] Part of the problem is simply the result of differences in interpretation, while much of the issue is that Colombia's internal complexities make simple descriptions difficult. Colombia's democracy has been described (in chronological order by publication date) as "oligarchical" (Wilde 1978), "consociational" (Dix 1980a; Hartlyn 1988), "exclusionary" (Pécaut 1989), "qualified" (Martz 1992, 22), "besieged" (Archer 1995; Bejarano and Pizarro

2002), "genocidal" (J. Giraldo 1996), "restricted" (Hartlyn and Dugas 1999, 251), "anocratic" (Jordan 1999), and "resilient" (Posada-Carbó 2004). As a change of pace, some authors have placed modifiers after "democracy" instead. For example, Kline titled his 1995 book *Colombia: Democracy under Assault,* and Taylor (2005a) wrote a recent chapter called "Colombia: Democracy under Duress."

Going beyond the formula of "fill-in-the-blank" democracy, we also find Colombia described as a "near-polyarchy" (Dahl 1971, 248),[2] "semi-democratic" (Mainwaring 1999), and "an inclusionary authoritarian regime" (Bagley 1984, 125). It would be remiss to fail to note, in this mosaic of descriptions, that Colombia is frequently described as a "narcodemocracy,"[3] a variant of which is Jordan's usage of "nacrosocialism," (1999, 158), while its state has been called "schizophrenic" (J. Giraldo 1999) and is generically considered "weak" (McLean 2002) or "partially collapsed" (Bejarano and Pizarro 2002; Bejarano 1994, 51).

All this stands in contrast to the self-proclaimed "participatory and pluralistic" democracy that one finds in the 1991 Constitution (Article 1). That there are deep contradictions in the very fabric of Colombian politics is indisputable, and hence neither the ongoing violence nor the history of successful electoral politics provides a sufficient point of departure for understanding Colombia. If anything, these great difficulties in picking appropriate adjectives to describe Colombia's democracy and state underscore the complexities involved in understanding the case. Certainly the panoply of modifiers indicates a lack of consensus over how to classify Colombia.

Even the basic problems associated with Colombian democracy are not straightforward. As with most aspects of Colombian politics and society, Colombia's democracy contains significant contradictory elements, such as increased political inclusion and the diminishment of protection of civil rights and liberties as noted by Bejarano and Pizarro (2002, 9–10). This tension is the result of the increased democratic access that political reforms, mainly the Constitution of 1991, have provided while simultaneously the state has continued to be unable to contain the ongoing political violence that has haunted the country for generations.

Defining Democracy

Beyond Colombia itself, part of the problem in classifying democracies is that there does not exist a clear consensus definition of the precise meaning of democracy as an analytic concept. There is a clear difficulty in defining democracy in an elegant fashion. The definitional enterprise is complicated by the fact that the ideal of democratic governance, when compared to *any* reality, exposes the inevitable shortcomings of actual regimes. The theoretical promises of democracy are impossible to fully achieve, hence Robert Dahl's suggestion of "polyarchy" (rule by the many, as opposed to rule by the people) as an alternative term of art.

Like Dahl, and Diamond more recently, the focus here is on the procedural elements of democracy and the degree to which, to use Dahl's terms, there is sufficient public *contestation* for control of government and *participation* by the public in that process.[4] By considering democracy on those terms, we find ourselves paying attention to the procedures in place that allow for the selection of members of the government, and the way in which they are empowered (or not) to formulate and execute public policy, and the degree to which the citizenry has ongoing, adequate input into that process.

The issue is not just elections, but elections that matter—elections that actually affect who governs. History is replete with examples in which "elections" took place, but involved little or no contestation for power and no true participation by the citizens in any meaningful way (examples such as the former Soviet Union, Iraq under Saddam Hussein, and Castro's Cuba all come to mind).

In fleshing out these concepts, and in trying to avoid too many modifiers, Diamond (1999, 7–12 and 15–17) provides the following useful categories: pseudodemocracies, electoral democracies, and liberal democracies (as well as nondemocracies, which itself represents a whole category of regimes).

Pseudodemocracies include some of the components of democratic regimes, such as multiple parties and some basic civil liberties (speech, press, assembly), but no real contestation for power exists. A key example would be Mexico under the Institutional Revolutionary Party (PRI).[5] Here we have the vestiges of democracy without true citizen input over who governs. Such regimes are ultimately nothing more than cases of soft authoritarianism.

Having set aside regimes that are clearly undemocratic (nondemocracies, i.e., various types of authoritarian regimes) and pseudodemocracies (authoritarian regimes dressed up to look like democracies), we are still left with a number of states that fall into that broad category of "democratic" but that nonetheless are clearly not identical (and hence we get back to the "democracy with adjectives" problem noted above). Even among countries with functioning electoral systems and basic rights, there are cases that are more functional than others, leading to the need for some sort of delineation. A minimal focus takes into account whether the government is actually elected in free contests, while a deeper focus also takes into account the degree to which the citizens actually have full access to their civil liberties and civil rights. It is possible for the government to be elected in a legitimate and democratic process without the state being able to fulfill all of its obligations to the citizenry. Given such a range of potential effectiveness, the delineation of electoral democracy as the basic minimum for defining a state as democratic, with liberal democracy being used as a more fully realized manifestation of democracy, is a helpful one.

Electoral democracies are those that conform to a minimal definition of democracy: power is contested in the public square, and free citizens participate in, and influence directly, the outcome of the contest; that is, those who govern are chosen in the electoral arena.[6] However, electoral democracies are flawed in some capacity. Indeed, it is the presence of these flaws that leads, in large measure, to the democracy-with-adjectives problem identified by Collier and Levitsky: how does one classify a case where free and fair elections occur in an otherwise flawed situation—especially when the nature of the flaws varies from case to case?

Liberal democracies are those that go beyond the procedural minimum of elections to fulfill the basic tenets of the democratic ideal as well as is possible in the real world, especially as pertains to the issues of citizens' rights. Diamond (1999, 11–12) details ten criteria that must be fulfilled to meet the ideal of liberal democracy, and specifically notes the need for strong constitutional order to be present. The ten components, and how well Colombia conforms to them, are discussed below.

As Diamond notes, "This four-fold typology [non-, pseudo-, electoral, and liberal democracies] neatly classifies national political regimes, but political reality is always messier" (17). Still, the basic categories are helpful, and are sufficiently broad to be applicable across cases. Further, this typology allows us a basis for discussing Colombian democracy—a case classified here as an electoral democracy struggling to be a liberal democracy.

Historical Overview of Colombian Democracy

For contextual purposes, table 2.1 summarizes the major eras of relevance to our discussion of Colombian democracy and my basic classifications of those eras using Diamond's categories.

While the main focus of this chapter is the evaluation of contemporary Colombian politics, it is useful to establish the basic context. During the first period listed we see in Colombia various types of voting to choose national leadership, all of which were limited in some fashion. From 1826 to

Table 2.1

Basic Chronology and Classification of Colombian Democracy

1819–1953	Pseudodemocracy: elections (many indirect) with limited suffrage[a]
1953–1957	Nondemocracy: military dictatorship of General Gustavo Rojas Pinilla
1958–present	Mix of electoral and liberal democracy: open competition for power, with citizen rights frequently marred by ongoing political violence

[a] See table 3.2, which details the suffrage issue and the fact that many offices were indirectly elected during much of this period.

1853 and from 1892 to 1904, the vote for president was done indirectly. From 1863 to 1884 the vote was by state. The 1857 and 1860 presidential votes were held under rules of direct election and universal male suffrage, although the 1860 election took place in the context of civil war.[7] Women were not granted the right to vote until 1954, which was not utilized until December 1, 1957 (the plebiscite that led to the National Front). Included in the 1819–1953 period are situations in which violence interrupted the electoral cycle, or wherein sitting presidents were deposed.

Given this brief sketch, it is clear that in the two periods prior to 1958, Colombia was at best a pseudodemocracy, with forays into nondemocracy.

The prevailing attitude toward the National Front (1958–1974) is that it was a form of restricted democracy, as it was a power-sharing agreement that split the government in two, giving a half to the Conservative Party and half to the Liberal Party. However, as will be discussed in detail elsewhere in this text, the restrictions on entering electoral politics were not as stringent as they initially appear. There were competitive elections for Congress during this period, and it was not at all illegal, despite the seeming limitations of the Front, for actors other than the PC and PL to participate in elections (they just had to finesse their entry to some degree).

It is legitimate to note, however, that during the presidential elections of the National Front period (1958, 1962, 1966, and 1970) democracy was incomplete, as the presidency was alternated between the two parties each cycle (PL, PC, PL, PC, to be precise) and the official nominee of the party always won (although in 1970 it would appear that an opposition candidate did win, but fraud forestalled his actual victory).

Ultimately, the congressional elections that were held were legitimate, and the successive governments were controlled by elected officials, making the period one of electoral democracy at a minimum. Indeed, the basic enjoyment of civil rights was largely unimpeded during the period, making it possible to consider the situation as one approaching liberal democracy. A detailed argument as to why the National Front should be considered less restrictive than is often argued is to be found in the next chapter.

The post–National Front period (1974 onward) has been one of a mix between liberal and electoral democracy. As violence has escalated, and as the state's capacity to control its territory and protect its citizens has waned, so too has the quality of Colombian democracy. The problems here are not about legalities or institutional arrangements, but rather about the inability of the state to control the violence that threatens the citizenry. A full discussion of the types of violence present, and their effects on democracy, is deferred until chapter 7, although specific statistical indicators that measure the violence are included in the discussion below. The remainder of the chapter is dedicated to the current state of Colombian democracy.

The Current State of Colombian Democracy

Within the context of the eras outline above, this work is primarily concerned with the post–National Front period—especially in terms of evaluating democracy. We can evaluate Colombian democracy using two different tools. One would be the Freedom House rankings and another would be to apply Diamond's basic criteria for liberal democracy (one of the types of democracy mentioned above).

Diamond's Criteria

Table 2.2 contains the ten criteria for liberal democracy that Diamond outlines in his work (1999, 11–12). I have subdivided the ten criteria into three categories: institutional design and function, civil liberties, and judicial/legal system. It should be noted that Diamond argues that these ten items imply an eleventh: a state constrained by a constitutional order. In any given case, an evaluation can be made as to whether the elements that Diamond describes are present or not and, if they are present, whether or not they are incomplete in any important way. This builds on a similar analysis done by Taylor (2005a, 502–504).

In examining these factors as they pertain to Colombia, the most striking theme that runs through the discussion is that Colombia's constitutions and basic traditions of governance are democratic in nature, but that the substantial presence of armed groups (guerrillas, narcotraffickers, and paramilitaries) hampers the state's ability quite considerably in terms of guaranteeing citizens the enjoyment of their rights and liberties. As a result, the design of the state and the written rights in question are quite

Table 2.2

Diamond's Ten Criteria for Liberal Democracy

Institutional Design and Function

1. Control of the state lies in the hands of elected officials.
2. Executive power is constrained.
3. Electoral outcomes are uncertain, with a presumption that some alternation of the party in power will take place over time.

Civil Liberties

4. Minority groups are not prohibited from expressing their interests.
5. Associative groups beyond political parties exist as channels of representation.
6. There is free access to alternative sources of information.
7. Individuals have substantive democratic freedoms (speech, press, association, assembly, etc.)

Judicial/Legal System

8. Citizens are politically equal under the law.
9. Liberties are protected by an independent, nondiscriminatory judiciary, whose decisions are respected by other institutions within the state.
10. Rule of law is sufficiently strong to prevent "unjustified detention, exile, terror, torture, and undue interference in citizens' personal lives not only by the state but also by organized nonstate or antistate forces" (1999, 12).

---

democratic (although far from perfect), while the main problem emerges in terms of the state's capacity to follow through on its promise of democracy, as is especially evident in the discussion of number 10, the rule of law.

Institutional Design and Function

The first three criteria deal with the institutional arrangements of power in a given state, which derive from the constitutional order and, more important, how well they function. It is one thing to have constraints on the executive on paper, quite another to actually have those constraints function properly.

1. Control of the State. Diamond cites the need for a liberal democracy to be controlled by elected officials and for those elected officials to be free from the control of unaccountable actors from outside (i.e., foreign powers) or internally (especially the military).

That the state of Colombia is under the control of elected officials is undisputable. What is disputable is the degree to which the state wholly controls its own territory. Indeed, in a strict Weberian sense, the argument can be made (and indeed has been made; see for example Bejarano 1994) that the Colombian state is incomplete, given that it clearly lacks a monopoly on the use of forces within its borders. However, where the Colombian state controls its territory, governing authority belongs to elected officials, from the president and the Congress down to mayors and municipal councils.

In regard to foreign influence, there is none that could be construed as controlling or influencing the functioning of the Colombian state in an undue way—certainly not in a way that would violate the notion that elected officials control the state. Yes, the United States has substantial pull in Bogotá, and that has been especially true with the Uribe administration. And while over the years Bogotá and Washington have had relatively warm relations, this relationship has had considerable ebbs and flows, as the Samper administration (1992–1996) in particular demonstrates.[8]

In regard to the military, it is also fair to say that it does not threaten democratic control of the Colombian state. While imperfect, civil-military relations in Colombia are historically atypical for the region; that is, the military has a long history of subordination to civilian control and has rarely asserted itself into the arena of governance. Military coups have been the rare exception rather than the rule in Colombia, with only three coup attempts[9] in the twentieth century—and only one of those was successful: the military takeover by General Gustavo Rojas Pinilla in June of 1953. Even if the net is cast to include the nineteenth century, only four successful military takeovers, in 1830, 1854, 1866, and 1900, can be added to the list.[10] Indeed, there is a history of the president being able to assert control over generals who overstep their boundaries in public. In 1965 President Guillermo León Valencia (1962–1966) fired the minister of war, General Alberto Ruiz Novoa, as the result of Ruiz's public calls for social reforms and apparent political ambitions. In 1975 the commander of the army, General Álvaro Valencia Tovar, was fired by President Alfonso López Michelsen (1974–1978) for his outspokenness on what the government's policy ought to be vis-à-vis the guerrillas. President Belasario Betancur Cuartas (1982–1986) fired the defense minister, General Fernando Landazábal Reyes, in 1983 for similar reasons (Dix 1987, 138–139).[11] At the time, President Betancur noted: "The President is the commander of the armed forces, which obey his decisions" (Riding 1984).

Of course, given the ongoing violence in Colombia, it is difficult for the military not to be seen as a key political actor. For example, there were resignation threats in response to military dissatisfaction over President Pastrana's ceding of a demilitarized zone to the FARC in 1999 (Watson

2005, 102). There is also the infamous case of the assault on the M-19-controlled Palace of Justice in downtown Bogotá in 1985, about which it has been speculated that President Betancur lacked sufficient control of the event (Hudson 1988).

It is noteworthy that since 1990 the defense minister in Colombia has been a civilian (prior to that point the position had been predominantly held by generals), including a female (Marta Lucía Ramírez de Rincón, 2002–2003).[12] Still, there is no formal political power afforded to the military, nor is there evidence of systematic undue influence over the state apparatus. On the problematic side of things, however, there are allegations of freelancing on the part of the military, specifically as it pertains to right-wing paramilitary groups.[13] Such actions underscore the ways in which the ongoing violence damages the ability of elected officials to adequately control the state. Such actions are not sufficiently dire to challenge the basic notion of control of the state by elected officials, but they do illustrate erosion of that control.[14]

Leaving aside, for the moment (see number 10 below), any discussion of how well the Colombian state controls its territory, there is no doubt that the state of Colombia itself is controlled by democratically elected officials.

Conclusion: Present.

2. *Constraint of Executive Power.* Latin America is well known for its overactive executives, and Colombia's presidency has been considered quite powerful. Indeed, one analyst referred to the office as that of a "demigod" (Cepeda 1985). To analyze the exact nature of executive power, and the degree to which it is constrained, we can look at the issue of emergency powers and the question of interbranch relations.

First, in regard to emergency powers, under the 1886 Constitution the president had rather significant decree authority. With only the consent of the cabinet, the president was able to declare a state of siege (*estado de sitio*) via Article 121 or a state of economic emergency (*estado de emergencia económica*) via Article 122 and thereby issue decrees that had the force of law (Carey and Shugart 1995, 141). The ease of that process resulted in the near-constant application of some sort of state of emergency from 1958 to the promulgation of the 1991 Constitution. Indeed, Archer and Chernick state, in an analysis of executive power from 1958 to the late 1980s, that "the power of the Congress, as a positive factor and instigator in the reform process, has diminished to the point that the first legislator of the country is not the Congress, but the President" (1989, 31).[15] They go on to point out that during that period of time the majority of legislation began as part of the president's emergency powers.

As dramatic as these powers appear, Archer and Shugart note that the capacity of the Congress to intervene was hardly nonexistent (1997, 141–142). The 1968 constitutional reform allowed the Congress the right to amend states of economic emergency, and as Archer and Chernick (1989) note, many of the decrees issued by Colombian presidents were later ratified into law by means of the regular legislative process. As such, Archer and Shugart conclude "that the 'emergency' decrees passed by the president did not deviate substantially from the congressional majority" (2003, 142). Of course, such actions could also be construed as congressional acquiescence in the face of an overbearing executive.

Still, the presence of institutional constraints, even those not used, such as the capacity to amend the constitution and remove presidential decree authority, does demonstrate the ability of other institutions to constraint the president as needed.

Under Article 213 of the 1991 Constitution, the president can declare a "state of internal disturbance" for a period of ninety days, with two ninety-day extensions and the second extension requiring senatorial approval. Decrees issued under this provision expire once the state of internal disturbance has expired, and may be extended for ninety days. The article contains explicit requirements for executive consultation with the Congress on the matter as well. Further, Article 214 requires that all orders and decrees issued under this power are to be referred to the Constitutional Court for review. It is noteworthy in the context of executive restraint that in 2003 this court went on to invalidate an extension of the state of emergency that Uribe had ordered (Robles 2003).

Article 215 provides for state-of-emergency powers when events occur "that disrupt or threaten to disrupt in serious or imminent manner the economic, social, or ecological order of the country or which constitute a grave public calamity." Under such circumstances, with the agreement of the cabinet, the president can declare a state of emergency for thirty days, with no more than ninety days total in a given calendar year. In such cases, decrees issued are to be reviewed by Congress for amendment or repeal.

As such, the 1991 document reigns in the president and empowers the Congress in comparison with the powers under the 1886 document. As Shugart notes, the presidency's decree powers have been curtailed, and congressional control over the process has been enhanced. Further, the ability of Congress to delegate its own responsibilities to the executive have been diminished under the new charter (2000, 12).

The president of Colombia still does have state-of-siege powers under the new constitution, but it is noteworthy that the Constitutional Court has review powers, and has struck down such orders, and that those rulings have been respected.[16]

A recent illustration of executive constraint and the proper operation of separation of powers and checks and balances in the Colombian context is President Uribe's attempt to instigate reform via referendum. One of Uribe's campaign promises was a set of referenda aimed at political reform. However, Uribe was constrained by the fact that he had to acquire congressional votes on the referendum package, and also had to submit to revisions of that package by the Congress. In addition to following the appropriate constitutional procedure (as spelled out in Article 378), the president's referendum package also went to the Constitutional Court for review. The court further modified the package by removing several questions from the slate.[17] Archer and Shugart (1997, 113–115) detail the attempts by presidents from 1958 to 1989 to engage in political reform via both the legislative process and their decree power. In each case Congress was not interested in reform, and the courts struck down the decree attempts. It was not until the 1989 decree by President Barco (which would eventually lead to the constituent assembly that would write a new constitution) that such a decree escaped being quashed by the courts.[18]

Other examples of checks and balances in operation regarding executive decree making include the 2002 actions of the Constitutional Court, which struck down as unconstitutional an antiterrorism law (Decree 2002), issued by Uribe under the state-of-siege powers, that would have allowed greater leeway for military action in specified zones (Wilson 2002).

In regard to the 2003 referendum, Uribe was unsuccessful in getting his measures passed because of low voter turnout. Still, the president abided by the results and did not seek to assert extraconstitutional authority. The failure of Uribe to achieve his own version of reform coupled with the Congress's ability to pass its own set of reforms (discussed in detail in chapters 5 and 6), which were at odds with Uribe's preferences, well illustrates that the president of Colombia is not as powerful as is frequently assumed.

In sum, we have numerous examples of capitulation of the executive to the Congress, the courts, and the citizenry, all by a president considered to be more hard-line than is the norm for Colombian politics. The combination of on-paper controls that dovetail with practical examples underscores that the executive in Colombia can be considered sufficiently constrained so as to fulfill this dimension.

Conclusion: Present.

3. *Elections.* Electoral outcomes in Colombia are uncertain, and campaigns are made up of actors truly contesting for power. As chapters 4, 5, and 6

will make clear, there is an active party system and elections demonstrate true competition, even though the Liberal Party was dominant during most of the post-Front period (a dominance that started to slip in the 1998 presidential elections and collapsed in 2002 in terms of both the legislature and the presidency).

Losers and winners alike abide by elections results, and it is not unusual for political outsiders and new parties to win elected office. Not only did 2002 bring an independent to the Casa de Nariño (Álvaro Uribe, a onetime member of the Liberal Party, ran as an independent), but the 2006 elections saw the success of several nontraditional new parties.

An oft-cited problem with Colombian elections is the lack of participation. Indeed, it is telling that the common metric used by Colombianists is not voter turnout but abstention rates. For example, García and Hoskin (2003, 8) note that the turnout rate for Colombian presidential elections from the 1940s through the 1990s was 40.74 percent as compared to a regional average over the same period of 56.9 percent. It should be noted that Colombia does not have an obligatory vote, while most countries in the region do; however, that fact should be not construed as a key explanation of Colombia's low participation rates.[19]

The next set of tables (2.3–2.5) provide turnout for Chamber of Representatives and presidential elections through 2006 as well as some comparative statistics for the region.

Of course, violence plays a role in this area as well. As García and Hoskin empirically demonstrate for the 2002 electoral cycle, the presence of violence (whether politically motivated or not) contributed to higher abstention rates: "At the departmental level, only homicide rates and guerrilla activity impact negatively on participation rates. One of the significant findings of this study suggests that non-political as well as political violence affects the involvement of Colombian citizens in the electoral process. Unlike the guerrillas, non-political agents of violence have not formulated a strategy to undercut the electoral process, but their actions discourage active citizen involvement" (22).

In short: there are free and fair, openly contested elections in Colombia. There have been incidences of fraud but only one case of likely major fraud, and political violence diminishes, if not wholly interrupts, the flow of elections in some parts of the country in a given election. Elected officials do govern, but in rural areas they have been known to be threatened by guerrillas, and politicians have been assassinated and kidnapped, even prominent national politics.

Conclusion: Present (but limited by the violence).

Table 2.3

Turnout of Registered Voters, Colombian Chamber Elections, 1945–2006

Year	Total vote	Registration	Vote/reg
1945	875,856	2,279,510	38.42%
1947	1,472,686	2,613,586	56.35%
1949	1,751,804	2,773,804	63.15%
1951	934,580	2,981,679	31.34%
1953	1,028,323	3,173,435	32.40%
1958	3,693,939	5,365,191	68.85%
1960	2,542,651	4,397,541	57.82%
1962	3,090,203	5,338,868	57.88%
1964	2,261,190	6,135,628	36.85%
1966	2,939,222	6,611,352	44.46%
1968	2,496,455	6,696,723	37.28%
1970	3,980,201	7,666,716	51.92%
1974	5,100,099	8,925,330	57.14%
1978	4,180,121	12,519,719	33.39%
1982	5,584,037	13,721,609	40.70%
1986	6,909,840	15,839,754	43.62%
1990	7,617,758	13,779,188	55.28%
1991	5,512,703	15,037,526	36.66%
1994	5,707,403	17,028,961	33.52%
1998	8,916,731	N/A	N/A
2002	9,561,952	23,998,685	39.84%
2006	8,533,169	26,595,171	32.09%

Source: National Registry of Colombia (Registraduría Nacional del Estado Civil): 1945–1990 numbers from 1990, 393; 1991 numbers from 1991, 240; 1994 numbers from author's calculations based on 1994 volume; 1998–2006, Registry website (www.registraduria.gov.co).

Civil Liberties

Well beyond the design of the basic governmental institutions is the issue of the rights enjoyed by the citizens of a democratic state, and the degree to which those citizens can influence, through constitutionally protected means, the actions of the state.

4. Freedom for Minority Groups. There are no legal prohibitions on the activities of minority groups. Suffrage in Colombia is universal—and has been since 1958. Indeed, the Constitution of 1991 establishes set-aside seats in the Chamber and Senate for racial and ethnic minorities. There are two seats set aside for "indigenous communities" in the Senate (Article 171),

Table 2.4

Voter Turnout, Colombian Presidential Elections, 1970–2006

1970	52%
1974	58%
1978	37%
1982	49%
1986	43%
1990	43%
1994, 1st round	34%
1994, 2nd round	43%
1998, 1st round	52%
1998, 2nd round	59%
2002	47%
2006	46%

Sources: Pinzón de Lewin (1991, 127) for 1970–1990 and Registraduría (various years) for 1994–2006.

and the constitution provides for legislation to set aside special seats for ethnic groups and political minorities (Article 176). The law currently allows for one indigenous seat and two for "black communities" in the Chamber.

As such provisions demonstrate, there is, in the common usage of the term *minority*, freedom for minority groups in Colombia. However, in the broader sense of the term there can be no doubt that belonging to an unpopular political minority can be a hazard. There is no doubt that leftists have been the target of violence and murder, although normally on an ad hoc basis.

Additionally, there is the dramatic example of the Patriotic Union (UP), the political wing of the Revolutionary Armed Forces of Colombia (FARC) in the 1980s. The UP was an attempt at establishing a political party of the left in Colombia, and for third parties was, by Colombian standards, moderately successful (see chapter 4 for a more complete discussion of third parties in Colombian political history). But members of the UP were systematically slaughtered by right-wing paramilitaries with collusion from some in the military.[20]

So, while there are formal protections in place for minority groups and there is no legal repression, as in many aspects of Colombian political life, the ongoing violence makes it impossible to state that all is well in this category.

Conclusion: Present (but limited by the violence).

Table 2.5

Regional Average Voter Turnout, Presidential Elections, 1940s–1990s

Venezuela	72.42%
Argentina	69.29%
Costa Rica	68.91%
Uruguay	68.40%
Bolivia	65.30%
Paraguay	55.15%
Mexico	51.62%
Ecuador	50.59%
Chile	50.26%
Peru	45.25%
Brazil	44.93%
Colombia	*40.74%*
Average	56.90%

Source: García and Hoskin 2003.

5. Interest Groups. There is freedom of association in Colombia, with interest groups able to form and function in civil society. Indeed, there has been a long history of such activity, with two of the most prominent examples being the National Association of Industrialists (ANDI) and the National Federation of Coffee Growers (FEDECAFE), which is the owner of the symbol of Colombian coffee, Juan Valdez. In addition to producer groups/guilds (called *gremios* in Colombia), there are also numerous active unions, including, for example, the main labor union, the Central Trade Union Federation of Colombia (CUT), and the teachers' union, Colombian Federation of Educators (FECODE).

As in the UP example cited above, however, political violence can hamper the ability of groups to form and to function—especially groups that are perceived as being of the left or being sympathetic to the guerrillas. For example: in 1997, gunmen linked to paramilitary groups broke into the home of Elsa Alvarado and Mario Calderón, researcher for the Center for Research and Popular Education (Centro de Investigación y Educación Popular, CINEP), and killed both them and Alvarado's father, Carlos Alvarado. Labor leaders have faced similar threats (and results).

As with all the problems besetting Colombia's democracy, the issue is not the lack of opportunity for interest groups to form, nor are there any legal strictures. Rather, the obstacles that do appear are the result of the violence.

Conclusion: Present (but limited by the violence).

6. *Freedom of Information.* There are, as Freedom House noted (2005, 152), concerns about the concentration of ownership of major media outlets, and it is true that major newspapers are linked to the major political parties (such as *El Tiempo*'s connection to the Liberals and *El Nuevo Siglo*'s connection to the Álvaro Gómez wing of the PC). There are no legal barriers to publication, nor are there any systemic attempts to curtail the dissemination of information.

As with most threats to Colombian democracy, the issue of political violence is relevant here as well. However, the threat of violence is not one that is exclusive to the press, and so while it should be taken into consideration in understanding freedom of expression in Colombia, it should not be construed as a specific prohibition on those rights. Certainly it is not a systematic one.

As table 2.6 demonstrates, being a journalist in Colombia is not the safest job in the world.

According to a 2004 report by the Fundación para la Libertad de Prensa, the violence was not aimed at a specific type of medium. During the 2002–2004

Table 2.6

Violence against Journalists, 2002–2005

Type of violation	2002	2003	2004	2005
Killed	3	5	1[a]	2
Killed while undercover	1	1	0	0
Deaths under investigation	4	1	2	n/a
Attempted attacks	10	1	2	n/a
Threats[b]	75	55	39	64
Wounded while undercover	0	1	0	2
In exile	n/a	7	5	6
Physical assault/inhumane or degrading treatment[c]	3	4	15	15
Kidnapped	12	11	0	1
Arrested or illegally detained	n/a	n/a	n/a	1
Obstruction of journalistic work	3	8	17	6
Attacks on communication infrastructure	n/a	n/a	n/a	6

Source: Fundación para la Libertad de Prensa 2004, 2005.

[a] In this case the target was a news vendor, not a journalist.

[b] This category includes multiple threats made to the same journalist.

[c] This combines "aggressions" and "torture" from the 2002–2004 study with the category "inhumane or degrading treatment" from the 2005 figures.

period under investigation, 37 percent of the violence affected print journalists, 31 percent radio, 27 percent television, and 6 percent other media (12). Also, the identifiable sources of the threatened violence spanned the spectrum of violent actors: 13 percent came from paramilitaries, 10 percent from the FARC, 5 percent from narcotraffickers, and 5 percent from other sources. The remaining 67 percent of all threats came from unknown sources (21).

On the positive side of freedom of information, it should be noted that Colombia has a long history of numerous leftist newspapers and magazines. Additionally there is a strong tradition of independent book publication, think tanks, and higher education.

Conclusion: Present (but limited by the violence).

7. Basic Democratic Liberties. Does the constitutional order protect the fundamental civil liberties needed to maintain democratic governance? These include freedom of speech, of the press, assembly, and so forth. On paper, these rights exist without question in Colombia, and normally are exercisable in reality as well. However, the relentless presence of political violence prevents full access to these rights by all citizens on a daily basis. This fact of life is made clear by the discussions above about elections, minority rights, and freedom of information.

Conclusion: Present (but limited by the violence).

Judicial/Legal System

Design and abstract ideals are both keys to democracy, but the ultimate question becomes the degree to which the citizens actually access the promises made in their constitution.

8. Political Equality. As a practical matter, the inability of the state to protect its citizens in all portions of the country does call into question the degree to which one can practically state that there is true political equality in Colombia. Violence has been known to hinder the ability of citizens to participate in the electoral process.

The same caveats apply here as apply in the section above on political minorities.

Conclusion: Present (but limited by the violence).

9. Independent, Relevant Judiciary. In looking at the question of executive constraint (number 2 above), it was demonstrated that the courts in Colombia have been able to act independently in the face of presidential influence. As those examples demonstrate, the courts have been able to assert their constitutional prerogatives.

Table 2.7

Violence Indicators, 1995–2005

Year	Population	Displaced (% of pop)	Kidnapped (% of pop)	Murdered (% of pop)
1995	36,200,251	85,000 (0.23%)	1,068 (0.003%)	25,398 (0.07%)
1996	36,813,161	181,000 (0.49%)	1,039 (0.003%)	26,642 (0.07%)
1997	37,418,290	257,000 (0.69%)	1,623 (0.004%)	25,379 (0.07%)
1998	38,580,949	308,000 (0.80%)	2,868 (0.007%)	23,096 (0.06%)
1999	39,309,422	288,127 (0.73%)	3,218 (0.008%)	24,358 (0.06%)
2000	39,685,655	317,375 (0.80%)	3,582 (0.009%)	26,540 (0.07%)
2001	40,349,388	342,243 (0.85%)	2,921 (0.007%)	27,841 (0.07%)
2002	41,088,227	412,553 (1.00%)	2,885 (0.007%)	28,837 (0.07%)
2003	41,662,073	207,607 (0.50%)	2,122 (0.005%)	22,199 (0.05%)
2004	42,310,775	287,581 (0.68%)	1,440 (0.003%)	18,888 (0.04%)
2005	42,954,279	310,387 (0.72%)	800 (0.002%)	17,331 (0.04%)

Sources: Population figures from the *CIA World Fact Book* (various years available online); displacement figures from CODHES (*www.codhes.org*); kidnapping figures for 1995 from U.S. Citizenship and Immigration Services (available online at *www.uscis.gov/graphics/services/asylum/ric/documentation/COL00001.htm*) and for 1996–2005 from Departamento Nacional de Planeación (available online at *www.dnp.gov.co/paginas_detalle.aspx?idp=562*); murder figures for 1995–2004 from *Forensis 2004*, 51, and for 2005 from *Forensis 2005*, 2 (both available via the Instituto Nacional de Medicina Legal y Ciencias Forenses, *www.medicinalegal.gov.co*).

However, a main problem with the courts has less to do with them directly (i.e., with their viability within the system), but rather with the ability of law enforcement to adequately police the territory and bring to the courts those who ought to be prosecuted and then, in turn, with the need for the law to be adequate to punish and deter the crimes in question. There is much criticism of the Colombian state on those issues, but these are problems of the executive and legislative branches, respectively. See, for example, the issue of impunity in the next section.

There is an ongoing question of the ability of the courts to do their jobs in the context of violence and the threat of violence, however. It is not unusual for judges and prosecutors to find themselves threatened. Indeed, beyond threats, some have been assassinated. As such, the Colombian judiciary finds itself under siege, like the rest of the Colombian state, and therefore its efficacy can be called into question.

Conclusion: Present (but limited by the violence).

10. Rule of Law Protects Citizenry. This is the area where the Colombian state fails substantially and clearly: it does not fully control its own territory, and cannot protect its population from arbitrary political and criminal violence. Indeed, the grave problems in this area lead to the limitations noted in seven of the variables listed above. As has been noted, violence has been an endemic part of Colombian politics for its entire history; however, in recent decades, the violence has been of such a level as to preclude the proper functioning of a number of the dimensions in this list.

Now, it is true that daily life in most urban centers is normally free of the political violence in question. However, given the high murder and kidnapping rates in Colombia, not to mention the hard fact that political assassinations do take place, it is impossible to say that there is full protection by the state of its populace.

If we look at indicators such as kidnapping, displacements, and murder, it is easy to see how the prevalence of violence in Colombia contributes to a significant degradation of the quality of life, and democracy, in the country. Table 2.7 details these key indicators from 1995 to 2005.

Generically, these figures demonstrate the substantial stress put on the Colombian state and its population in recent decades by a combination of the fight among the state, the guerrillas, and paramilitary groups as well as drug trafficking and other forms of organized crime. The figures show a peak in the violence from the late 1990s into the early 2000s, with a seeming easing in the last several years. Perhaps the most dramatic indicator in the chart is that of internal displacement, which peaked at 1 percent of the overall population in 2002.

The homicide rate paints a grim picture, as figure 2.1 illustrates. A striking feature of the numbers is that if one looks at the 1948–1958 period, which is the main period of *La Violencia*, and compares it to the period from the late 1980s into the 2000s, it is clear that despite the infamous nature

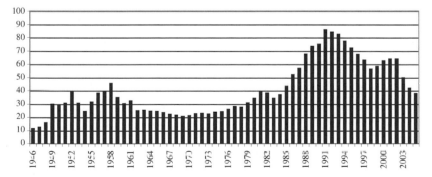

Figure 2.1. Colombian Murder Rate, 1946–2005 (Values on the y-axis represent murders per 100,000 people.) *Sources:* Braver, et al. 2004: 15–16 and Forensis 2004: 51 and 2005: 2.

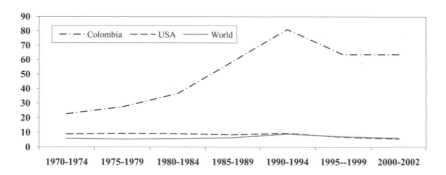

Figure 2.2. Comparative Murder Rates, 1970–2002 (Values on the y-axis represent murders per 100,000 people.) *Sources:* Brauer, et al. 2004, Forensis 2004, FBI, UNODC, and Bunivić and Morrison 2000.

of the earlier period, more recent decades have been far more deadly. Figure 2.2 puts the Colombian murder rate in global comparison, noting the rates for Colombia, the United States, and worldwide from 1970 to 2002.

Given these indicators, and the intractable nature of the violence in Colombia, it is impossible to say that the citizens of Colombia who live in or near zones of conflict are, in fact, protected from the ongoing violence.

Beyond the acts themselves, the ability of the Colombian state to bring malefactors to justice is clearly limited. As a 1999 report from OAS' Inter-American Commission on Human Rights (1999, chap. 5) noted:

> In June of 1996, the Superior Council of the Judiciary reported that between 97% and 98% of all crimes go unpunished, and that 74% of crimes go unreported. Other State authorities provide similar statistics. According to information issued by the National Police, 90% of all crimes go unpunished. According to the 1996 report of the Commission for the Rationalization of Public Spending and Finances, the level of impunity in all cases has reached 99.5%. That organization asserts that only one out of every 100 crimes reaches the trial stage of criminal proceedings. Another sign of impunity is the inability of the State to carry out arrest warrants against defendants. As of January 1998, State entities reported that there existed 214,907 outstanding arrest warrants which had not been executed.

Clearly these figures underscore a severe lack of institutional capacity. These numbers are from the apex of the most recent violence, but even with moderate improvements in the number of crimes, the ability of the state to adequately deal with these issues remains poor.

A summation of this situation is not easy. On the one hand, it is true that the majority of the population can go through their daily lives without having the violence affect their ability to do so—and this is especially true in the urban centers. However, there is no place in the country that the violence cannot reach at any given moment. And ultimately it is clear that there are areas in which life is shaped by the violence on a day-by-day basis.

Conclusion: Absent in large portions of the country.

Summarizing the Diamond Variables

Having reviewed the variables, one can see that Colombia has the foundations for electoral democracy but lacks stability in key areas that would allow it be considered a liberal democracy. Table 2.8 summarizes these issues.

The dominant theme is that the institutional and structural parameters needed to fulfill each of the dimensions exist, but that the violence precludes their realization. All these factors culminate in the simple fact the activities of guerrillas and paramilitary groups, and organized (as well as petty) criminal activity, have created a set of problems that the state cannot affect. These problems have been getting worse in the last two decades but have existed for over four. It is necessary to recognize that the Colombian state has to function in the context of a great deal of well-funded chaos. The confluence of antistate actors, drugs, and landowners willing to take matters into their own hands is a volatile one. That mix directly challenges the ability of the state to control its own territory.

Both the problems noted in table 2.8, and indications that conditions have worsened since the 1980s, are reflected in the Freedom House numbers

Table 2.8

Diamond's Ten Variables and Colombia

1.	Control of state by elected officials	Present
2.	Executive power is constrained	Present
3.	Electoral outcomes are uncertain	Present—but limited by the violence
4.	Minority groups not repressed	Present—but limited by the violence
5.	Free association/group formation	Present—but limited by the violence
6.	Freedom of information	Present—but limited by the violence
7.	Basic democratic liberties	Present—but limited by the violence
8.	Citizens equal under the law	Present—but limited by the violence
9.	Independent judiciary	Present—but limited by the violence
10.	State protection from violence	Absent in large portions of the country

on Colombia.[21] Freedom House issues annual reports on the state of basic democratic freedoms in two categories: political rights and civil liberties. These categories comport well with the Dahlian formulations of public contestation and public participation as noted above, and also mesh with Diamond's four-part classification of regimes, also noted above. Indeed, in his book (1999, 12) Diamond notes that his ten components overlap in large measure with the variables examined by Freedom House. He further notes that "[t]he 'free' rating in the Freedom House survey is the best available empirical indicator of liberal democracy" (12).

In terms of both reputation and reality, Colombia's democracy has degraded since the 1980s. Indeed, if one looks at the Freedom House classifications for Colombia from 1972 to 2007, one can seen the degradation. Figure 2.3 charts civil liberties and political rights as measured by Freedom House over the period in question. (Using those measures, it is not difficult to see a correspondence to Diamond's liberal democracy and electoral democracy categories.) On both Freedom House scales, the lower the number, the more free the state, and the higher the number, the less free the state. The two scores are averaged to produce a composite score on a scale of 1.0 to 7.0 (1 is the highest level of freedom and 7 the lowest).

Freedom House categorizes countries as "free" if they score from 1.0 to 2.5 on the composite scale, "partially free" if they score from 3.0 to 5.5, and "not free" if they score from 5.5 to 7.0.[22] Colombia was categorized as free from 1972 to 1987, when the country slipped from a 2.5 composite score to a 3.5. By the late 1990s the country was scoring a consistent 4.0 composite score, with some positive movement starting in 2006.

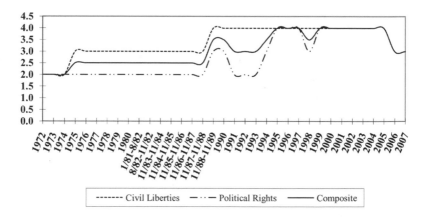

Figure 2.3. Colombia's Freedom House Scores, 1972–2007

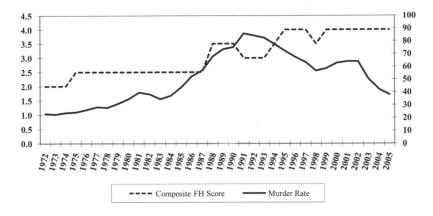

Figure 2.4. Murder Rate and Composite Freedom House Score, 1975–2005

If we take the composite index of Colombia's Freedom House score and compare it to the murder rate over the same period, we see that as the murder rate took a dramatic upward tick, so too did the Freedom House composite (fig. 2.4). While a crude measure, the homicide rate in the Colombian context is a proxy for the activities of guerrillas, narcotraffickers, and paramilitary groups, as well as the state's response to those groups. And, of course, it is the nexus of violence and response that has led to the diminution in Colombia's Freedom House rankings.

In looking at figure 2.4, it is noteworthy that it was only in the mid-2000s that the murder rate started to return to the range it was occupying before the Freedom House composite began moving upward in the 1980s. Thus there is some hope that the recent diminishment of violence might aid in the improvement of the variables that make up the Freedom House score. Indeed, in both 2006 and 2007, Freedom House moved Colombia's score to a 3.0 in both political rights and civil liberties, suggesting that the decrease in the murder rate in the early 2000s is indicative of a general improvement in the basic lives of Colombia citizens, and therefore in the quality of Colombian democracy.

Basic Conclusions on the State of Colombian Democracy

Colombia has a flawed democracy. It clearly contains key elements giving it the potential for being a liberal democracy, while also falling far short of the mark in terms of the state's capacity to protect its citizens and to assert its will. As such, it is an electoral democracy in search of status as a liberal democracy.

This chapter sets the stage for the remainder of our discussion. It demonstrates that it is fair to term Colombia an electoral democracy aspiring to become a more liberal one, and that in order to understand the development of that democracy, it is necessary to focus on its institutions. This chapter has also established that the main threat to Colombian democratic development has been the prevalence of violence, which will also be examined later in the book.

Colombia's best hope of improving the quality of its democracy, assuming that the violence does not evaporate any time soon, is to make institutional adjustments that will allow for more responsive parties and better policy making that is representative of the needs of the population. Given these assumptions, plus Colombia's substantial history of constitution writing and the significance of political parties to its political development, the focus from here is heavily on parties and elections.

CHAPTER 3

Cartas de Batalla

*In Colombian history when crises have become so bad that society seems to
be breaking up, when civil wars get extremely serious, or impunity overcomes
the institutions, when public order becomes lack of order, and when the
governmental branches are powerless to do anything, Colombians begin the
clamor for a constituent assembly.*
    —*El Tiempo*, April 24, 1990 (trans. Kline 1999, 154–155)

The history of our parties during the past century is the history of our civil wars.
    —Baron 1915, iii (my trans.)

THE STRUGGLE FOR a stable constitutional structure for the Colombian
state has been a key theme of the country's political development since
even before it achieved full independence from Spain. Hernando Valencia
Villa (1987) gave his book on Colombian constitutional development the
evocative title *Cartas de Batalla*, literally, charters of battle. This is an apt
description of the development of the Colombian polity, that the fights
that existed in the state as it sought to define itself were manifested on
parchment. As table 3.1 notes, each of the nineteenth-century constitutions
was drafted in the context of substantial political turmoil. Although the
current constitution (that of 1991) was not drafted as the direct result of
civil war, it was drafted in the context of ongoing fighting, and was written
in an attempt to find some resolution to the ongoing clashes within the Colombian state. Thus, the theme of conflict and violence alongside accord
and rule making is central to Colombian political development.

The fact that violence was often associated with the establishment of a
given constitutional order highlights the contradictory synergy between
the impulse to violence and the impulse to democracy in the fabric of Colombian politics. More than simply symbolic, the constitutional struggles
have set down key markers in the political history of the country, as well as
set the institutional parameters for the evolution of the political system.

The early struggles over centralism and federation were played out in the
nineteenth century, to eventually settle on a unitary state in 1886. Further,
the struggle over the constitutional order was part of the development of
the traditional party system in the mid-1800s, and certainly the reform to
the 1886 Constitution that created the National Front, and the replacement

Table 3.1

Context for Constitutional Change in the Nineteenth Century

1821	War for independence
1830	Decree by Bolívar in the context of his two-year dictatorship, 1828–1830
1832	Resignation of Bolívar and the dissolution of Greater Colombia (the leaving of Ecuador and Venezuela), coup in 1830
1843	Civil war (War of the Supremes), coup in 1842
1853	Civil war
1858	Civil war
1863	Civil war
1886	Rebellion leading to decree nullifying the 1863 Constitution

of the 1886 Constitution in 1991, have been of monumental importance to the evolution of democracy (and party politics) in Colombia. Further, aggrieved actors within Colombian politics have often cited their perceived (if not real) exclusion from the prevailing rules of the game as a reason for taking up arms.

To set the stage for the overall discussion of Colombian political development, this chapter provides an overview of the institutional development of the Colombian state as it evolved through a changing constitutional structure. In this chapter, the various eras of constitutional conflict (and constitutional stability) are examined. The first several eras are dealt with in summary fashion, and are included to provide an overall picture of Colombian political development, as well as to underscore the degree to which Colombia's entire postindependence history has been one of political conflict exemplified by a struggle for an acceptable constitutional order.

The discussion is properly divided into five segments: 1810–1886, 1886–1953, 1957–1974, 1974–1990, and 1991 to the present. These segments are not of equal significance to the overall purpose of the book—indeed the latter three are of most use in understanding contemporary politics in Colombia.

First Era: 1810–1886

Like most of postindependence Latin America, Colombia spent much of the nineteenth century sorting itself out. During the century there were eight constitutions that governed various incarnations of Colombia.[1] The lack of a settled institutional order is hardly surprising, given that the country did not fully settle its national territory until 1903 and changed its name numerous times during this same period as well.

In terms of the geography issue, the original version of Colombia included Ecuador, Venezuela, and Panama (all part of the Viceroyalty of New Granada). Ecuador and Venezuela struck out on their own in 1830, and Panama seceded (with help from the United States) in 1903. In terms of name, the country was originally the Republic of Colombia.[2] With the 1830 Constitution the country was known as New Granada, and it remained such until the 1863 Constitution, when it was dubbed the United States of Colombia. The 1886 Constitution returned to both a unitary state structure and the name Republic of Colombia. Table 3.2 details the constitutions of the nineteenth century and includes some key information about each.

Even before full independence from Spain was achieved in 1819, there were conflicts within the Viceroyalty of New Granada that would foreshadow Colombian political conflict for much of the rest of the century. While the Spanish Crown was busy dealing with Napoleon and his allies starting in 1808, there was much mischief among the creole elite in the Americas. During this period, two portions of what would become Colombia moved toward independence from Spain. One proceeded in a confederal direction, while the other preferred a more centralist mode, with each writing a constitution in 1811 to fit its political aims (Valencia Villa 1987, 106).[3] One portion—the United Provinces of Gran Colombia—was a loose confederation made up of Antioquia, Cartagena, Neiva, Pamplona, and Tunja. Meanwhile the other portion, consisting of Bogotá and Cundinamarca, formed its own state under its own constitution, which was centralist in orientation. That entity was called Cundinamarca.

Conflict arose between these two portions of what would become Colombia, mostly because of aggression by Cundinamarca. However, the United Provinces were able to capture Bogotá in 1814. All this occurred in the context of formal declarations of independence from Spain, the Spanish reconquest, and the eventual expulsion of the Spanish from the former Viceroyalty of Nueva Granada. This led to the establishment of the first Republic of Colombia, also known as Gran Colombia.

After independence, a total of eight constitutions would be promulgated in the nineteenth century (1821, 1830, 1832, 1843, 1853, 1858, 1863, and 1886), for a new constitution roughly every eight years. On the one hand, this demonstrated substantial fissures within the body politic, which often resulted in political violence if not civil war. On the other, this series of documents indicated an abiding belief in the need for a proper constitutional and legal order. As Safford and Palacios observe: "[t]o a greater degree than some other Spanish American countries, New Granada, and later Colombia, in the nineteenth century operated in some approximation of constitutional rules" (2002, 131).

Table 3.2

Basics of the Nineteenth-Century Constitutions

Name of state	Type of state	Suffrage	Notes on government
		1821	
Republic of Colombia (aka Gran Colombia)	Unitary	Male; property/income requirements for voting; no literacy test until 1840	Indirect election of president and Congress
		1830	
Republic of Colombia (aka Gran Colombia)	Unitary	Male; property/income requirements for voting; no literacy test until 1840	Indirect election of president and Congress
		1832	
State of New Granada	Unitary	Male; income requirement for voting; movement of literacy requirement to 1850	Indirect election of president and Congress; president's powers diminished as compared to 1821 and 1832 Constitutions; enhanced powers of provincial governors
		1843	
Republic of New Granada	Unitary	Male; property or income requirement; literacy requirement for any who turned 21 on or after January 1, 1850	Indirect election of president and Congress; enhanced presidential powers

Table 3.2 (*continued*)

Name of state	Type of state	Suffrage	Notes on government
		1853	
Republic of New Granada	Unitary (with federal elements)	Universal male suffrage	Direct election of president and Congress
		1858	
The Granadine Confederation	Federal	Universal male suffrage	Direct election of president and Congress
		1863	
United States of Colombia	Federal	Left to the states: most revoked universal male suffrage and returned to literacy or income requirements (Bushnell 1993, 122–123)	President indirectly elected by electors in each state, with each state having one vote; manner of choosing members of Congress left to the states
		1886	
Republic of Colombia	Unitary	Male; income/employment requirement	Indirect election of president; Senate elected by departmental assemblies; House directly elected; autonomy of local government eliminated

Second Era: 1886, Part 1 (1886–1953)

It was not until 1886 that a more or less stable constitutional order can be said to have been established. Indeed, the 1886 Constitution would go on to be the longest-serving constitution in the Western Hemisphere after only the 1789 Constitution of the United States. The 1886 Colombian Constitution's eventual longevity is not indicative that political (or constitutional) struggle ended in Colombia with the 1886 document, just that some of the basic rules of the game, such as a central, unitary state, had finally been established. Indeed, the necessity of dividing the discussion of the 1886 document into three distinct eras demonstrates this fact.

The 1886 Constitution did not put an end to violent political conflict—indeed, like its predecessors it came into being itself as a result of significant political conflict. Rebellions had led to the issuing of a state-of-emergency decree by President Rafael Núñez, which, in turn, cleared a way for him to void the 1863 Constitution. The new, 1886 document radically reversed the hyperfederal nature of the prior charter and created a unitary state in Colombia.[4] Even after the installation of the new constitution, there was the War of a Thousand Days (1899–1902), *La Violencia* (1948–1953), and the Rojas dictatorship (1953–1957).

Noteworthy is the fact that the 1886–1953 period did not result in any further replacements of the constitution itself. There were a number of amendments, most especially those of 1910, and the document itself was recompiled in 1936 and 1945.[5] Table 3.3 details a selected set of reforms made to the constitution, most of which relate to the development of Colombia's democratic institutions.

Third Era: 1886, Part 2, the National Front (1957–1974)

For the purposes of this study, the story gets truly interesting at this point, as the referendum of 1957 institutionalized a power-sharing agreement called the National Front. The Front was part of the political solution crafted to deal with the partisan fighting of *La Violencia* and to allow the removal of Rojas by a bipartisan action.

The Rojas dictatorship was short-lived, as the utter loss of control of the Colombian state by the elites of the traditional political parties was sufficient to jar them into an accord while in exile. The return of the Liberals and Conservatives to power meant the restoration of the 1886 Constitution to its full power, although the pact that brought civilian government back to Colombia required alterations to that document.

Table 3.3

Selected List of Reforms to the 1886 Constitution, 1886–1953

Legislative Act No. 5 of 1905
- Abolished offices of the vice president and the designate (*designado*)[a]

Legislative Act No. 3 of April 8, 1910
- Shortened presidential term from six to four years
- Abolished reelection of president
- Required that the president be selected by popular vote (instead of indirectly)
- Reduced Senate terms from six to four years
- Reduced Chamber terms from four to two years
- Reestablished the *designado*
- Shifted representation in the Senate from three seats per department to a system based on population[b]

Legislative Act No. 1 of August 5, 1936
- Increased state powers in economic affairs
- Removed requirements that public education be Catholic in orientation

Legislative Act No. 1 of February 16, 1945
- Instituted universal male suffrage[c]

---

[a] The designate was a person designated to replace the president if needed, much like a vice president. However, the designate was not part of the electoral ticket but was rather appointed after the elections. For most of the twentieth century Colombia had a designate, not a vice president. The vice presidential role was restored in the 1991 Constitution.

[b] As Gibson notes: "and thus another vestige of federalism . . . was ended" (1948, 356).

[c] The 1936 codification of the 1886 Constitution is unclear on the male-specific nature of the right to vote (see Article 14). However, the 1945 codification inserted the clause "the right to vote and eligibility to popularly elective office are reserved to male citizens" (Article 15). Indeed, the 1936 codification, in the text of Article 14, specifically allowed women to hold elective office.

On December 1, 1957, a referendum was held to ask for the endorsement of a power-sharing agreement that would become part of the Colombian constitution. The National Front was accepted by the population with 4,169,294 voting in favor, 206,864 voting against, and 20,738 blank votes (i.e., "none of the above") (Dix 1967, 133). Safford and Palacios (2002, 330) note that 73 percent of those over twenty-one years of age voted on the question.[6] The confirmed text was then ratified as an amendment by the Congress in 1958.

The National Front agreement, which emerged out of negotiations[7] between the Liberals and the two main factions of the Conservatives (the

Gomez and Ospina factions[8]), created a power-sharing agreement that allowed for a return to civilian rule in Colombia. The Front was driven by the principles of parity and alternation. Parity meant that the Colombian state would be essentially divided in half, with offices (elected and unelected) going half to the Conservative Party and half to the Liberal Party. Alternation referred to the office of the presidency, the electoral plum of the system. This office was to alternate between the PC and PL from 1958 until 1974, when electoral contests would return to normal. Every four years the presidential elections consisted of Liberals versus Liberals or Conservatives versus Conservatives (an "official" candidate and "dissident" ones).

The basic tenets of the agreement, which was made part of the constitution, were as follows:

- *Alternation.* For sixteen years the presidency of the republic would alternate between the Liberals and Conservatives.[9]
- *Parity in Legislatures.* Representation in all "public corporations" (i.e., Congress, departmental assemblies, and municipal councils) was to be split evenly between Liberals and Conservatives.
- *Parity in Appointed Posts.* The roles of governors, mayors, cabinet members, Supreme Court justices, and all nonmilitary, non–civil service positions would be filled in equal measure by PL and PC members.
- *Legislative Supermajorities.* All nonprocedural votes in the Congress would require a two-thirds majority for passage of the measure in question.

The plebiscite also[10]

- confirmed women's suffrage (declared by Rojas in 1954 but not put into effect until the referendum vote);
- stated that Supreme Court appointments were for life;
- reaffirmed the official status of the Catholic faith (reversing a modification made in 1936);
- promised that as of January 1, 1958, at least 10 percent of the national budget would be dedicated to education;
- legalized the post-Rojas military junta until August 7, 1958;
- prohibited partisan activity by the civil service except for voting.

The National Front is often characterized as being a closed system—and, on paper, it would appear to be the case that electoral competition was exclusive during this period, limiting ballot access to only Liberals and Conservatives. However, one of the long-standing characteristics of Colombian politics has been its fragmented, clientele-based political parties.

As such, the fact that the Front allowed factionalized lists for congressional elections undercuts the notion that it was truly rigid in terms of competition. Indeed, the rules under the Front simply allowed the already fragmented traditional parties to maintain their fractured ways.

Certainly, parity meant that there were some limitations to full contestation of seats in Congress and in local legislative bodies. Similarly, alternation meant that the president was chosen in a manner not fully contested. Without a doubt the National Front period was not one of complete democracy. Table 3.4 demonstrates the lack of competitiveness during this time (with the clear, obvious, and problematic exception of 1970). It is fair to call Colombia during the Front period a limited electoral democracy, but it does not qualify as a nondemocracy during that time.[11]

Table 3.4

Presidential Elections during the National Front

Candidates	Total popular vote
1958	
Lleras Carmargo (PL)	2,482,948
Leyva (PC)	614,861
Others	290
1962	
Valencia (PC)	1,633,873
Leyva (PC)	308,814
Lopez Michelsen (MRL)	624,863
Rojas Pinilla (PC-ANAPO)	54,557
Others	494
1966	
Lleras Restrepo (PL)	1,881,502
Jaramillo Giraldo (PL-ANAPO)	741,203
Others	589
1970	
Pastrana Borerro (PC)	1,625,025
Rojas Pinilla (PC-ANAPO)	1,561,468
Betancur (PC)	471,350
Sourdis (PC)	336,286

Source: Bushnell 1993, 291.

The presidential elections demonstrate a few key issues about both the rules of the Front and the traditional parties. First, it is noteworthy that despite the framework of the Front, a Conservative (albeit a fairly unimportant one) was allowed to run in 1958, which was the PL's year. Further, in 1962, the PC's year, a dissident Liberal group, the Liberal Revolutionary Movement (MRL), led by the son of President Alfonso López Pumarejo (1934–1938, 1942–1945), also ran. Even more interesting is the run by Rojas Pinilla,[12] the ex–military dictator, who ran as a PC candidate under the factional label of the National Popular Alliance (ANAPO). Note, too, the flexibility of the labeling rules, as the candidacy of José Jaramillo Giraldo demonstrates. In 1962 and 1970 Rojas was ANAPO, running as a PC candidate. In 1966 Jaramillo was PL, but also ANAPO.

While there was a clear lack of full competition for the presidency, the case for the Congress also being under substantial constraint is far more difficult to make. It is true that the National Front agreement split the Congress down the middle, with half the seats going to Liberals and half to Conservatives, but there was still substantial competition within the parties, and indeed, because of this allowance for factional lists, the ability of third parties to enter the fray was not truly curtailed.

Table 3.5 illustrates the fact that the parity arrangement under the Front did not simply consist of the PL and PC leadership submitting slates of candidates who automatically received the allotted seats. Rather, there was substantial factionalization within the parties, including even competing "official" lists. This factionalization was especially acute within the Conservative ranks, which started the Front divided between the Ospina and Gómez factions.[13] Only in 1964 did the PC present a unified electoral front. Table 3.5 also illustrates how the factions identified with specific presidential candidates in the 1970 election.

Beyond factions within the mainline parties, lists were submitted that represented third-party formation (and won seats). The two most prominent examples of this activity were ANAPO and the MRL. Both exploited the Front's rules to run their own lists of candidates for the Congress. Because of the strictures of the Front system, these parties were referred to as "movements" rather than political parties (a linguistic and legal category that still exists in Colombia);[14] however, in terms of political analysis, an entity that declares its own unique label and seeks to place its own members into office is a political party. Indeed the MRL, although led by Alfonso López Michelsen, son of a former Liberal president, represented a clear deviation from mainline Liberal politics, including an alliance with the Colombian Communist Party for a time.[15]

As such, the electoral system under the Front was not as closed as is frequently stated. That the system constrained competition is clear, especially in terms of the selection process for president, where voters really did not have much choice. Yet it is difficult to argue that congressional elections were not essentially competitive. Parity, while distorting the national vote, was not as much a deviation from normal Colombian electoral politics as it might seem (especially when one factors in the factionalization and dissident lists discussed above). Ultimately, the only real strictures that this arrangement placed on the system in terms of the ability of candidates to compete for votes was that factional lists had to be at least nominally associated with one of the two major parties. In terms of affecting representation, congressional elections were contrived so as to inflate the influence of Conservative voters. To wit: Conservative lists were awarded half of the seats, yet they consistently polled less than 50 percent of the vote.[16]

So what can be said, in general, about the Front? First, the main political actors in Colombia prior to the Front were the two traditional parties; limiting electoral access to those two actors was more a case of hardening existing political relationships and behaviors than of clear exclusion. Second, and more important, the factionalized nature of the party system meant that not only were "dissident" lists offered in the contests for Liberal and Conservative seats, but those lists could actually be new, third parties. Indeed, ANAPO's ability to effectively function as a third party by playing within the loose nature of the Front's rules illustrates that calling the system a closed one is simply incorrect.

Of course, letting dissidents run in contravention of the spirit of the pact was one thing, as was letting such factions win seats in the legislature. Letting such a dissident win in the presidential election was quite another. If there was a clear cornerstone to the National Front, it was alternation of the presidency. If Rojas had won the 1970 contest and bested the official candidate, Misael Pastrana Borrero, it would have abrogated the Front. Further, if the former dictator had won, it would have undermined the traditional relationship between the parties and the state.

Although it has not been conclusively proven, the circumstances surrounding the 1970 election are such to lead one to the conclusion that electoral fraud was perpetrated by the Lleras administration to guarantee a Pastrana win. First, there is the highly suspicious fact that on the night of the election the government halted the transmission of poll results, with the winner being announced the next morning by President Lleras, who also ordered a curfew in the major cities (Safford and Palacios 2002, 331).

Table 3.5

Chamber of Representatives—Seats and Votes via Partisan Factions, 1958–1970

Party	Factional lists	Votes	(faction's % of party)	Seats	(faction's % of party)
		1958			
Liberal	Oficialistas	2,105,171	(100.00%)	74	(100.00%)
Conservative	Unionistas	340,106	(22.03%)	17	(22.97%)
Conservative	Laureanistas	915,886	(59.33%)	45	(60.81%)
Conservative	Independientes	287,760	(18.64%)	12	(16.22%)
		1960			
Liberal	Oficialistas	1,100,000	(78.57%)	56	(73.68%)
Liberal	MRL	300,000	(21.43%)	20	(26.32%)
Conservative	Unionistas	600,000	(55.30%)	37	(48.68%)
Conservative	Laureanistas	400,000	(36.87%)	37	(48.68%)
Conservative	Independientes	85,000	(7.83%)	2	(2.63%)
		1962			
Liberal	Oficialistas	1,081,103	(64.24%)	59	(64.13%)
Liberal	MRL	601,926	(35.76%)	33	(35.87%)
Conservative	Unionistas	794,688	(61.97%)	50	(54.35%)
Conservative	Laureanistas	487,733	(38.03%)	36	(39.13%)
Conservative	ANAPO	115,587	(9.01%)	6	(6.52%)
		1964			
Liberal	Oficialistas	738,437	(51.68%)	59	(64.13%)
Liberal	MRL	666,904	(46.67%)	31	(33.70%)
Liberal	ANAPO	16,495	(1.15%)	1	(1.09%)
Liberal	MIL	7,129	(0.50%)	1	(1.09%)
Conservative	Unionistas /Laureanistas	794,000	(73.03%)	65	(70.65%)
Conservative	Independientes	1	(1.09%)		
Conservative	ANAPO	293,183	(26.97%)	26	(28.26%)
		1966			
Liberal	Officialistas	1,120,824	(68.74%)	69	(72.63%)
Liberal	MRL	369,956	(22.69%)	21	(22.11%)
Liberal	ANAPO	100,898	(6.19%)	4	(4.21%)
Liberal	Independientes	24,026	(1.47%)	1	(1.05%)
Liberal	Others	14,940	(0.92%)	—	—
Conservative	Unionistas	474,397	(36.53%)	36	(37.89%)

Table 3.5 (*continued*)

Party	Factional lists	Votes	(faction's % of party)	Seats	(faction's % of party)
Conservative	Lauro Alzatistas	346,664	(26.69%)	24	(25.26%)
Conservative	ANAPO	422,204	(32.51%)	33	(34.74%)
Conservative	Leyvistas	7,485	(0.58%)	1	(1.05%)
Conservative	Independientes	40,106	(3.09%)	1	(1.05%)
Conservative	Others	7,771	(0.60%)		
	1968				
Liberal	Oficialistas	988,540	(74.40%)	77	(75.49%)
Liberal	Oficialistas Disidentes	196,457	(14.79%)	17	(16.67%)
Liberal	MRL	55,984	(4.21%)	2	(1.96%)
Liberal	ANAPO	82,294	(6.19%)	6	(5.88%)
Liberal	Others	5,351	(0.40%)	0	
Conservative	Unionistas	578,485	(49.85%)	49	(48.04%)
Conservative	Independientes	199,330	(17.18%)	19	(18.63%)
Conservative	ANAPO	319,609	(27.54%)	28	(27.45%)
Conservative	ANAPO				
	Lauro-Alzatistas	48,087	(4.14%)	5	(4.90%)
Conservative	Others	14,937	(1.29%)	1	(0.98%)
	1970				
Liberal	Pastranistas[a]	1,051,666	(51.69%)	57	(54.29%)
Liberal	Rojistas	563,614	(27.70%)	28	(26.67%)
Liberal	Belisaristas	137,069	(6.74%)	6	(5.71%)
Liberal	Sourdistas	156,877	(7.71%)	9	(8.57%)
Liberal	Others	125,316	(6.16%)	5	(4.76%)
Conservative	Pastranistas	589,234	(30.50%)	30	(28.57%)
Conservative	Rojistas	849,138	(43.95%)	43	(40.95%)
Conservative	Belisaristas	300,223	(15.54%)	19	(18.10%)
Conservative	Sourdistas	185,686	(9.61%)	13	(12.38%)
Conservative	Others	7,881	(0.41%)	—	—

Sources: Figures for 1958–1964 are from Dix 1967, 140 and 142; for 1966–1970 are from the Registraduría Nacional del Estado Civil official publication of electoral statistics for the years in question.

[a] In 1970 the Registraduría listed the factional lists by the presidential candidate that the list supported, rather than by factional labels.

Additionally, there were some statistically unlikely outcomes in several of the later reported ballot boxes.[17]

Rojas accepted defeat, and in 1971 he established ANAPO as an independent political party, as opposed to being a dissident "movement" (see above) within either of the traditional parties. His failing health led to his handing over the reigns of leadership to his daughter, María Eugenia, and her husband, Samuel Moreno Díaz.[18] The party won seven Senate seats (6.25% of the chamber) and fifteen Chamber seats (7.54% of the chamber) in the 1974 elections, the first post-Front congressional contests. The party would not win another seat in Congress until 1994, when Rojas' grandson, Samuel Moreno Rojas, would win a seat in the Senate.[19]

Also of note, the guerrilla group known as M-19, or the April 19th Movement, formed in response to what its founders perceived to be the electoral fraud of April 19, 1970, which had denied Rojas the presidency. M-19 will be dealt with elsewhere in the book as both a guerrilla group and a political party.

Fourth Era: 1886, Part 3, the *Desmonte* (1974–1990)

The dismantlement (*desmonte*) of the National Front began during the Carlos Lleras Restrepo administration (1966–1970), the last of the Liberal National Front presidents. Specifically, the administration shepherded through a set of constitutional reforms, which were approved as Legislative Act No. 1 of 1968.[20] The reforms of 1968 altered the Front in the following ways:

- Removed the two-thirds supermajority requirement for regular legislation
- Ended parity in local assemblies in 1970
- Extended the term of office for local assemblies and Congress to four years
- Extended parity in the cabinet, for governors and mayors, and in bureaucratic offices until 1978

After 1978, parity would end in the president's cabinet, but the party in power would be expected to invite members of the minority into the cabinet. Specifically, Article 120 of the constitution stated that "adequate and equitable" representation in the cabinet (as well as in governorships, mayoralties, and bureaucratic posts) should be given to the major party distinct from that of the president. That party would not be required to accept offices in the cabinet, although there were seats given to the opposition party in all post-Front cabinets until the Conservatives decided to forgo the offer during the Barco administration (1986–1990), creating the first government-opposition scheme in the post-Front period.

This period saw the establishment and escalation of the drug problem in Colombia, and the escalation of left-wing guerrilla violence. Numerous attempts in the 1980s were launched to address the challenges facing the state. Many of these manifested in political decentralization in an attempt to strengthen local administrative power (see Gaitán and Moreno 1992). A key reform along these lines was the move to allow the popular election of mayors (Law No. 1 of 1986). Other reforms included laws governing political parties such as partial public financing of campaigns and provisions for the use of radio and television for parties during campaigns (Law No. 58 of 1985) (see Pinzón de Lewin 1987).

With Law No. 1 of 1986, the Congress of Colombia sanctioned the popular election of mayors for the first time in Colombian history. Prior to that, mayors had been appointed by the governors, which had in turn been appointed by the president. This practice was part of the centralized control of the nation by the capital and by the party that controlled the capital; it was also a means by which the ruling party could maintain client ties in the various regions of the nation.

Fifth Era: 1991–Present

As was observed above in the overview of the nineteenth century and the subsequent reforms of the 1886 Constitution, the notion of addressing problems via institutional reform has a long tradition in Colombian political history. The most recent major attempt in that area was the replacement of the 1886 Constitution, the longest-serving one in Latin American history, with a wholly new constitution written in 1991 by an elected constituent assembly and promulgated on July 4 of that year.

Getting a New Document

In the context of seemingly endless violence (what Bejarano called "the long Hobbesian night of the 1980s" [1994, 47]), the idea of serious constitutional reform emerged in the late 1980s and culminated in a series of referenda that, in turn, produced a National Constituent Assembly (or *Asamblea Nacional Constituyente*, NCA) that was to promulgate a new constitution for Colombia. The series of events that led to the assembly's convocation in 1991 were unusual, not to mention of questionable constitutionality.

Institutional constraints made revising the 1886 Constitution difficult, as Article 13 of the plebiscite of 1957 (which had established the National Front) had forbidden constitutional reform via referendum, leaving only the constitutionally prescribed process of amendment via the vote of two consecutive sessions of the Congress. Specifically, the article stated: "constitutional reforms can only be made by the Congress via the process established in Article 218 of the Constitution."[21]

A memorandum written by then–presidential adviser Manuel José Cepeda to President Virgilo Barco Vargas (1986–1990) noted that an assembly could be called constitutionally either through congressional action or via a referendum to alter Article 13 of the 1957 plebiscite or Article 218 of the 1886 Constitution (Cepeda 1993, 213–218). The memorandum did note that the "procedure of minimal risk" (214) was the congressional route. The administration initially sought a referendum that would alter the Article 13 strictures to be held in conjunction with local elections on March 13, 1988; however, the Council of State declared the move unconstitutional (Kline 1999, 156). From there the administration attempted to achieve limited reform via the congressional route in 1988 and into 1989, but the results were naught.[22]

Using the logic that Article 2 of the 1886 Constitution placed sovereignty "exclusively" in the nation, a movement emerged among students who sought to have a constituent assembly called to write a new constitution, regardless of the aforementioned constitutional barriers. The movement ultimately manifested in the inclusion of the "*septima papeleta*," or seventh ballot, in the March 11, 1990, elections. The 1990 elections were the last in Colombian history wherein non-state-produced ballots were used—voters cut the ballots out of newspapers or had ballots distributed to them by parties. Each office had its own ballot, and so the inclusion in the voting envelope of an additional (in this case a seventh) ballot was possible.

Although unofficial, the seventh ballots were counted, and the favorable results provided the basis for President Barco to issue, under his state-of-siege powers, Decree 927 of 1990, which proclaimed that, in conjunction with the May 27 presidential elections, voters would decide the question of whether or not a national constituent assembly should be convoked (Cepeda 1993, 231–232). With the success of the May 27 referendum,[23] an additional decree was issued (Decree 1926 of 1990), which provided for a vote on December 9, 1990, that would again ask whether there ought to be a constituent assembly and whether delegates should be elected to it—to serve from February 5, 1991, until July 4, 1991, for the express purpose of producing a new constitution for Colombia (Cepeda 1993, 233–249).

Ultimately the Article 13 problem noted above was surmounted by citing that, per Article 2 of the 1886 Constitution, sovereign power was held in the hands of the people and that, per Article 45 of that same document, the citizens had the right to petition government. Hence, the legal justification was that those two statements, combined with the president's Article 121 decree powers, could be used to override Article 218 and the clear letter of the amendment process. The institutional acquiescence of the Supreme Court helped as well (see its Sentence 54 upholding presidential Decree 927 in Programa Democracia 1990, 180–198).

Although the ultimate constitutionality of the process seems doubtful—a plain reading of Article 13 of the 1957 plebiscite and Article 218 of the 1886 Constitution leaves one with no other interpretation—it is still quite noteworthy that the process that led to the 1990 calling of the NCA was still made with a significant amount of energy being directed at finding an institutionally viable process.

The NCA Process

Once a procedure had been devised to call the assembly, elections were held to select the delegates. Those elections were held on December 9, 1990, and consisted of 116 electoral lists on a ballot that itself was nonpartisan (each list had a number and the name and picture of the list's head), although the affiliations of the lists were known. Seventy seats were up for grabs, selected from one national electoral district with seats being distributed via the Hare quota.[24]

The results of the election were quite interesting and significant in and of themselves. First, the list to win the most votes was that of former guerrilla leader Antonio Navarro Wolff, whose Democratic Alliance/M-19 (AD/M-19) unified list won 992,613 votes, which translated into nineteen seats. The second-largest winner in terms of a single list was Álvaro Gómez's National Salvation Movement (MSN), which won 574,411 votes and eleven seats. However, in terms of seats, the Liberal Party won the most with twenty-two. It did so by offering multiple party lists that were able to win both by quota and also via multiple largest remainders. The Conservatives (functioning then under the label Social Conservative Party) won a mere seven seats. The remaining eleven seats were distributed among a number of smaller parties (see table 3.6 for a complete breakdown).

These results were of striking significance for numerous reasons. The most obvious (and dramatically felt at the time) was that traditional control by the two main parties was ruptured by this process: of the seventy elected seats, only twenty-nine (or 41.4%) were controlled by the PL and

Table 3.6

NCA Election Results—Seats by Party

Partido Liberal	22
Alianza Democrática/M-19	19
Movimiento de Salvación Nacional	11
Partido Social Conservador	7
Unión Cristiana	2
Unión Patriótica	2
Unidos por Colombia	2
MAIC (Mov. de Autoridades Indígenas de Col.)	1
Movimiento Estudiantil	1
ONIC (Organización Nacional Indígenas de Col.)	1
Nueva Colombia	1
Por Nuevo Pais	1
Total	70

Note: Four additional seats were allocated after the election as part of the peace process. The EPL was awarded two voting seats, and the PRT and MQL each were awarded one seat with voice (but no vote).

PC. Further, the showing by the AD/M-19 meant that it would be given one-third of the assembly's presidency along with the PL and MSN. The P(S)C[25] was cut out of direct leadership.

The idea that a new constitution could, and would, be written under such circumstances was a watershed in Colombian political development, insofar as the prior politics of the twentieth century had been dominated by the traditional parties. If one thinks simply in terms of *La Violencia* and the National Front, the significance of this new political reality, even if it was not to hold (at least in terms of the AD/M-19), is quite striking.

Another significant element from this election that should be noted, and that will be further examined in chapters 4 and 5, is the degree to which the Liberals were able to adjust to the rules of the NCA election with great strategic success. The usage of multiple lists (the so-called Operación Avispa, or Operation: Wasp) to win more seats with fewer votes (their 903,984 to the AD/M-19's 992,613)[26] was both an example of the political acumen of the Liberals and a foreshadowing of a tactic that would help the PL maintain majority status well into the next decade, even with the advent of rules that were supposed to help minority parties.[27]

The symbolism of the NCA was quite significant as well. For example, one of the copresidents of the assembly was Álvaro Gómez, who had been a kidnap victim of M-19 in 1988; he served alongside another copresident,

Antonio Navarro Wolff, who had been a leader of M-19. The fact that the document produced by this constituent assembly was not the direct result of *bipartidismo*, but rather a multipartisan effort, was also of great importance.

A New Document

So what did the new constitution bring? The fruit of the NCA's labor can be both overstated and understated. Certainly the original response to the document was overly optimistic. The Constitution of 1991 retained much of the basic design of the state from the 1886 Constitution, that is, a presidential system with a bicameral Congress and a unitary state. Within that basic framework, some of the changes in structure and procedure can be seen in table 3.7.

Table 3.7

Comparing Major Elected Offices, 1886 vs. 1991 Constitutions

Office	1886	1991
President	Single-round plurality needed to elect. Nonconsecutive reelection possible.	Absolute majority needed to win office; runoff required if no majority winner in the first round. No reelection before 2005 reform; now two terms possible.
Vice President	*Designado* selected by Congress; played no role in electoral competition.	Runs on same slate as president (must be same person in both rounds).
Senator	Elected from territorially based electoral districts; 112 seats in 1974 and 1978, 114 seats 1982–1990.	A total of 102 seats: 100 chosen from one national electoral district, 2 seats from a special national district for *indígenas*.
Deputy	Chamber: 199 seats.	Chamber: 161 seats in 1991, 163 in 1994, 166 in 1998 and 2002.
Governor	Appointed by president.	Popularly elected.
Mayor	Appointed by governor (until 1988).	Popularly elected.

Source: Adapted from Taylor 1996, 127.

The most essential issue for the new constitution, as part of the grand narrative of Colombian politics, is whether or not it set the appropriate stage for further democratic development within the Colombian state. I would argue that while the NCA and its product were neither the beginning nor end of this process, the events that brought about the 1991 Constitution very much furthered the evolution of party politics that has brought Colombia to its current electoral epoch.

Chapter 4 addresses the basics of the Colombian party system and addresses the issue of how best to understand and discuss that system. Chapter 5 directly deals with the question of how the specific constitutional periods, and their commensurate electoral rules, affected party behavior in the late twentieth and early twenty-first centuries, and therefore the very shape of the party system, which is currently undergoing interesting and serious change.

CHAPTER 4

Rethinking the Traditional Parties

The organization and functioning of Colombia's traditional parties . . . explain a great deal about Colombian politics, including the likely directions of political change.
—Robert Dix (1967, 231)

INTERMESHED WITH THE constitutional question has been the role of traditional political parties—the Liberals and the Conservatives. They have been the basis for both governance and civil strife from almost the beginning of the republic. It is difficult to find another party system in Latin America as intricately interwoven into the fabric of sociopolitical development as has been the case in Colombia.[1] Beyond that, as in any electoral democracy, the parties are the main vehicle through which political organization takes place. As such, one of the keys to understanding Colombian politics and its development over time is its party system. Specifically, too, the overarching theme of institutional change is directly linked to the parties, as it is party system change and behavior in response to electoral and other institutional reform that is a major theme of this inquiry.

To assess the role of the parties, several issues must be addressed. First, it is necessary to lay out a basic overview of the traditional party system that originated in the nineteenth century, components of which continue to operate into the twenty-first. Second, there is a need to take stock of the dominant thinking regarding these parties, especially as it pertains to the conventional wisdom on the effect that the National Front had on them. From there we need to look in-depth at the responses of the party system to the various institutional reforms of the twentieth and twenty-first centuries.

This chapter deals with the first two points and lays the foundation for the discussion of system change that is found in chapters 5 and 6. A major part of the argument in this chapter is that there is a need to rethink our understanding of the traditional parties so as to better comprehend the changes that the system has experienced (and continues to experience). This "rethinking" is aimed at the conventional wisdom that prevails in the literature on Colombia, which focuses heavily on the idea that the parties were radically affected by the National Front, which led to a "crisis" of the parties that persists to the present period.

In summary, this chapter will provide an overview of the traditional parties (origins and main characteristics), a definition and critique of the dominant approach to the parties, and an assessment of what a "rethought" approach to the party system should look like.

Foundational Issues

Colombian political life, whether we are talking about governing or warring, has been dominated until recently by *bipartidismo*—the dominance of the two traditional political parties: the Conservatives and the Liberals. It is important to understand that *bipartidismo* does not translate as "bipartisanship" (which would indicate cooperation between two parties in policy formulation) but rather more accurately as "two-partyism" and can be conceived of as the dominance of electoral politics, and thereby the government, by two key parties over time (in other words, rule by the two main parties). The term can be both a neutral description as well as one that carries a critical connotation. Some (indeed, many) consider the prevalence of *bipartidismo* to be a major component of Colombia's problems.[2]

Certainly much of the analysis of Colombian politics has been undertaken through the lens of *bipartidismo* for reasons that are not hard to understand, given that the political violence of the nineteenth and early twentieth centuries was fundamentally partisan in nature. Further, two of the most prominent phenomena of Colombia's political history, the partisan civil war known as *La Violencia* and the power-sharing agreement known as the National Front, were both party-based at their core.

While one of the central theses of this book is that the political system of Colombia should no longer be understood in terms of *bipartidismo*, it is nonetheless quite important to be familiar with this phenomenon before undertaking an examination of the profound institutional changes that have led to an evolution of the party system itself.

The first step in addressing this topic is to examine the basic origins of the parties and their long-term historical significance. From there this section will examine the main factors that need addressing in any assessment of Colombian parties.

Origins

As the discussion of Colombian constitutionalism in chapter 3 should have made clear, the first century-plus of Colombia's political history was marked by pseudodemocracy at best. Given that women did not effectively receive the franchise until the late 1950s, the notion of even full electoral democracy is impossible to defend prior to that point. Nonetheless, in terms of relative historical context, Colombia's politics have long been democratic and did revolve around a party system—although a party system with neofeudal elements.[3] That is to say that the parties were the creatures primarily of landed elites and those who worked the land and supported their patrons at the polls (and sometimes on the field of battle).

The basic tale of party formation in Colombia is that the two traditional parties emerged from the political conflicts of two of the country's early leaders, with the Conservative Party emerging from Simon Bolívar and the Liberal Party from Francisco de Paula Santander.[4] Of course, as with most political narratives, that is an oversimplification—but it does make for a dramatic story.

Not long after independence, conflict arose between President Bolívar and Vice President Santander, forming the groundwork for this idea that the partisan split in Colombian politics can be traced back to these two key leaders the way the U.S. parties trace their lineages to Jefferson and Lincoln. In the lead-up to the crisis that would see Bolívar claim dictatorial powers, the opponents of the Liberator, who coalesced around Santander, often called themselves "liberals" because of their support for the constitution over the personalism of Bolívar (Safford and Palacios 2002, 122). Of course this origin story, despite its elegance, is mostly mythos.

In terms of their formal founding, one can place both parties' origins in the 1848–1849 period. Not only did these years see the publication of the first party platforms; the 1849 election was the first major mobilization of the two parties for electoral purposes.[5] As Bushnell (1993, 115) notes, the advent of universal male suffrage (temporary as it was) in the 1850s was the first time that the parties had a structural incentive to recruit large numbers of rank-and-file members.

The specific issues that emerged as key points of contention between the two parties were state structure, trade policy, and the role of the Catholic Church. The Conservatives favored a unitary, centralized state, protectionism, and an official role for the church. Liberals preferred federation, free trade, and separation of church and state. Indeed, the clearest manifestation of the differences between the two sides in the nineteenth century was in the struggle over the constitution and the question of whether the Conservative vision of a unitary state would be codified or whether the Liberals' desire for federation would win out (see table 3.2). As Dix describes, the Conservatives drew much of their perspectives from Iberian traditionalism and the Liberals from classical liberalism (1967, 232–239). Dix also notes that these "differences sometimes appear[ed] to be more of tone and approach than of actual behavior" (1967, 238).

While the ideological foundations of the parties were distinct, it should also be noted that the parties were both clientelistic in nature and often quite personalistic, with regional issues and needs often trumping philosophy. Certainly the rank-and-file adherents of the two parties were loyal not out of ideological attraction but because their patron was affiliated with a given party. As will be underscored below, clientelism is a far more important element than ideology in terms of understanding the traditional parties. The parties have long been particularistic rather than programmatic in their governing behavior.

The Consociational Elements

Beyond just longevity, the centrality of the traditional parties in Colombia has long been cultural. For most of Colombian history, one's party affiliation was part of one's identity. For a rural, traditional society with significant patron-client networks, the connection to party is perhaps not surprising. What is striking, however, is the intensity of those connections until well into the latter half of the twentieth century. Kline describes the relationship as follows: "the masses of Colombia were 'organized,' not in the sense of a European mass political party, but in an emotional sense. The effect of the emotional organization was similar to that of the European mass-party organization: the masses were obedient followers of the party leaders" (1980, 62). The emotion in question was clearly driven and solidified by the ability of party leaders to provide patronage.

The connections that existed in the patron-client relationships within the parties, as well as regional consideration, led to a deep-seated party identification within the Colombian populace well beyond normal partisan attachments. Ample reference has already been made to the two most well-known manifestations of these tendencies, the National Front and *La Violencia*; however, those are far from the only coalitions and internal wars undertaken by these parties. Kline (1983, 40–41) notes eleven examples of coalitions between the parties/factions of the parties from 1854 to 1949. Of course, none of these were as dramatic as the National Front. They were, as Dix notes, "generally short-lived, and most were at the bottom intended only to be temporary, seen as truces or as a means of effecting the transfer of power from one party to the other by gradual and therefore less threatening stages" (1980a, 306). Similarly, one can identify at least ten significant civil conflicts in the nineteenth century wherein the traditional parties, or their factions, were involved.[6]

The persistence of the two parties, and the fact that they did form the ongoing basis for cooperation and conflict, demonstrate their penetration of Colombian politics and society. The importance of these parties has been so profound that several authors (Wilde 1978; Dix 1980a and 1987; Hartlyn 1988) have considered the relationship between the parties (at least in the past) as being of a consociational nature—a term usually reserved for power-sharing arrangements built around ethnic or religious differences (see Lijphart 1977).

In other words, the ties that most Colombians felt to their party were so profound that, as Hartlyn put it: "The country's two major political parties, the Liberal and the Conservative, came to represent functional equivalents of the segmental divisions among religious, linguistic or ethnic lines identified in other consociational cases" (1988, 16). Dix notes that these ties were handed down from parent to child and were linked to the prevalence of patron-client relationships in Colombia, wherein the partisan affiliation of one's patron was therefore one's own (1967, 210–211). Further, the antagonisms between the parties were so intense and lasting that they constituted "hereditary hatreds" (Dix 1967, 211). As in other divided societies, these tensions led both to the aforementioned civil conflicts and to the need to have formalized coalitions as a means of diffusing the profound political conflicts that arise between such actors.

One can thus see the intertwined significance of *La Violencia*, an interparty civil war that claimed hundreds of thousands of lives, and the National Front, a clear power-sharing agreement in the consociational mold. Not only were they culminations of long-term historical patterns; they represent the apex of conflict and coalition, respectively. It is also easy to see how those two events directly influence the political analysis of Colombia and Colombian parties, leading to a treatment that often sees the entire situation as sui generis, which clouds the analysis. The exact significance of the National Front is at the heart of any analysis of the traditional parties, and especially the paradigm that dominates the current literature on Colombian parties.

Other Major Themes

Three other major themes emerge in almost any discussion of Colombia's party system—elitism (and elite-driven factionalism), clientelism, and abstentionism—and therefore need to be addressed here. All three are descriptively true of the system, as there is no disputing the fact that the traditional parties have long been parties of notables who have thrived on clientelistic practices. Beyond that, there is no denying that the voter turnout rates for Colombian elections have been unimpressive by regional standards (although not all that different from those for the United States). These three themes are addressed here, therefore, for two key reasons. The first is because they do point to important features of the party system, and therefore serve a descriptive purpose. The second is because all three are typically cited in the literature in a way that amounts to criticism of the traditional party system itself. Such issues will be more directly addressed in the next section of the chapter. Here, however, it is necessary to outline the three themes in question.

First, the traditional parties are, without a doubt, parties of elites and have been from their inception.[7] Key families have persisted throughout the history of these parties, with party factions often coalescing around specific caudillos from those families. In fact, Dix called the nineteenth-century violence "warfare among rival caudillos" (1967, 77). The significance of factionalism within the parties is underscored by the fact that it was quite common for specific factions of the parties, especially in the PC, to be identified by the name (usually the last name but sometimes the first) of the factional leader. For example, in the PL, the followers of the Lleras wing of the party were referred to as Lleristas, while the Turbay supporters were called the Turbayistas. Such designations were sufficiently institutionalized that they were used, in some cases, in official electoral statistics during the National Front period to designate different slates of candidates. While the practice of identifying currents within the parties with specific persons continues to some degree in the Colombian press, the dominant usage of such identifiers has waned since the late 1970s and early 1980s. Certainly since the advent of the officially produced ballot in 1991, the usage of overt factional designations based on familial ties has died out.

Perhaps there is no better illustration of the historical importance of elites to the party system (and to Colombian politics writ large) than the fact that Rojas could not have come to power had there not been a fracturing of the elites prior to 1953, and that it was the alliance of those previously estranged elites that ousted Rojas via several pacts four years later. In other words, the only military coup of twentieth century took place in the context of a fractured elite, and the transition away from military rule took place because of the reunification of those elites. The pacts in question led to the installation of the National Front, a system that extolled the individual party leaders even further by allowing personalized electoral lists for institutionalized intraparty competition (as was noted in chapter 3).

The fact that the parties have been so elitecentric has long been used as a criticism of the system, as it has meant that despite the substantial electoral success of the two parties, their orientation has been less directed to the public good (as interpreted by each party) than might otherwise have been the case with truly mass-based parties. Nonetheless, the parties have been (as noted above) capable of mass mobilization. This capacity is linked to the cultural significance of the parties as noted in the previous section and to the importance of patron-client networks.

So, a second theme to address is clientelism.[8] As Archer (1990) notes in his excellent work on the evolution of clientelism in Colombia, the patron-client relationship has evolved from traditional clientele networks to brokered clientelism, wherein the main goal is for the patron to funnel the largesse of the state in the direction of localities. In the initial stages of Colombian political development we saw the traditional types of patron-client relationships, with local caudillos providing protection and support for peasants in exchange for loyalty. This relationship has evolved into one based more on the ability of individual patrons to act as brokers between the central government and the localities as a means of distributing the largesse of the state to those localities. Understanding the prevalence of clientelistic practices is central for comprehending that the Colombian party system has long been particularistic rather than programmatic. The term *particularistic* means that the parties have been oriented toward particular interests and the private good of their clientele network and their allies within their voter base. *Programmatic* parties are oriented toward the furtherance of a specific version of the public good (i.e., a program). That view of "the good" likely also serves a specific set of interests, but it is based on a philosophical/ideological perspective, rather than being simply oriented toward accessing state resources for specific distribution. It is not assumed that programmatic parties never engage in pork-barrel spending, but rather that the distribution of pork is not their main raison d'être. Further, clientelism has rewarded more rural, and therefore more conservative, parties at the expense of urban voters (as Nielson and Shugart [1999] argue).

A number of key institutional features allowed for the fostering of brokered clientelism within the party system. The first was the ability under the 1968 reform of the 1886 Constitution for members of Congress to engage in directed pork-barrel spending called *auxilios parliamentarios*, which could manifest as specific public spending on a particular public work (such as a new bullfighting ring) or scholarships to students back home. Although *auxilios* were banned under the 1991 Constitution in an effort to curtail explicit clientelism, they have continued in less public forms (Cárdenas, Junguito, and Pachón 2006, 30).

Ballot structure also played a key role in fostering clientele networks. Prior to 1991, elections for office were held on candidate-produced ballots (or *papeletas*) that represented specific factions of the mainline parties.[9] The factional list would typically be headed by the regional patron, the candidate for the Senate, and would go on to include lists for the Chamber, the departmental assembly, and the municipal council. As such, a vote for the patron was a vote for the entire network of subpatrons (although a given *papeleta* could be split up to allow for cross-list voting). Starting with the presidential election of 1990, and then with the election of the first Congress under the new Constitution of 1991, all voting was conducted via state-produced ballots that no longer linked all the members of a given network on a single ballot. Instead, there was a separate piece of paper (called a *tarjetón*) for each office in the election.[10]

Also, the centralized nature of the state, with substantial appointment power vested in the president (including presidential appointment of mayors until 1988 and governors until 1991), encouraged the fostering of patron-client networks. Given the lack of multiple channels of access to obtain state goods, one needed a connection within the existing power structure either via the executive branch or directly from the Congress. For example, since fiscal policy was centralized, localities had to depend on the central government's budget for funding for local projects.[11] In such a context, the emphasis on clientele networks that were oriented toward access to the central government is understandable.

A third key topic is abstentionism.[12] As noted in chapter 2, voter turnout rates in Colombia have been far from impressive (see tables 2.3, 2.4, and 2.5), to the point that within Colombian politics it is more common for commentators and analysts to speak of abstention rates instead of turnout figures. This is typically considered evidence of problems (if not a "crisis") within the Colombian electoral/party system. For example: Valencia states, in regard to the abstention rates in the immediate post-NF period, that it is "impossible to image a comparable crisis of legitimacy" (1978, 117–118). Peeler states that "[h]igh abstention rates have been pointed out by some analysts as an indication of political crisis in Colombia" (1976, 219). Such arguments, however, are tautological, insofar as the abstention numbers themselves are considered to prove the crisis, while the crisis is what supposedly fuels the abstention. That the turnout rates are unimpressive is an indisputable fact. However, as will be noted below, the actual significance of those numbers is worthy of more debate; in themselves they are not sufficient for making hard and fast conclusions about the system. Nonetheless abstentionism remains a key theme in discussions of Colombian elections.

Summing Up the Foundational Issues

To put all the basic pieces together, one should note that the traditional parties have deep roots in both the history and culture of Colombia. Further, the parties have a long history of elite focus and clientelism, and Colombian elections have long had poor voter turnout. From here the question is how to intermesh these issues with an understanding of the National Front regime as well as to consider the general origins of these behaviors.

Addressing the Conventional Wisdom: Definitions and Critiques

Given that the traditional parties are longtime, central players in Colombian political development, it is hardly surprising that when it comes to diagnosing Colombia's numerous ills, the parties have been a central focus for blame. Certainly, there is room to assert that policy problems in Colombia should redound to the parties, as they are the basic vehicles of governance. Further, as noted above, the parties have rightly been criticized for being overly oriented toward the interests of the elite class, as well as having been interested more in particularistic activities (i.e., feeding clientele networks) than in working on behalf of serious programmatic solutions to Colombia's manifest woes. It is likewise understandable why voter turnout is not higher, given the issues of policy performance and also the pervasive violence that has existed for decades.

In allowing for the obviously reasonable notion that the parties deserve criticism and a share of blame, the issue becomes how we should evaluate the party system in this context. Before that can be done, it is necessary to examine the prevailing views on the parties that can be found in the literature. Those views will be presented and critiqued along with a discussion of how to deal with party labels in the Colombian context, which then allows for some rethinking of how to analyze Colombian politics.

The place to start the discussion of the dominant view of the parties is with what I call the "crisis thesis" and from there to address the question of how to evaluate the role the National Front played in the development of the party system. The section concludes with a discussion of how we ought to look at party labels in the Colombian context—specifically that there has been a tendency to simplistically categorize parties and candidates under the Conservative and Liberal rubrics.

Two basic arguments will be made in detail in the following pages. First is that there is a remarkable overemphasis in the literature (in English and in Spanish) on the notion that the Colombian party system is "in crisis."[13] If anything, the most fundamental rejoinder to this idea is definitional: a crisis is an acute, temporally delimited event; so to speak of a constant crisis over the course of multiple decades is to be describing normality, not a crisis. It may well be that the normality in question is an unpleasant one, but a crisis it is not (if we use the word properly). The second argument is that much of the literature is simply wrong about the effects that the National Front had on the party system (which, in turn, has further fueled the crisis thesis).

The Crisis Thesis

Before applying the idea of crisis to the traditional parties themselves, it is worth noting that there is a long tradition in the literature on Colombia of deeming the situation to be one of "crisis."[14] While the ongoing bloodshed noted in detail in chapter 2 might encourage one to consider the whole society as being in crisis, as noted above, after a while one has to reclassify a continuing situation as simply being an undesirable version of normal.[15] The predilection to write about the crisis in Colombia is indeed such a general, holistic one, but there is also a deep strain in the literature on Colombian parties that specifically notes their "crisis" status.[16] The crisis is sometimes termed one of legitimacy or one of governance but is just as likely to be "crisis" à la carte. The basic notion here is that the traditional party system has been unable to deal with the problems that have beset the Colombian state and therefore there must be something fundamentally wrong with those parties. The assumption has been that the parties will at some point cease to function, as a result of their inability to adequately represent the population and to make public policy to solve the seemingly intractable problems of violence and development within Colombia.

Some of the fundamental elements of this thesis link up with the basic ingredients of the party system described above: that the parties are elite focused, and hence ignore the actual policy needs of the country; and that they are more interested in providing pork to their client base, and hence broad national policy is not formulated. Additionally, the high voter abstention rates are seen to be an indication of the general attitude of the population in regard to these problems. Further, as we will see below, the argument has been that the National Front in particular is responsible for this sorry state of affairs. The prevailing assumption, then, is that a crisis of the parties exists, and that presumably it will come to some sort of dramatic conclusion—the death of the traditional parties.

We can trace such arguments at least as far back as the later 1950s and one of the first major English-language books on Colombian politics, Vernon Fluharty's *Dance of the Millions* (1957). Fluharty argued that *La Violencia* and the subsequent Rojas dictatorship had led to the death of "hyperpartisanship" and to the "obliteration of the traditional system" (155). Ironically, within a year of the book's publication, with its dramatic pronouncements about *bipartidismo*, the parties emerged like the phoenix via a series of elite-level pacts to restore the PC and PL to their place at the center of the Colombian state in the guise of the National Front.[17]

Still, between *La Violencia*, the Rojas dictatorship, the extraordinary nature of the National Front rules, and then the problematic election of 1970 (see chapter 3), it is not surprising that by the 1970s many thought that the time had come for the parties to fade into the sunset. Peeler notes that the literature at that point was split between those who viewed the parties "apocalyptically" and those who viewed them "fatalistically"—in other words, those who saw their coming doom and those who saw the parties as problematic but entrenched (1976, 204). Two years later Ruhl noted: "For nearly two decades observers of Colombian politics have been predicting the demise of the nation's traditional political parties" (1978, 29). However, this clearly did not happen. Although the traditional parties have undergone substantial changes since the 1991 Constitution, as we enter into the second decade of the twenty-first century they persist as important political actors in Colombian politics. Regardless, the view that the parties were (and remain) "in crisis" is a persistent theme in the literature.

One approach to rethinking the parties is to focus not on the crisis notion but rather on their resilience. Not only can these parties trace their lineage back over a century and a half (making both of them older, for example, than the Republican Party in the United States); they have also weathered civil wars (the War of a Thousand Days and *La Violencia*, to name two), the Rojas coup, and numerous institutional changes over the decades. The Conservatives have even had a number of recent electoral setbacks, yet continue to persist (that issue will be addressed in the next chapter). Colombia faces a number of very serious problems; however, political parties that are about to conflagrate at any moment is not one of them.

On balance, the notion of the parties being in crisis has been linked in large measure within the literature to the advent of the National Front regime (described in chapter 3). The next section deals with that assertion.

The National Front, Parties, and the Conventional Wisdom

Apart from the vague application throughout the literature of the *crisis* label to the traditional party system, there is a more specific narrative that points directly to the National Front as the source of all things crisis-oriented in regard to the traditional parties. Specifically this line of reasoning states that the National Front was an exclusionary regime that resulted in the inability of new actors to access the state, forcing some actors to utilize violence as a means of participation. The notion can be found in the literature from the 1970s (e.g., Leal 1973) to the 2000s (e.g., F. Giraldo 2003).[18]

Essentially the argument goes that the institutionalization of the National Front regime led to the exclusion of new voices from politics while simultaneously making the existing parties less responsive to voters. Thus the parties are considered to be unrepresentative and therefore unable to deal with the country's woes. Further, key to the discussion is how the exclusionary rules of the Front led to the Left taking up arms. A very recent iteration of this idea can be found in Cárdenas, Junguito, and Pachón:

> The agreement between Liberals and Conservatives excluded other sectors, most relevantly the left, which did not have access to a democratic channel for participating in the political process. Guerrilla activity became more intense, and the political system started to lose credibility due to patronage, corruption, and the entry of drug money into the political process. The exclusionary nature of the system, along with the lack of authority and presence of the State in parts of the country, eroded the *Frente Nacional*'s popular support, resulting in high rates of abstention. Guerrilla groups—such as the M19, EPL, ELN and FARC—as well as labor and social movements gained momentum in urban and rural areas. (2006, 9)

In sum, the argument is that the rules of the Front broke the traditional parties *and* led to the defection from mainstream politics of leftists, which therefore created a protracted guerrilla conflict that has wracked the country since the early 1960s. Following this basic line of reasoning, the majority of Colombia's problems are seen to be the result of the Front itself and its lingering effects on all things political. To understand the deeper components of the argument regarding the effects of the Front, and thereby to understand the essential elements of the dominant paradigm formed by this view of the National Front, we need to specifically examine the way the argument is laid out in the literature.

A succinct presentation of this approach can be found via Dugas, who outlines what he argues are four important negative consequences to the traditional parties of the Front (2000, 87–94, and 2001, 5–7). These negative consequences, which are not unique to Dugas' work but are representative of mainstream discussion on the Colombian parties, are as follows: depoliticization, increased fragmentation, increased clientelism, and decreased representativeness. If we add these four elements to the general argument about exclusion noted above, then we have the major components of the prevailing view of how the National Front led to a crisis of the traditional parties and, thereby, exacerbated (if not created) the generic crisis that we see in Colombian today.

However, it is my contention in this work that such assertions overestimate the effects of the Front. Moreover, they ignore questions of how to make appropriate comparisons between different historical eras, and they lack as well sufficient analysis of institutional effects on party behavior. In short, the conventional wisdom regarding the traditional parties, especially as it pertains to the NF, needs to be rethought. The purpose here is to detail and assess the components of the argument. It should be noted that the goal is not to utterly discount the issues raised by the conventional wisdom but to reassess how we should think about them.

The place to start this discussion is to ask a question about comparisons and comparability. Thinking for a moment in terms of a simple process model, the dominant argument is that the traditional parties from the pre-Rojas era were put into the black box of the National Front, which transmogrified them into a damaged set of actors (in terms of behavior and ability) by 1974. For example, Dugas states: "The established thesis generally accepted by analysts is that the political crisis was the result of the bipartisan regime provided by the National Front" (1993a, 16).[19] Scarpetta argues that "[a]fter the government of the National Front ended, the national institutions faced a progressive crisis of legitimacy" (1991, 1162).[20]

Such arguments assume on their face that the party system of the pre-Rojas era was somehow substantially different from (and, by extension, better than) that which emerged from the Front. Starting from that premise we need to ask two questions: first, are the two periods comparable? and second, to what degree are the party systems of the two eras substantially different from one another? The first question can be addressed by a review of the relevant history, while the second can answered by looking at Dugas' four consequences of the Front. My critique of the conventional approach to the effects of the Front will conclude with a direct assessment of the "exclusion" argument.

Comparability

In regard to the first question, there are some comparability problems that are not addressed by the conventional wisdom. One needs to consider what preexisted the Front before it can be determined what the Front did or did not change.

Looking back to the Colombian party system before the breakdown of democracy[21] raises important issues of comparability with the post-Front era. The broadest net we could cast would take us back to 1914 and the beginning of the usage of the popular vote (rather than election via indirect processes). However, in terms of comparing specific historical segments of the electoral system, going back that far is problematic, as the method for electing the Congress was not set to a version of list-PR until 1929.[22] Losada argues that "only two presidential elections (1942 and 1946) and five congressional elections (1939, 1941, 1943, 1945 and 1947) can plausibly be compared to the National Front elections because the two parties participated" (1980, 89–90).[23] The 1930 presidential contest was one of a Liberal versus two Conservatives, so we could add that to the list. Considering both the changes in the electoral system and the lack of a large number of competitive elections for comparative purposes, the 1930s and 1940s do not appear to be a legitimate era to use in asking the question of what the Front did or did not change. Yet the literature that subscribes to the conventional wisdom's view of the Front tends to hark back to that period, both by implication and by explicit reference.[24]

However, are the 1930s–1940s a good sample to compare with the post-Front era? Does looking at that period and then to the 1970s tell us how the Front changed the parties? The claim, when scrutinized, is a dubious one. The states of Colombian society, and Colombian democracy, were quite different in the 1930s versus the 1970s. Let's consider some basic demography: not only did the Colombian population grow considerably from the later 1930s to the end of the National Front (from 8.7 million to 22.9 million in 1974), but also, even more significantly, the percentage of the populace living in urban areas almost doubled in the same period, from 30.9 percent in 1938 to 59.5 percent in 1973.[25] Furthermore, there is the basic suffrage question: in the 1930s women were not allowed to vote, yet starting with the referendum that approved the Front (in 1957), universal suffrage was in place. Building on both the general trends in population and the inclusion of women, it is worth further noting that Colombia went through a number of demographic changes from the 1930s to the 1970s, including infant mortality rates, fertility rates, illiteracy rates, and elementary school enrollment (among other indicators).[26] The substantial shift to urban centers, the inclusion of women, and overall social development meant that by the time the Front had done its work the electorate had been substantially changed. In short: Colombia was a different place in the 1970s, making direct comparisons with the 1930s–1940s problematic.

Going beyond the questions of the party system, basic politics, or the demography question is the issue of political violence. If we look to the pre-Rojas period, do we see a situation in which political violence was an unusual manifestation? Clearly, this is not the case. Not only was *La Violencia* a main provocation in motivating the Rojas coup, but violence has long been a political tool in Colombian history. Additionally, although the FARC was formally established in 1966, it has its genesis in peasant fighting groups from the *Violencia* period (i.e., prior to the Front).[27] Indeed, the leader of the FARC, Pedro Antonio Marín (aka Manuel "Sureshot" [Tirofijo] Marulanda Vélez), was fighting as early as 1950–1951 (Safford and Palacios 2002, 354–355).[28] The notion that leftist political violence can be linked to the advent of the Front is therefore problematic from a historical perspective.

Overall, it is questionable as to whether the two historical periods provide directly comparable circumstances that allow for a definitive assertion that the Front changed the parties—given that the context in which the parties were operating had changed considerably. Even if we set aside the comparability issue, there is still the question of whether the behaviors of the post-Front parties are really sufficiently different from the behaviors of the past to warrant the conclusions of the conventional wisdom. There is a great deal of fundamental continuity that can be noted, which damages the notion that the NF fundamentally changed Colombian politics. To deal with that issue we can go on to consider the actual behavior of the parties post-NF.

The Alleged Consequences of the Front

To address the question of party behavior, we can look at what Dugas has termed the four negative consequences of the National Front (depoliticization, increased fragmentation, increased clientelism, and decreased representativeness). Really, two issues emerge here—one descriptive, the other causal. First, is the description of these consequences an accurate reflection of the condition of the party system from 1974 onward? Second, if the description is accurate, can the Front itself be appropriately blamed for the conditions in question? Let us consider the four issues one at a time.

1. *Depoliticization.* To start with, there is something surreal about the suggestion that *political* parties could be depoliticized.[29] Nonetheless, the argument is made by various authors, and it proceeds as follows: the need to decrease points of conflict between the PL and the PC (i.e., to flush out any chances of reigniting the hereditary hatreds that sparked violence) forced the Front to turn political competition from an interparty activity to an intraparty one, and hence managed to "depoliticize" the parties. For example, Leal writes of the loss of "the function of channeling the political expressions of the civil society to the state" (1990, 30) as a result of the Front, and he specifically argues in another work that the NF led to the "depoliticization" of the parties (1973, 187). It is argued that this "depoliticization" of the parties fed abstention and disengaged citizens from the electoral process. As such, the notion is that the Front did its job of detaching voters from the parties too well.

The manifestation of this process is supposed to be lack of electoral participation and decrease in party identification. On the descriptive front, it is true that voter turnout in Colombia is hardly stellar, as table 2.3 shows. And it is true that the three pre-Rojas congressional elections had a higher average voter turnout (52.63%) than that of the Front period (50.74%) and the 1974–2006 period (42.73%). Of course, the pre-Rojas set of elections occurred prior to universal suffrage, and the number of cases is only three, as opposed to seven for the Front era and ten for the post-Front era. In terms of party identification, it stands to reason that the aforementioned urbanization process would diminish partisan ties (a point that Dugas makes in this context [2000, 89]), as such shifts normally diminish traditional political ties. Hence it is wholly unclear that one can blame either low voter turnout or decreased party identification on the National Front.

Beyond the question of whether the parties were, in fact, "depoliticized" is the question of whether they were ever as politically responsive as this notion would suggest. Given the basic conditions of democracy in the 1930s (such as limited suffrage), it would seem that Leal and others are overly romanticizing the pre-Rojas era. There is also a question to be addressed here over how to distinguish between the notion of "depoliticization" and "decreased representativeness" as discussed below. Surely the notions of mass mobilization, party identification, and voter turnout are all linked to how well parties represent mass publics?

2. Increased Fragmentation. There is no doubt that the NF rules encouraged greater factionalization of the parties. However, as has been noted, the Front did not create such behavior. For example, the politician whose assassination sparked *La Violencia* (Jorge Eliécer Gaitán) ran on a "dissident" Liberal list in 1929 (Sharpless 1978, 57), and Payne notes that in the 1949 Chamber elections, Liberals ran an average of 2.2 lists per department, and Conservatives 1.1 (1968, 202).[30] Further, intraparty fragmentation along familial lines, as noted above, was not new either. It is true that list proliferation increased under the Front as a matter of strategic necessity (i.e., because the elections were essentially intraparty during that period), but it also true that the strategic usage of lists was endemic to the electoral rules that Colombia functioned under until 2003 (as will be explored in chapters 5 and 6).

The fragmentation process can certainly be seen as exacerbating a lack of ideological and programmatic cohesion within the PL and PC (which might, in turn, be said to contribute to the "depoliticization" of the parties, at least as defined by the conventional wisdom). Of course, the parties had never had much cohesion in the first place. On the other hand, the nature of the fragmentation meant that any electoral entrepreneur could form his or her own list. The ease of fragmentation did discourage the creation of large, coherent parties. The degree to which the Front specifically is at fault, however, is questionable.

It is worth noting that there is a certain irony in pointing to fragmentation as a negative consequence of the Front: it contradicts the exclusion arguments that undergird the crisis thesis, as the ability of the parties to offer multiple lists under the Front allowed more access to the electorate (e.g., the ANAPO lists) than would have been available if the rules of the Front had insisted on unified lists from the PL and PC in all elections.

3. Increased Clientelism. The basic argument here is that the Front exacerbated clientelism in a way that would not have taken place if the Front had not been adopted. Clientelism was hardly new to Colombian politics in the 1958–1974 period. Indeed, the institutional structure of the Colombian state under the 1886 Constitution encouraged clientelistic practices, especially in the rural and underdeveloped segments of the country. A unitary and centralized state meant that largesse had to flow through Bogotá, and therefore actors in the localities needed to send emissaries to the capital to obtain state resources. Further, presidential appointment powers located a great deal of authority in the hands of the president with or without the Front (e.g., governors and mayors were appointed by the president under the 1886 charter, not to mention other offices). As such, the institutional arrangement of the Colombian state along with traditional political patterns meant that clientelism would have flourished in the 1960s with or without the Front.

Now, there is a case to be made that the 1968 constitutional reforms with the *auxilio* feature (discretionary funds that legislators could spend on their departments) are an example of substantially enhanced broker clientelism in Colombia. Further, one could argue that the purpose of the reform at that stage was to enhance the political grip of the traditional parties as the Front was coming to a close.

Even allowing for the effects of those reforms, traditional clientelism was a hallmark of Colombian politics prior to the Front, and was hardly unusual in an early-twentieth-century Latin American republic with an agrarian economy and oligarchic political parties. Hence, while the 1968 reforms may have enhanced clientelistic practices, it is far from certain that (a) the change was a substantial departure from the general Colombian mode of politics, and that (b) such a mechanism could only have been installed via the Front.

4. Decreased Representativeness. A substantial problem with this pillar of the argument is determining exactly what "representativeness" means in this context (along with "depoliticization" above). The linkages in the literature tend to be along the lines of either class or policy performance, although there is a general lack of theoretical clarity on the subject.

In terms of class, there is the question of whether or not the parties are representing the upper classes at the expense of the lower classes. Such discussions often echo, sometimes very directly, the language of the populist politician of the 1930s and 1940s Jorge Eliécer Gaitán, who used to refer to the political class (meaning upper class oligarchs) as the *país político* and the people as the *país nacional*—the underlying logic behind the terms being that those in politics were representing themselves, not the interests of the Colombian people. Such language finds its way into the political science literature, with the most prominent usage being by Hoskin (1980, 1994, and 1995, for example) as well as by others (Murillo 1999 and Restrepo 1992). Of course, the notion that traditional parties, especially those with nineteenth-century origins, would be more oriented toward the wealthy in their practical activities is not surprising. So, again, the notion that the Front had a direct effect on this situation is highly questionable from an empirical perspective.

If we couple the "depoliticization" argument from above with the "representativeness" discussion, and we link them both to the fact that the authors who focus on these types of issues frequently look back to the 1930s and 1940s as a superior period of party behavior, we likely have a general answer as to what the authors in question are pointing toward. Likely it is a combination of looking back with nostalgia to *Gaitanismo* (or the populist, anti-upper-class rhetoric and politics of Gaitán) as well as to the *Revolución en la Marcha*, the New Deal–like social reforms of the first López Pumarejo administration (1934–1938). Ironically, while this set of policies may be construed as being more representative of general social needs in Colombia at the expense of the upper classes, López won office in 1934 essentially uncontested.[31] Such circumstances raise the question as to whether that political era is a very good example of an electoral process producing "representativeness" (unless "representativeness" has nothing to do with elections, per se, but rather with who benefits from policies).

Further, if the basic process that has driven much of Colombian party politics has been the provision of pork to narrow constituencies, it is questionable to what degree such a system lacks "representativeness"—as surely it is representing the interests of its constituents, even if the net result is not policy aimed at key national problems. So, rather than being evidence of a system in crisis, it would seem that the post-Front system worked exactly as one should have expected (even if the outcomes could be construed as negative by the given observer). One might prefer that the system produce different policy outcomes, but that would be a normative criticism, not empirical evidence of a crisis. Certainly, there is a key criticism to be made of Colombian parties in terms of their lack of programmatic behavior and their penchant for particularism (i.e., clientelistic practices in lieu of more serious policy proposals). However, there is little evidence to suggest that this is in any way a function of the National Front; rather it has been endemic to the electoral system used in Colombia until 2003.[32]

There seems to be an assumption in much of the writing on this topic that the masses are seeking radical change but have been denied that change by the oligarchs in the parties, and so they have had to turn to guerrilla warfare to achieve their goals. However, if such a general attitude toward the state of politics in Colombia has in fact been in place, then why has there never been sufficient popular support for the various revolutionary groups that have roamed the Colombian countryside since the early 1960s? While there are plenty of examples of policy inadequacy that one could note, they are not unique to Colombia, but rather are common to much of Latin America (e.g., in the areas of public health, education, infrastructure, and so on). Most of these problems are attributable to Colombia's level of development in terms of national wealth, not to the lack of the "representativeness" of the parties.

Getting back to the general question of how representative the NF era was, one could argue that the Front actually expanded representativeness in the Colombian state by insisting on partisan parity within the state, as the Liberals were an electoral majority and could have dominated the state via elections and executive appointments sans the Front.[33] Further, the Front guaranteed a Conservative president every other term, something that would likely not have happened if elections had been predicated on unregulated competition. One can easily argue that the system was insufficiently democratic, but it actually increased the broad representation of the two parties within the state.

The Exclusion Question

We are left, then, with the exclusion question: exactly how exclusionary was the NF, and to what degree can we blame the ongoing guerrilla violence on the argument that such actions were their only recourse? Did the Front exclude the masses in favor of the oligarchy, leading to both an increase in guerrilla violence and a lack of progressive third-party choices at the ballot box?

The best argument for this line of reasoning is the Movement of the 19th of April and its relationship to the 1970 presidential election. As noted in the previous chapter, serious questions surround the 1970 contest, and a substantial argument can be made that electoral fraud boosted Misael Pastrana of the PC to victory in lieu of Rojas, the ANAPO candidate. M-19 started its guerrilla campaign against the state for the stated purpose of protesting that event and took its name from the date of the election, April 19, 1970.

Of course, to use M-19 as an exemplar of the notion that exclusion led to violence is to ignore the fact the other major guerrilla groups had started fighting in the 1960s, with the FARC really able to trace its roots back to Liberal partisan fighters during *La Violencia*. Further, M-19 did not start operations until 1973, when the Front was coming to a close. Beyond that, the fact of the matter was that given the loose rules of the Front, dissident lists were allowed on the ballot. The exclusion argument is especially difficult to maintain given that there were leftists directly involved in electoral politics, such as the alliance, at one point during the Front, between the Communist Party of Colombia and a dissident Liberal group, the Revolutionary Liberal Movement (Dix 1980b, 135). Indeed, there is a simple test to be applied here: could candidates find a way onto the ballot using a unique label, and could voters freely choose those candidates? The answer is yes.

There are really only two caveats. First, under the strictures of the National Front, a Conservative vote tended to count slightly more than a Liberal vote. Is this enough to declare the system undemocratic, closed, or oligarchic? The fact that some voters are more favored than others by a given system is not uncommon in circumstances that are typically considered democratic. Think, for example, of any federal system in which an upper house of a bicameral legislature has seats allocated based on some function other than population—in such a case there will be some places where votes count for more than they do in other parts of the country. In the United States, for example, each state has two seats in the Senate regardless of its population. Thus the influence of a voter in Wyoming, with a small population, is some sixty-nine times greater in a Senate election than that of a voter in California, with a huge population.

Second, the alternation of the presidency during the National Front did create an important problem insofar as the leading candidate, spared from an interparty challenge, was likely to face no real competition. Still, dissident candidates could run. Indeed, the 1970 race has the virtue (if one can use the term in this context) of illustrating that the actual voting system was not preordained to produce a particular outcome. In other words, the 1970 elections did not start with the game fixed for Pastrana, but once it became clear that he was going to lose, then the mad scramble took place to fix the situation at the last minute (if we are to interpret the end result as one of fraud).

Given these factors, it is difficult to maintain that (1) the system was so exclusionary that violence was the only route opposition actors could pursue, and (2) the violence in Colombia is directly traceable, in any substantial way, to the Front. As Berry and Solaún put it: "in terms of past Colombian electoral and civil rights history, the National Front cannot be considered to have been unduly restrictive; it was a liberalizing departure from the post-1949 developments. In the past the basic political dilemma involved the alternatives of high competitive participation with *violencia* or peace with low participation" (1980, 441).

Summing Up the Issue of the Front

If we consider the comparability question, examine Dugas' four factors discussed above, plus evaluate the general exclusion hypothesis, the conventional assessments of the Front's effects on the parties are left wanting. Not only is there a major problem in comparing the pre-NF party system with the post-NF system, there is little solid evidence to suggest that the

Front itself created any of the shortcomings attributed to it. It is clear that the Front exacerbated the existing factionalization of the traditional parties and that the 1968 constitutional reform provided a new tool for pork-barrel politics. However, that does not amount to confirming the standard argument that the National Front created a "crisis" for the party system.

Further, it should not be forgotten that the Front was the mechanism that allowed for the return of civilian rule and democratic institutions to Colombia. The Front and its effects are therefore better viewed as part of the natural progression of the party system rather than as a rupture in the natural flow of Colombian politics. In others words, the Front did not introduce anything radically new into Colombian party politics—at worst it exacerbated existing tendencies that might have been amplified even without the Front's existence. There is no reason to assume that factionalization, clientelism, abstensionism, and the like would not have grown even without the parity and alternation requirements of the Front. Indeed, as chapter 5 will argue, factionalization was a logical response by power-seeking actors given the institutional parameters created by the personal list–PR system in place in Colombia *before* the Front.

Rethought

The rethinking proposed here may appear to be only subtle, but it is nonetheless quite important. If one blames Colombia's problems on a difficult to define "crisis" that eludes solution, then one focuses analytical time and energy in the wrong place. If the crisis thesis is correct, there were once more vigorous parties in Colombia that engaged in a mode of politics that had a real chance of solving Colombia's various problems. If this is true, the quest should be restoration. However, if such parties never existed (as the discussion above demonstrates), the issue is not the corruption of a prior party system, nor is the solution a return to some mythical past. If the main problematic behaviors, however, have other origins and causes, then that is where we should place our energies, in terms of both understanding them and devising solutions.

The conclusion to be reached by this discussion is that several basic tenets of the conventional wisdom regarding Colombia's party system should be rejected. The overarching notion to be rejected is that of crisis. The parties are not in crisis; indeed they have been, historically, among the more persistent political parties in the Western Hemisphere. Second, the National Front did not alter the parties as much as the conventional wisdom argues. Yes, the Front accelerated the factionalization of the parties, and a specific Front-era constitutional reform enhanced the capacity of politicians to dole out pork. However, the basic post-Front political behaviors (clientelism, abstentionism, etc.) are deeply rooted in Colombian politics and were not created by the Front. Third, the exclusion hypothesis lacks merit. While it is true that several key guerrilla groups emerged during the Front era, there is little evidence to suggest that the reason they emerged was because of the rules of the Front. Yes, the M-19 (a post-Front group) emerged in response to alleged electoral fraud in 1970, but the FARC had its origins in pre-Front violence, and the rules of the Front were such that it was possible for even leftist politicians to acquire ballot access. Hence there are serious empirical problems with the claim that excluded groups had to turn to violence as their only means of political recourse.

So where does this lead us? A better way to look at the evolution of the party system is not to allow the lens of *bipartidismo* be the main means by which we view the development of the party system. The parties are not the independent variable here, affecting all other aspects of the system. Rather, they should be viewed as a dependent variable reacting to the institutions and the incentive structures created by the rules of those institutions.

Working along those lines, chapter 5 examines the long-term evolution of the electoral rules and other pertinent state structures to explain why the parties have developed as they have. Chapter 6 goes on to look in detail at strategic choices made by the parties post-Front and especially at key reforms in the 1991 Constitution (which was further modified in a significant way in 2003): reforms involving the election of the Senate and how those reforms have affected party behavior.

CHAPTER 5

Parties: Reform and Adaptation

> *The world changes, societies and nations also change, and consequently, political parties, unless they want to perish, have to change, in order to adapt to the society in which they are active.*
> — *Semana*, August 29, 1955 (as quoted by Fluharty 1957, 259)

IF, AS ARGUED in the previous chapter, we should downplay the notion that the National Front led to a crisis of the party system, how should we understand the behaviors of political actors within that system? The answer is that a far better approach is to look at the long-term interactions between politicians and the incentive structures created by the electoral rules. This chapter takes a mainly narrative approach to describing the prevailing rules that have been in place in Colombia during the twentieth and into the twenty-first centuries. What have those rules been, and what have been the basic responses of political actors to those institutional parameters? Chapter 6 will take the themes generated from the discussion in this chapter and examine the specific behaviors and strategies that the parties utilized to navigate the Colombian political landscape.

From Duverger through Rae, Lijphart, Cox, and Taagepera and Shugart, it is has been empirically demonstrated that electoral rules have political consequences, influencing the way voters cast their ballots and the strategic choices politicians make as to how to pursue office.[1] The tools used to analyze these behaviors all start with some simple data: the numbers of votes won by candidates and parties, and the commensurate numbers of seats garnered by those votes in accordance with specific sets of rules. Given such information about rules and results, a key place to start answering the question of why a party system looks as it does, and why its constituent elements behave as they do, is to look at the electoral rules under which those actors operate.

The basic theoretical assumption that undergirds this chapter is that actors enter politics seeking power and that as they seek access to it, a major influence over the behavior is the prevailing rules of competition. As noted in chapter 1, the concept of "power" being used here is very generic, and it is assumed that the precise motivation for a given candidate or party will vary greatly.[2] In a democratic setting, power seekers must understand the electoral rules and adapt to them in a way that enhances the given power-seeking actor's access to the levers of government via the process of elections. While given actors may make miscalculations along the way, it is assumed that the basic shape of the system will derive from the collective responses of power seekers to the system that they have to work within. As such, the party system, as defined by the number of consistent participants in electoral contests, is a response to the basic rules of the game. Certainly these are not the sole factors that affect behavior, but they are the ones primarily being addressed here.

This chapter has two main sections. The first is an overview of the electoral rules in Colombia over time, with a detailed discussion of the 1958–2006 period. The second section looks at how those rules have shaped the behavior of power-seeking actors, and thereby the shape of the party system. The time under scrutiny in that section is 1974 and onward, as we have already dealt with the National Front previously in the text. There is also a concluding section that examines the shape of the party system as of the 2006 elections.

Electoral Rules over Time

While we are ultimately concerned with the evolution of the party system after the end of the National Front, it is worthwhile to understand the broad history of elections in Colombia. The following contains a look at the basic evolution of the process of legislative election in Colombia as far back as the nineteenth century. Understanding where the system was prior to the Front (which is often where most discussions of Colombian politics start), we can know what kinds of deviations were introduced. Further, it is worth noting that conflict over electoral rules has a long history in Colombia, which is ultimately not surprising given that, as has already been noted, political parties and the constitutional order have both been of great importance to the political development of the state.

After the discussion of the early rules, we move to a specific detailing of the rules and their changing from 1958 onward, covering the Front but with specific emphasis on the post-Front era: the dismantlement period (1974–1991), the new rules instituted by the 1991 Constitution (1991–2003), and the post-reform period (2003 onward).

The Early Rules

From independence to 1905, Colombian congressional elections functioned under various simple majority systems (Eastman 1982, 226). From

1822 to 1888 the main type of system was called the *voto en bloque* ("block vote"), in which the party list that won the plurality of the vote in a given district won all the seats in that district—although, during the federal era, different departments had the option of using different methods for electing members of Congress. From 1888 to 1905 the system was one of single member districts with plurality winners.[3]

In keeping with the basic narrative of Colombian political development, the electoral process was a point of contention, as the *voto en bloque* system in particular was one in which it was possible for one party to utterly dominate the legislature. Indeed, one of the issues that led to the War of the Thousand Days was the fairness of the electoral system.[4] The postwar electoral reforms responded to that issue, leading first to a system that guaranteed minority representation in Congress and then to the proportional representation system that would remain in place until the early twenty-first century.

In 1905, President Reyes decreed that in all popular elections for legislative bodies the right of the minority to be represented would be recognized (Dix 1967, 130). This declaration led to Legislative Act No. 8 of 1905, which created what was called the *voto incompleto* ("incomplete vote"), wherein the numbers of seats in electoral districts were divisible by three, so that two-thirds of the seats went to the party list with the most votes and the remaining one-third to the list with the second-highest number of votes.[5]

The constitutional framework for the Colombian electoral system was established by Legislative Act No. 3 of 1910, which set down the basic parameters for the electoral processes that were legally permissible.[6] This amendment allowed for a menu of options, specifically the usage of the *voto incompleto*, the *cuociente electoral* (electoral quota with largest remainders), the *voto acumulativo*, or whatever system that would assure *representación proporcional* of the parties. The 1910 amendment left it up to the law to determine which was to be used (Eastman 1982, 227). An interesting footnote in the history of the *voto incompleto* is that some Conservatives figured out that they could offer multiple lists in a given district, allowing both the first- and second-place winners to be from the PC and hence returning some districts to the same outcomes as the *voto en bloque*. This practice was banned via Law 13 of 1920 "by specifying that parties, not lists, had to be represented in Congress" (Mazzuca and Robinson 2006, 38). However, the offering of multiple lists representing party factions would be a very significant practice in Colombian legislative elections during much of the twentieth century. This strategizing was a foreshadowing of

Box 5.1

SIMPLE EXAMPLE OF THE HARE QUOTA

Consider a district with a district magnitude (M) of five seats and a vote total of 100,000 votes (V). In such a situation under the Hare quota ($q = V/M$), the distribution of seats would be as follows, with the majority of the seats being quota seats (QS), and a handful being largest remainder seats (LRS).

List	Votes	QS	LRS	Total seats
Party A	49,000	2 (40,000 votes used)	0 (third-largest remainder of 9,000 votes, no seats left)	2 (both QS)
Party B	33,000	1 (20,000 votes used)	1 (first largest remainder of 13,000 votes)	2 (1 QS + 1 LRS)
Party C	11,000	0 (not enough votes for a QS)	1 (second-largest remainder of 11,000 votes)	1 (1 LRS)
Party D	7,000	0 (not enough votes for a QS)	0 (fourth-largest remainder of 7,000 votes, no seats left)	0
Totals	100,000	3 QSs allocated	2 LRSs allocated	5 seats allocated

Source: Adapted from Lijphart 1994, 155.

party behavior later in the century. Not only would it be an occasional practice prior to the Rojas dictatorship; it would also become a key feature in the institutional fabric of the National Front. Further, as will be argued below, it would become a practice that very much encouraged Colombia's party system to remain primarily of the two-party variety well into the 1980s despite the proportional electoral system installed after 1929.

Law 31 of 1929 instituted the use of the quota with largest remainders, with the provision that no party could win more than two-thirds of the seats. This basic system would remain in place until 2003. The quota employed was the Hare (*quota = votes/seats*), with seats being allocated to lists first via quota, with any remaining seats assigned to the lists with the largest remainders (box 5.1 illustrates how the system works). The lists were closed, meaning that voters could vote only for a list, not for their preferred candidate on a list. But, as noted above, the practice of offering multiple lists per party per district would be a major feature of this system, starting especially with the Front and accelerating into the 1970s. As such, the system was technically one of closed list–PR, and it is better described as personal list–PR. The significance of that fact will be discussed in greater detail below.

Having established some historical context and the basics of the system, we can move to examine the specifics under the National Front, the dismantlement period, the 1991 constitutional changes, and the changes made by the 2003 reforms.

The National Front (1958–1970)

The 1957 plebiscite, which became Legislative Act No. 1 of 1959, expressly required (in Article 2) the usage of the quota for districts with more than one list competing for PL or PC shares of seats in that district (Eastman 1982, 235). Article 6 of that document also addressed the issue. Legislative Act No. 1 of 1968 (Article 50) enshrined the quota-with-largest-remainder system into the Constitution of 1886 (Article 172), removing the power of the legislature to determine the type of PR system to be used in Colombia (Eastman 1982, 237).

Box 5.2 details the overall electoral system for the National Front period, which was identical to that of the pre-Front era save for the key aspects of alternation of the presidency and parity in other offices.

The Desmonte and Onward (1974–1991)

The post-Front period is often referred to as the "dismantlement" (*desmonte*) and began in earnest with the 1974 elections, which were the first since before the dictatorship to function without the strictures of alternation for the presidency and parity in all other elected offices.

The first several presidential administrations after the Front were termed a period of dismantlement because it was one of transition from over a decade of a specific set of institutional parameters and because, as a result of the 1968 constitutional reform, some of the elements of the Front were slowly removed, rather than being abruptly ended. Specifically, Article 120 of the 1886 Constitution was amended to require that parity in the cabinet, governorships, mayoralties, and the civil service would remain in place until 1978. Additionally, that article was further amended to require that starting in 1978 the cabinet and other aspects of public administration should be filled in a way that would create "adequate and equitable representation" for the party distinct from that of the president.[7] Through such measures, a certain amount of the flavor of the Front was constitutionally mandated for that period. Of the post-Front administrations only the Barco administration (1986–1990) had a unipartisan cabinet, as the Conservatives declined the cabinet posts that Barco offered.[8]

Box 5.2
BASIC ELECTORAL RULES, 1958– 1970

Executive Offices
President
- Plurality election.
- No immediate reelection.
- PC and PL alternated control of the presidency. (Each contest was made up of an official candidate and a number of "dissident" candidates, i.e., any non-"official" list offered under the PL or PC, which could be factional lists or third-party lists like those offered by ANAPO.)

Vice President
No vice president (instead, an appointed designate).

Governors
Appointed by president, half to PC and half to PL.

Mayors
Appointed by president, half to PC and half to PL.

Legislative Offices
Congress, Departmental Assemblies, and Municipal Councils
- Process of election in all cases: Personal list–PR (i.e., closed lists with multiple lists per party allowed) using the Hare quota with largest remainders (see box 5.1).
- During the Front each chamber was divided equally, with 50% of the seats going to the PL and the PC respectively. Party factions competed for the seats.
- Congress (Chamber and Senate) elected in department-based districts.

Ballots
Party produced (often by specific factions).

Box 5.3 shows that during this period the basic rules were identical to those in effect during the Front period, save for the elimination of parity and alternation. The very end of the period marked a shift to the popular election of mayors and eventually a move to replace the 1886 Constitution and thereby to changes in some of the electoral rules. Thus, from 1930 to 1991, there was a great deal of continuity to the electoral rules. Still, the end of this epoch in Colombian politics did see the beginning of alterations to the institutional structure of Colombian democracy. The ability for local voters to choose their own mayors, along with other decentralization

Box 5.3
BASIC ELECTORAL RULES, 1974–1990

Executive Offices
  President
  • Plurality election.
  • No immediate reelection.
  Vice President
  No vice president (instead, an appointed designate).
  Governors
  Appointed by president.
  Mayors
  • Appointed by president (1974–1988).
  • Plurality election to two-year terms (1988–1990).

Legislative Offices
  Congress, Departmental Assemblies, and Municipal Councils
  • Process of election in all cases: Personal list–PR (i.e., closed lists with multiple lists per party allowed) using the Hare quota ($q = V/M$) with largest remainders.
  • Congress (Chamber and Senate) elected in department-based districts.

· Ballots
  Party produced (often by specific factions).[a]

  [a] Starting with the 1990 presidential elections, state-produced ballots were introduced.

moves, was an attempt to increase local power and to encourage participation in politics so as to provide a strengthening of the existing institutional order and to lessen the appeal of revolutionary change as promised by guerrilla groups. The political decentralization of the mayoralties also diminished the patronage power of the president, who previously had appointed those officers. Another change of note at the very end of this period was the move to state-produced ballots. A detailed discussion of the evolution of the ballot in Colombia, along with examples, can be found in appendix 1.

The 1991 Constitution, Phase One (1991–2003)

The new constitution brought a number of changes to the electoral order in Colombia (see box 5.4). In terms of the executive branch, the election of

---

Box 5.4
BASIC ELECTORAL RULES, 1991– 2002

Executive Offices
President
- Absolute majority required for election (runoff if needed).
- No reelection.
- Four-year terms.

Vice President
Elected as part of presidential slate.

Governors
Elected via plurality vote (three-year terms).

Mayors
Elected via plurality vote (three-year terms).

Legislative Offices
Congress, Departmental Assemblies, and Municipal Councils
- Process of election in all cases: Personal list–PR (i.e., closed lists with multiple lists per party allowed) using the Hare quota ($q = V/M$) with largest remainders.
- Chamber elected in department-based districts (plus special districts for specific set-aside seats).
- Senate elected in two national districts (one with 100 seats, and a special national district with 2 seats for indigenous persons).

Ballots
State produced: one ballot per office.

---

the president was moved from a plurality system to one that required an absolute majority, hence necessitating a runoff provision. The process of political decentralization that began in the 1980s was furthered as governors, along with mayors, were moved from the realm of the appointed to that of the elected.

In terms of the legislature, bicameralism was retained, but the sizes of both chambers were contracted. The most significant change, which will be dealt with in greater detail in chapter 6, was the transformation of the Senate into a body that was elected primarily from one national electoral district. Set-aside seats were also created for minorities—specifically for indigenous persons and blacks.

Box 5.5

BASIC ELECTORAL RULES, 2003 ONWARD

Executive Offices
President
- Absolute majority required for election (runoff if needed).
- Reelection allowed (with a maximum of two terms total).
- Four-year terms.

Vice President
Elected as part of presidential slate.

Governors
Elected via plurality vote (three-year terms).

Mayors
Elected via plurality vote (three-year terms).

Legislative Offices
Congress, Departmental Assemblies, and Municipal Councils
- Process of election in all cases: D'Hondt method (see box 5.7). Each party limited to one list per office. Parties have the option for the lists to be open or closed.
- Chamber elected in department-based districts (plus special districts for specific set-aside seats).
- Senate elected in two national districts (one with 100 seats, and a special national district with 2 seats for indigenous persons).

Ballots
State produced: one ballot per office.

The 1991 Constitution, Phase Two (2003 onward)

The start of the twenty-first century saw two key electoral reforms—one that affected legislative elections and one that changed the number of terms that the president could serve (see box 5.5).

The most significant electoral reform in the history of Colombia was instituted via Legislative Act No. 1 of 2003 (the key aspects of which are detailed in box 5.6). It did away with the two most important elements of the electoral system most responsible for the shape of the party system: it replaced the Hare quota with the D'Hondt method (called in Colombia the *cifra repartidora*; see box 5.7) and also forced parties to offer only one list per office. Those two fairly simple changes have set Colombia's party system

---

Box 5.6

KEY ELECTORAL REFORMS, LEGISLATIVE ACT NO. 1 OF 2003[a]

- Requires parties to offer only one list per office (Article 263).
- Institutes the D'Hondt method (*cifra repartidora*) for legislative elections (Article 263).
- Installs an electoral threshold (*umbral*) for legislative elections
    - For the Senate: 2% of the valid vote (votes for candidates + blank votes).
    - For the Chamber and other offices: 50% of the electoral quota (i.e., $q = V/M$).
- Forbids simultaneous membership in more than one party (Article 107).
- Parties lose their legal status (*personaría jurídica*) if they win less than 2% of the vote (Article 108).

[a] Full document is available online at http://*www.secretariasenado.gov.co/leyes/ ACL01003.HTM*

---

onto a substantially new path that will allow for what the critics of the system have long desired: the formation of serious and long-lasting electoral alternatives to the traditional parties. Further, the new rules installed an electoral threshold of 2 percent of the vote or 50 percent of the quota.

While it is true that the reforms that had culminated in the 1991 Constitution had already created substantial changes to the party system, those alterations had not fomented a long-term and clear change to the influence of the traditional parties, especially the Liberals. The new conditions set in motion in 2003, however, have already created a clear effect on the party system, as the 2006 congressional elections have demonstrated.

These changes have radically altered the calculations of power-seeking actors in Colombia (and removed some of the electoral strategies that have been employed in the past, as discussed in detail in chapter 6).

The Evolution of the Party System

The question then becomes, what effects have the above rules had on the shape of the Colombian party system? If, as argued above, power-seeking actors will adapt to the rules of a given electoral game to create, over time, a party system, what has been the reaction of the political actors in Colombia to the rules, and how have changes to the rules altered the behaviors in question?

We know that the basic history of Colombian parties has been one dominated by *bipartidismo* (i.e., the supremacy of the two traditional parties, the

Box 5.7

EXAMPLE OF THE D'HONDT METHOD

The D'Hondt method is a system of allocating seats to an electoral list using a set of divisors (1, 2, 3, 4, ...) to determine the highest averages. Consider a district with seven seats, five parties, and 10,000 votes. Using the D'Hondt method, the allocation would work like this:

	Votes/1		*Votes/2*		*Votes/3*		*Votes/4*		*Seats*
Party A	4,850	(1st)	2,425	(3rd)	1,616.67	(4th)	1,212.5	(7th)	4
Party B	2,900	(2nd)	1,450	(5th)	966.67		725		2
Party C	1,400	(6th)	700		466.67		350		1
Party D	750		375		250.00		187.5		0
Party E	100		50		33.33		25		0

In the first column we have divided the votes won by each party by the first divisor (*1*); we then allocate the first seat to Party A, as it has the highest average. We then divide the votes by the second divisor (*2*) and look at both columns to allocate the next two seats: the second seat to the second-highest average (Party B) and the third seat to the third-highest average (Party A). We then divide the votes by the third divisor (*3*) and look at the averages in all three columns to allocate the next three seats, and so forth until we have allocated all seven seats.

Note: Table adapted from Taagepera and Shugart 1989, 32. For the specifics of the Colombian usage of the process see http://www.registraduria.gov.co/Elecciones/refor_elect.htm.

Conservative Party and the Liberal Party). Yet, does that tell us enough? A cursory review of the electoral rules would suggest that a quota system with largest remainders should produce a multiparty system—so why did strong *bipartidismo* sustain itself for so long, and what finally caused that to change?

The Number of Parties

The place to start the discussion, and to easily track the evolution of the system, is to look at the number of parties represented in the Congress and their relative strength in terms of seats. Table 5.1 provides three different metrics for this purpose for the post–National Front period. The first is the Laakso-Taagepera effective number of parliamentary parties index,[9] the second is a raw count of the number of parties with seats, and the third is the percentage of seats belonging to the two traditional parties, the Conservatives and the Liberals.[10]

What we see is a fairly stable two-party system under the 1886 constitutional regime (i.e., 1974–1990).[11] The advent of the 1991 Constitution, however, sees an initial move into a multiparty system that substantially expands by 2002 and 2006 (and note that in 2006 a new set of electoral rules was in place).

It is worth noting that during the 1974–1990 period a handful of third parties offered lists, and some of those lists did win seats. However, they were inconsequential in determining the shape or behavior of the legislature—especially given the PL's continued majority status in both chambers until the 2002 elections.[12] The high-water mark for third parties in this period was the 1986 Congress, where third parties controlled 10.6 percent of the seats of the Chamber and 11.4 percent of the Senate—and those numbers owed much to the fact that Luis Carlos Galán's New Liberal Party had split from the mainline Liberals.[13] A clear shift takes place in all the metrics starting in 1991, when a new Congress was elected under the new constitution (the mandate of the Congress elected in 1990 having been revoked by the National Constituent Assembly). The 2006 elections show a change in the absolute number of parties holding seats, which speaks to the decrease in fractionalization brought about by the rules instituted under the 2003 reform.

That the Colombian party system is evolving and responding to new rules and political circumstances is empirically clear. However, the what and the why of the changes require further explanation. Before moving on

Table 5.1

The Evolution of the Party System in the Colombian Congress

	Effective number of parliamentary parties (N_S)		Number of parties holding seats		Percentage of seats held by the PC + PL	
	Chamber	*Senate*	*Chamber*	*Senate*	*Chamber*	*Senate*
1974	2.28	2.17	4	4	90.0%	92.8%
1978	2.06	2.01	4	3	97.5%	99.1%
1982	1.98	2.04	4	4	99.0%	98.2%
1986	2.46	2.47	13	9	89.4%	88.6%
1990	2.20	2.24	18	11	91.0%	91.2%
1991	3.03	3.10	19	20	70.0%	63.7%
1994	2.82	2.90	27	23	78.5%	74.5%
1998	3.27	3.56	40	27	69.6%	64.7%
2002	7.39	9.19	56	47	46.1%	41.2%
2006	7.60	7.10	23	12	38.6%	35.3%

to the issue of how given rules influence the way office seekers behave, the issue of party label and how it influences counting (and therefore the empirical measure of system change) needs to be addressed.

Party Label in the Colombian Context

Counting the number of political parties running for office and the seats they win is a fundamental staple of electoral studies and is usually a straightforward affair: the basic delineator is the unique party label. The choice of party label is a clear and very public choice made by a power-seeking actor in an electoral context as a shorthand for differentiating candidates in terms of their likely behavior if elected. Indeed, I would argue that party label and the seeking of votes in the hopes of winning office are the two main constituent elements of a political party. The choice of label (and thereby party membership, broadly defined) is a strategic one aimed at enhancing the chances that the given actor will win elective office. Indeed, labels serve a number of key functions including signaling to voters how one is likely to behave in office, with whom a given candidate will caucus in the legislature, as well as whom that candidate will support to control the executive. As long as it is assumed that power seekers enter elections for the purpose of winning votes to win office, and to then seek certain outcomes once in office, we should treat the selection of party label as purposeful and meaningful.[14] To ignore or downplay signals from political actors is to remove from analysis a clear attempt at public communication by those actors.

For example: the choice of party affiliation can lead directly to victory or defeat. A specific example of this would be U.S. representative Ron Paul from the Fourteenth District of Texas. Paul describes himself as a "libertarian" and was the 1988 presidential candidate of the Libertarian Party. However, during Paul's stints in the U.S. Congress (1976, 1979–1985, and 1997–2009[15]) he has always run as a Republican (and, indeed, in 2007 declared himself a candidate to be the Republican Party's presidential candidate). What we see in the case of Paul, especially in his second campaign for Congress (given his 1988 candidacy as a Libertarian), is a strategic choice of label. Many of Paul's positions fit the Libertarian party platform better than the Republican, but had he run in 1996 as a Libertarian, holding those same views he had as a Republican candidate, there is little doubt that he never would have been elected to the U.S. House. Ironically, Paul defeated another party switcher in the 1996 GOP primary. Greg Laughlin had been the representative from the Fourteenth District as a Democrat, but because of the Republican takeover of the House in the 1994 elections, Laughlin decided to switch parties; he then lost to Paul in the Republican primary. So, in the Laughlin case, we see a strategic choice that did not play out as expected.

Now, the above examples are pretty straightforward: Libertarian or Republican, Republican or Democrat, and so forth. In regard to Colombia, however, the issue of label has historically created problems for analysts in terms of methodology (i.e., simply how best to count), which, in turn, created analytical questions about the evolution of the party system. These problems manifest in four specific ways, three of them quite concrete and the fourth somewhat abstract. The three concrete issues are the modifiers used by traditional party candidates, the creation of splinter parties with variations on traditional labels, and the creation of partisan coalitions. The more abstract issue has to do with the tendency within Colombian political culture to associate a candidate or group with a traditional party even after that person (or persons) has left that party (basically: once a Liberal/Conservative, always a Liberal/Conservative). More specifically, the first issue is that within the mainline parties it was not unusual for individual lists to add modifiers to the traditional party label (e.g., "Convergencia Liberal" [Liberal Convergence] rather than just "Liberal"). The second is that some political actors have struck out on their own and created parties that used a modified version of the traditional label in a way that may be difficult to differentiate from the first example (e.g., "New Liberalism" or the "National Conservative Movement"). The third is that of the existence of coalitional lists that often contain one (and sometimes even both) of the mainline parties (e.g., the PL + UP list that won a Chamber seat in 1986—a coalition of the Liberals and the Patriotic Union). All these issues create questions about how these labels ought to be classified in terms of the number of parties.

In the case of modifiers tacked onto the traditional party labels, this is not an unusual occurrence in Colombian politics. The problem is easily overcome methodologically by the fact that when the National Civil Registry counts the votes, it ignores such modifiers and simply pools those lists under either the PC or PL headings.

However, there are also cases where what appears at first glance to be nothing more than another modifier being applied to a traditional label ends up being a new party. The most famous example is Nuevo Liberalismo or "New Liberalism," the party formed when Luis Carlos Galán split from the mainline PL in the early 1980s to run congressional lists as well as to launch a presidential bid in 1982 (which led to a split vote between the PL and NL, and therefore to a PC victory).[16] Again, the easiest way to deal with whether such labels constitute different parties is whether the candidates in fact differentiate themselves from the traditional parties and therefore whether the Registry counts their votes separately.

Another problem is dealing with electoral coalitions—the combination of two or more parties endorsing a specific electoral list. Counting coalitions is tricky, and one can reasonably go in more than one direction. For example, one could simply count all lists that contain the name of a traditional party as belonging to that party, so that all PL + X lists would go to the PL (of course, the PL-PC coalitional list that won a seat in the 1990 Senate would give anyone following this procedure counting fits). Another option is to consider coalitional lists as unique strategic choices and therefore count them as unique parties for the purpose of a given election, which is how they are treated in this work. Regardless of how they are counted, their numbers are quite small, and therefore have only a marginal effect on calculations. Their biggest effect is to inflate the count of individual parties holding seats in the middle section of table 5.1.

In some cases the coalitional lists do raise questions, such as the case of Fabio Valencia Cossio, a senator who ran under the Progressive Force label in 1991 and then under a Progressive Force–Conservative Party coalition in 1994 and 1998, and was part of the PC leadership during that period. An argument could be made that since Valencia had a prominent role affiliated with the PC, the coalitional nature of his list should be ignored. However, the issue here is not about what a power seeker does once elected but, rather, what choices are made in the pursuance of office. Indeed, one could argue that the flagging PC turned to Valencia at least in part because of his demonstrated electoral prowess in Antioquia (as well as nationally).[17] Therefore, to treat his strategic choices as nonexistent fails to take into account that conscious choices had been made by the candidate and his allies. At a minimum, the Valencia case does illustrate the fluidity of party label in some cases in Colombia and does explain why some observers choose to simply see most political actors in shades of red (the PL) and blue (the PC). It is simply easier in many cases to do so.

As for the abstract element of party identification, there is a propensity in the political science literature, and in the press, to view almost all partisan political activity in Colombia as taking place within the two broad categories of "traditional" and "nontraditional." By traditional is meant "Liberal" or "Conservative," and by nontraditional is meant truly new political actors. The problem comes in that any action by a so-called traditional politico is considered "Liberal" or "Conservative" even if the actor in question is deviating from the traditional label, often using a wholly new label. For example, in 1994 and 1998 Andrés Pastrana ran as an independent candidate for the presidency (winning in 1998).[18] On the 1994 ballot he was listed simply as "Andres Presidente" and in 1998 under the label "Gran Alianza por Cambio" with the slogan "El Cambio es Andres" as his party symbol[19]—nevertheless he is frequently identified as the Conservative candidate. Now, it is true that the PC endorsed his candidacy in both elections and that the younger Pastrana ran for, and won the mayoralty of, Bogotá in 1988 as a Conservative.[20] More to the point, his father, Misael Pastrana, was a Conservative when he served as president in the 1970–1974 period and was subsequently a key figure in the party for years afterward. However, when we look at the younger Pastrana's political career after his two-year stint as Bogotá's mayor, we see that he clearly and strategically eschewed the PC label. In 1991 he headed a list of Senate candidates under the banner of a new party, the New Democratic Force—a label he did not use in his presidential bids. What we see here is a clear set of strategic choices in regard to party label that Pastrana made because he believed they enhanced his electoral chances.

The real problem emerges, in terms of proper identification and analysis, when observers conflate pure PC and PL candidates and winners with other candidates who have made the strategic choice to run under unique labels. It is not unusual to encounter seat counts that include clear PC and PL winners with other lists that the compiler of the seat count believes to fit into one of the two traditional camps—this is especially true of various splinter parties related in one way or another to the PC. For example, in a table summarizing the breakdown of the Senate, Dugas (2000, 83) attributes 29 seats to the PC in the 1998 Senate, while the calculations used above for table 5.1 assign only 17 seats to the PC. Dugas takes the 17 seats that won under lists with the PC label and adds 12 other seats won with various other labels: the Progressive Force (4), the National Conservative Movement (4), the New Democratic Force (2), Independent Conservatism (2), the National Salvation Movement (1), and a coalitional list (1).[21] There are numerous examples of this type of accounting in the literature.[22] Some authors try to solve this problem by classifying third parties as belonging to either the Conservative or Liberal "families"—which at least allows the unique labels to be noted (see, for example, Muñoz 2003).

This propensity to use "Liberal" and "Conservative" as a cultural über-label often manifests in the press as well—and not just over issues like candidacies or seat counts. A rather clear example would be a 2007 obituary in the Bogotá daily *El Tiempo* of a sitting Colombian senator, which ran under the headline "Liberal Senator Luis Guillermo Vélez Dies of a Heart

Attack."[23] The only problem with such a designation was that the senator in question had been elected under the label of the new party called the Party of National Social Unity (la U). Indeed, he had publicly split with the PL. Nevertheless, in Colombia, once a Liberal (or Conservative), always a Liberal (or Conservative)—at least in the eyes of many.

The desire to pigeonhole new parties as "belonging" to either the PC or PL misses a fundamental point about how new parties might be formed in the context of new rules created in an existing party system: many of the new parties will come out of the old. In other words, to count new label creation as really being nothing more than the old politicians using a new name is to miss the significance of the fact that the established politicians believe that there is a strategic advantage to be had by using a new label. If we look at the old-line Conservative who adopts a new party label and say to ourselves, "Oh, that's just the same old fellow using a new name, so really it is just more of the same," we miss the fact that for such behavior to really be "more of the same," the politician in question *would still be using the old label* and seeking votes the old way. The fact that old guard politicos decide that changing the way they do business is needed is a sign that the system is evolving. While we would obviously expect an evolving party system to see truly new actors entering the fray, the fact that old dogs decide that they must learn new tricks is significant in and of itself and should not be dismissed out of hand.

It is worth noting that some of this confusion is a legacy of the National Front and the fact that the legal status of political parties, and therefore control over labels, was not settled until the 1990s. If we look back to the discussion of the National Front, the ability of candidates to offer "dissident" lists and the idea of "movements" within parties emerged as part of the basic political lexicon in Colombia. Even ANAPO, which was its own party, had to run under the Front's rules as ANAPO-PL or ANAPO-PC. As such, it should be no surprise that there is a long-term mind-set that sees all politics as bracketed by the PL and PC.

Although political parties had been mentioned in Colombian legislation as early as 1905, they were not legally defined until the passage of Law 58 of 1985 (Hernández 2006, 335–336). The codification was integrated into the Constitution of 1991 and further elucidated in Law 130 of 1994. Because parties were granted legal control over their labels and further because legally recognized parties were entitled to partial public financing of campaigns, it became a matter of legal record as to whether a specific label actually constituted a separate political party.[24] After the passage of the 1994 law, candidates had to receive official permission to use a specific label.

The Rules and Adaptation

The conventional wisdom, as discussed at length in the previous chapter, has long contained the argument that the National Front's legacy was to cut off political expression by other actors and therefore has led to violence. However, I would submit that the Colombian political system, even during the National Front, has always been open to entry by nontraditional actors (again, defined as other than the PC and PL). Several factors have curtailed the success of such actors, with clientelism leading to entrenched power by long-standing elites certainly being one of them. The inherent conservatism of rural voters is another (and the malapportionment that has long favored those rural voters). However, a key factor that has made it historically difficult for new forces to achieve electoral success in Colombia has been the very nature of the electoral rules themselves. While the laws have not specifically favored the PL and PC in some codified or overt fashion, elements of those rules have long made it advantageous for politicians to affiliate with one of the traditional parties.

Several institutional ingredients were mixed together to create the conditions that shaped the Colombian party system. The recipe was altered in 1991 and then again in 2003. At each alteration, we can see a clear change in the behavior of power seekers as measured in multiple ways in table 5.1. The question then becomes, what specific arrangement of ingredients led to a specific configuration of actors? When speaking of "ingredients," we are dealing with the general institutional structure of the state in terms of where power resides and how it is accessed. We then have to look at the specific electoral alchemy of the system: the transformation of votes into office.

Ultimately the question comes down to what one has to do under the rules to win a seat and therefore what kind of behavior a power seeker must engage in to win. Can that actor go it alone using a unique label and organization, or must that actor join up with a far larger organization to have a chance to win office and influence the government? The basic question becomes whether the given set of ingredients encourages a two-party system or a multiparty system.

Let's consider: what is the advantage of forming one's own party? Presumably this is done because a given power seeker believes that he or she would be a better officeholder than someone else (or that his/her copartisans would be better in office than some other slate). The problem is, of course, can that candidate win? It is the kind of dilemma faced by Ron Paul as noted above: a serious chance to win as a Republican trumps a guaranteed loss as a Libertarian any day (even if Paul better "fits" the Libertarians).

And even if one wins as a third-party candidate in a two-party dominant system, one is often shut out of the advantages that come with belonging to a large party. To enhance his or her ability to influence policy, a hypothetical third-party legislator might caucus with a large party, but the degree to which that legislator would be granted access to all the benefits that members of the larger party enjoy would be in question (such as committee assignments, seniority, and so forth)—of course, much would depend on how much the larger party needs the vote of the third-party legislator!

1974–1991

As one notes the strength of the two parties during the 1974–1991 period, one is tempted to look solely at history and political culture for explanations. After all, as noted in the previous chapter, Colombians were born into parties and saw those parties as part of their identities. Additionally, the two most significant political events of the first six decades of the twentieth century were based on the parties: *La Violencia* and the National Front. However, as compelling as the forces of history may be, they are insufficient to explain the party system, especially in the post-Front era.

In looking first at the 1974–1991 period, we should remember that Colombia was a presidential system, with a unitary state where governmental largesse flowed from the national budget through the hands of the legislators down to the localities. Further, the president held appointment power for local executives—and while the Colombian presidency was not as abused an office as perhaps others in the region, there were decree powers to be had for the person who occupied the Casa de Nariño.[25] A further aspect of the presidential prize is that, in the career paths of major nominees during this period, a stint at the cabinet level is a common denominator.[26]

In this general context we must also remember that clientelistic practices were a key political process and that connections to senators and representatives were essential parts of any such clientele network.[27] This relationship is well illustrated in the discussion of the ballot format during the 1974–1990 period in appendix 1. In looking at the 1974 ballot in figures A.1 and A.2, one can see how the different offices are linked in one long ballot, with the senatorial candidate being a key departmental political leader, the representative being perhaps more localized, and then from there the assembly and council candidates being local leaders. Although voters could separate out the ballot into smaller ballots and mix and match different candidates to different offices, the structure of the ballot lent itself to factional slates being voted on together. In other words, while split-ticket voting was possible, straight-ticket (indeed, straight-faction) voting was encouraged by ballot format. As such, aspiring politicians in given departments needed political patrons on whose lists they could ride. Otherwise they might find themselves entirely without a clientele network and unable to bring home the bacon to the voters.

During this period there were really only two main electoral prizes within the Colombian state: the presidency and a majority in Congress. Indeed, the only other elected offices in Colombia were the relatively weak departmental assemblies and municipal councils—and they were linked, as noted above, to congressional candidates and their networks. In such a system, if a group of power seekers were looking at what they needed to do to control as many of the resources of the state as possible, they would have to be able to build either a stand-alone majority party or a coalition of like-minded parties. The fact that the system was presidential made the former option more attractive, as it is more difficult to share the presidency with coalition partners than it is to share the government in a parliamentary system.

From here we can see how the electoral rules specifically worked within this institutional context to promote a two-party system. The procedure to elect the president was one of plurality: the candidate with the most votes won the presidential prize. For Congress, the process was one of list proportional representation with largest remainders.

On the face of it, that type of electoral process should contribute to multiple parties, because winning seats in the legislature in such a system does not require coming in first, and so parties do not have to be large in size to achieve representation (as the example in box 5.1 shows). Typically in such systems each party submits one list of candidates per district, and then the seats are allocated to each list based on the votes received under the quota formula being used. If a list receives enough votes for four seats, then the fifth candidate and on down the list are out of luck. Now suppose that this fifth candidate believes that she could win a seat by herself should she form her own party; in that case a list PR system provides an incentive for such behavior in a way that a single-member–district, first-past-the-post system like that in the United States does not. Indeed, a fifth-place finisher in the United States is simply a loser who, if she wishes to have any influence in the political system, needs to become active in one of the two major political parties.

If the opportunity for politicians to strike out on their own had always existed in the Colombian system, then why did so many power seekers remain with the two dominant parties? The answer lies in the fact that under

Colombian list PR, parties were allowed to offer as many lists as they liked. The basic result of this factor in the system, as it applied to maintaining the two parties, was that candidates like our hypothetical fifth-placer above could have their cake and eat it too: they could remain in the party *and* have their own, personalized electoral vehicle. And while the tendency for the parties to offer factional lists was encouraged by the National Front, it should be reemphasized that this was not a practice that started with the Front (as noted above). The precise strategic impact of personal lists will be dealt with in more detail in the next chapter.

In sum, the 1974–1991 period is marked by a dominant two-party system because all the incentives in regard to accessing power made it more advantageous to operate within two large electoral collectives. Further, the exigencies of the system for legislative elections (i.e., the ability to offer personal lists, yet to remain in the traditional party framework) provided a safety valve for those political actors who wanted some autonomy in issues such as nominations for down-ticket offices and even some variation in label. Colombian politicians could, under this system, have their own lists and still be in the mix to be associated with the governing party. Why be fifth or tenth on someone else's list when one can be first on one's own list?

The incentive to remain with one of the dominant electoral collectives was especially strong for Liberals, as it seemed as though their party was destined for permanent majority status in terms of both winning the presidency and maintaining legislative majorities.[28] Indeed, the only time during the era under discussion that the PC won the presidency was in 1982, when Galán's failure to win the PL nomination led to the formation of New Liberalism and thereby the fracturing of the PL. The entire experiment with New Liberalism taught the PL that they needed to stick together, and indeed after the new party's short existence (in 1982 at the presidential level and in 1986 at the congressional) Galán returned to the fold and was the leading candidate for the PL presidential nomination for the 1990 contests until he was gunned down on the campaign trail in 1989.

Certain segments of the Conservative Party started to realize that they were in a seemingly permanent minority status, and as a result the forces of cohesion started to weaken: many would-be power seekers began to question the usefulness of remaining under the PC umbrella. For example, in the 1986 congressional elections, the National Conservative Movement ran its own lists as a separate party and won a Senate seat and three Chamber seats.[29] More prominent was the formation of the National Salvation Movement by Álvaro Gómez, who had been the PC's presidential candidate in 1974 and 1986. Gómez ran as the MSN's presidential candidate in

1990, winning almost twice the votes of the PC candidate, Rodrigo Lloreda Caicedo. The MSN went on to have a prominent role in the National Constituent Assembly (as noted in chapter 3 and discussed below) and had a congressional presence, albeit small, in the 1990s.

The very end of this period—indeed, almost as close to the end as one can possibly get—foreshadowed changes to come when, on December 9, 1990, the country elected a National Constituent Assembly (NCA), which was tasked with writing a new constitution. This election, held using the personal list–PR rules noted above, in one national district of 70 seats, was the most multipartisan election to that point in Colombian history. The process clearly demonstrated that it was at least possible for nontraditional actors to win substantial numbers of votes, as the Democratic Alliance/ Movement of the 19th of April list won the most votes and the second-largest number of seats (19 to the PL's 22). The elections also highlighted the tendency of Liberals to compete via large numbers of lists (36 out of 116 lists for 70 seats) and of Conservatives to segment into multiple parties, with the National Salvation Movement of Álvaro Gómez winning more seats (11) than the mainline PC (which won 7 and was called at that point in time the PSC or Social Conservative Party). The effective number of parliamentary parties for the NCA was 4.75, well over twice the average in either chamber during this period. If anything, the NCA elections illustrate that changes in rules could lead to changed behaviors and outcomes and that new entrants (i.e., the M-19) could have success.

1991–2002

Table 5.1 clearly shows that the behavior of voters and power seekers changed after the implementation of the new constitution, which was promulgated on July 4, 1991. Several key changes were put into practice that altered the calculations of those seeking elected office.

The presidential prize was diminished by the creation of popularly elected mayors and governors. The election of mayors was a reform that predated the new constitution, although only two such elections had been held (1988 and 1990) before the installation of the new constitution. The most obvious diminution of the presidency in this regard is simply the fact that the office now appoints fewer posts than it did in the past, a fact that lessens, to some degree, the richness of the office as an electoral prize. The loss of these appointments has also affected the pathways that politicians now take to the Casa de Nariño. In the past the only way for a potential candidate to add any executive experience to his or her political résumé was via presidential appointment to a governorship, mayoralty, or the cabinet. Indeed, as noted above, if we look at presidential candidates in the post–National Front period, we find that in their career paths service in the cabinet was a key element. Under such a system, belonging to one of the major parties was a plus for anyone who might want to be president someday.

The ability to be elected to local executive office, however, gave power seekers a new entrée and diminished the direct reach of the presidency into the localities. In other words, these new centers of power diminished the presidential prize in the sense that presidential appointment was no longer the only way that a potential candidate could demonstrate his or her executive bona fides. With the creation of popularly elected executives at the departmental and municipal levels, the new system created a new method for building one's pre-presidential résumé. In the presidential elections from 1991 onward, there is evidence to suggest that this route has been recognized by power seekers. Of the three presidents elected in this period, two (Pastrana, 1998–2002, and Uribe, 2002–2006, 2006–) had no prior cabinet experience but did have experience as elected executives (Pastrana was the first elected mayor of Bogotá, and Uribe was the elected governor of Antioquia for the 1995–1997 period).

It should also be noted that the decree powers of the presidency were curtailed versus those in the 1886 Constitution. This would mark yet another diminishment of the presidential prize—although certainly not one that would dissuade politicians from seeking the office.

The method of selecting the president was changed under the new constitution in a way that provided power seekers with more options for acquiring the office, which, in turn, further weakened the traditional parties' advantage as being the main pathways to the presidency. The process of electing the president was changed from winning a plurality to requiring an absolute majority to win the office. This changed the calculus for those seeking the presidency. For one thing, the two-round structure allowed for candidates to run in the first round and need only a second-place finish to live to fight another day, as long as the first-place finisher did not win an absolute majority. Depending on how fragmented the first round was, it might not take an overwhelming number of votes to move on. Further, even if one's first-round bid was unsuccessful but one showed some voting-winning ability, the possibility of aligning with one of the top two finishers was present. Indeed, had this system been in place in the 1980s, would more voters have opted for Galán in the first round in 1982? Would there have been more incentive for Galán to have built New Liberalism into a long-term proposition if it had a legitimate chance of being a second-place finisher in the first round? It is impossible to know, but one can look back and think how both candidates and voters might have viewed that contest differently if the rules had not been what they were.

There are only three presidential elections to analyze for this period—1994, 1998, and 2002—but we do see some important changes from the previous period even with just these three cases. For one thing, the PL's dominance of the presidency ended. The PL did win in 1994 when Ernesto Samper bested Andrés Pastrana, but it lost in 1998 (when Pastrana defeated Horacio Serpa) and again in 2002 (when Álvaro Uribe beat Serpa).

Pastrana's two campaigns took on a conscious pluripartisan strategy that sought to create an electoral alliance of Conservatives with other parties. Indeed, while Pastrana was endorsed by the PC in both races, he was not a PC candidate in terms of campaign symbols nor as listed on the ballot (as noted above). In 2002 Uribe's candidacy was an independent run that gained such momentum that there was no need for a second round; Uribe won in the first round with 53 percent of the vote.

The baseline rules for electing Congress did not change, but there was a very important change to the process of electing the Senate. Instead of the body being elected from territorially delimited electoral districts based on the departments, it was elected in two national districts: one hundred seats were chosen from one national district and two additional seats were set aside for indigenous communities, also elected in one national district. The large national district was conducive to new party formation, as it eliminated any malapportionment that favored the large, traditional parties and it also meant that any given list could collect votes from all corners of the country. The strategic opportunities under personal list PR also meant that the large parties, especially the PL, could offer reams and reams of lists to capture a large number of seats via largest remainders and thereby lessen the chances of some of the smaller parties to win seats. The specifics of this strategy will be discussed at length in the next chapter.

The Chamber and the Senate were reduced in size under the new constitution. The Chamber went from 199 to 161 (166 by 2006). The Senate went from 114 to 102. Malapportionment in the Chamber was increased under the 1991 Constitution by the promotion of several national territories to the status of department. In Article 309 of the 1991 Constitution, four districts (*intendencias*)—Arauca, Casanare, Putumayo, and San Andrés—and five police districts (*comisarías*)—Amazonas, Guaviare, Guanía, Vaupés, and Vichada—were converted into full departments, raising the total number to thirty-two. The new departments accounted for 18 out of the 161 department-based seats in the Chamber (11.18 percent), while under the 1886 constitutional order they accounted for 6 of 199 seats (3.01 percent).

A new ballot format also de-linked the specific party bosses from their subordinates. The effect here was to further fragment the parties, as candidates who might have otherwise seen the necessity of seeking out an electoral patron could, instead, simply offer his or her own list within the party (given that the parties were quite liberal in allowing usage of their labels, even after the 1994 law gave them clear legal control over them).

The general upshot is that we see an increased fragmentation in the party system as more and more independent actors offered lists. The PL, however, maintained itself as the dominant collective for most of the decade of the 1990s, but once it no longer appeared to be the gateway to the presidency, the collective started to fracture—as we see in the 2002 congressional election. Indeed, in all three elections in the 1990s the PL maintained absolute majority status in both chambers of the legislature. It appeared, in fact, that the rest of the party system was a fractured shambles by 1998 with the PC being the second-largest party, but it was literally one-third the size of the PL in terms of seats won. The fortunes of the PC were so anemic that its 2002 presidential nominee, Juan Camilo Restrepo, decided to withdraw his candidacy.

Indeed, the inability of the PL to win the presidency starting in 1998 and the PC's inability even to field its own unique candidate after the 1990 election both indicate that as the 1991–2002 period was coming to a close, the incentives for remaining in the two traditional parties, at least as they related to seeking and winning the presidency, had seriously eroded, if not evaporated. And hence by 2002 the traditional-party share of seats in Congress had fallen to 46.1 percent in the Chamber and 41.2 percent in the Senate—numbers that would have been unthinkable in the previous period. Indeed, had just the PL by itself fallen into the 40 percent range there would have been assumptions that something was seriously wrong with the party.

Uribe's election, and the lack of a clear majority party starting in 2002, meant that new legislative coalitions needed to be formed to work with the new president, and a number of politicians from various parties ended up working to form an Uribista bloc in Congress. Further, the desire to capitalize on Uribe's popularity, as well as the desire to be in line for some of that popularity to rub off once it came time to be Uribe's successor, has led to the formation of new parties or the strengthening of existing ones. These circumstances made it possible for a set of reforms to be enacted, which included a substantial change to the method of electing legislative bodies in Colombia as well a constitutional amendment to allow for the president to be elected to a second consecutive term.

2003 and Onward

The single most important reform in terms of Colombia's party system is the adoption of the D'Hondt method for electing legislative bodies. This method, unlike the Hare quota, contains no incentive for list proliferation, as the system does not reward extremely small remainders as the Hare quote does if there are no formal electoral thresholds.[30] Additionally, the new rules instituted an electoral threshold, which means that lists with very small vote totals could not garner a seat. The new rules also instituted a requirement that each party can submit one, and only one, list per office per district (although, again, D'Hondt creates those conditions in strategic terms by itself). This move utterly eliminated the interest that many power seekers had for remaining in the traditional parties, as the ability to be part of a big party yet run one's own slate of candidates evaporated. (As we will see in the next chapter, the PL in particular had become a party predicated on large numbers of individualized lists.) It also changed the calculation in terms of votes needed to win. Under the old system, candidates could win seats based largely on remainders, whereas the new system (D'Hondt) removed the ability for a large number of candidates to win with very small remainders. Indeed, the D'Hondt method slightly favors the consolidated lists of larger parties—a reversal of the incentive structure present under the old system.

The ability of the president to be reelected also brought about some changes in the party system, at least in the short term, insofar as it encouraged power seekers to attach themselves to his political popularity, which meant the formation of new parties. The most conspicuous example would be the Party of National Social Unity (Partido Social de Unidad Nacional), whose symbol is a capital U with a circle of red, yellow, and green, and which goes by the nickname of the Partido de la U or, more simply, la U. There is also Democratic Colombia (Colombia Democrática), which is headed by Uribe's cousin Mario Uribe Escobar, and whose Web page claims Uribe as a founder.[31] Further, the PC revitalized itself for the 2006 electoral cycle by supporting Uribe, and the previously microscopic Radical Change (Cambio Radical) was able to find substantial electoral success in 2006 by supporting Uribe.[32]

Hence by the end of the 2006 electoral cycle we find a true multiparty system made up of several moderate-size parties (such as the PL, PC, CR, and la U) where before we had either a strong two-party system or a fragmented multiparty system made of numerous microparties. Although this new party system has not fully consolidated, the bottom line is that the incentives for power seekers to cast their fate with large electoral collectives no longer exist. The elimination of personalized political lists and the alteration of the presidential prize means that we should expect the multiparty system to continue in the 2010 electoral cycle and onward.

Conclusions

From examining the evolution of the electoral rules of Colombia and the commensurate behaviors of power-seeking actors, it is clear that this case demonstrates that rules matter and can matter quite a lot.

Ultimately this is a story of how the reconfiguration of the rules over time has lead to the diminution of what were two of the most dominant political parties in the hemisphere for over a century. Figure 5.1, which charts the vote shares of the PL and PC in elections for the presidency and

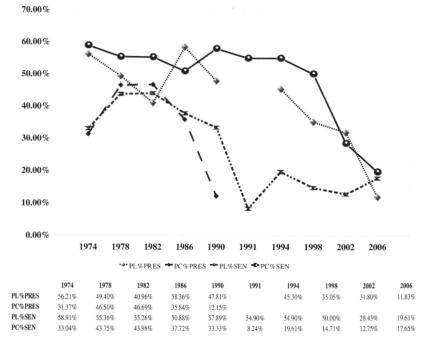

	1974	1978	1982	1986	1990	1991	1994	1998	2002	2006
PL%PRES	56.21%	49.40%	40.96%	58.36%	47.81%		45.30%	35.05%	31.80%	11.83%
PC%PRES	31.37%	46.50%	46.69%	35.84%	12.15%					
PL%SEN	58.91%	55.36%	55.26%	50.88%	57.89%	54.90%	54.90%	50.00%	28.43%	19.61%
PC%SEN	33.04%	43.75%	43.98%	37.72%	33.33%	8.24%	19.61%	14.71%	12.75%	17.65%

Figure 5.1. Trends for the Traditional Parties in Presidential and Senatorial Contests, 1974–2006

the Senate during the 1974–2006 period, dramatically shows this change. From 1974 to 1986 the two traditional parties practically control the entire vote. The PC starts its decline first, which is quite prominent after 1986, the last year it was a viable force in presidential elections, and it hits its nadir of 8.24 percent of the Senate vote in 1991. The PL appears to be maintaining itself as a majority or near-majority party until it starts to slip with the 1998 presidential contest, and then the bottom falls out in terms of the Senate.

The diminution of the electoral appeal of the traditional parties as a result of the strategic options created by changes in the rules led to the capturing of substantial portions of the vote, and thereby of government, by a combination of truly new parties such as the Alternative Democratic Pole (Polo Democrático Alternativo) or parties such as Radical Change and Democratic Colombia, among others, made up of mostly long-term politicians who have decided that their paths to political influence no longer remain with the PL and PC.

The next chapter examines some of the specific strategic moves discussed in narrative form above—specifically demonstrating how the usage of personal lists was key to the pre-2003 system.

CHAPTER 6

Parties, Rules, and Strategic Choices

Electoral rules can make or break a party—or even a country.
—Rein Taagepera and Matthew Søberg Shugart (1989, 2)

A KEY QUESTION, as we look at the Colombian party system, is why did it go from a strong two-party system (1974–1990) to increasing atomization (1991–2002) to seeming consolidation in a multiparty system (2006)?[1] Chapter 5 details the shift in electoral rules over this period of time, as well as changes to the institutional features of the state, especially the presidency, as an overarching explanation for this shift. However, to fully understand this evolution one must look at two factors. The first has to do with the effects on the system of electoral lists, and the second has to do with the changes made to the election of the Senate under the 1991 Constitution.

This chapter amplifies an argument made in the previous chapter, which is that one of the major reasons that the Colombian electoral system did not spawn a multiparty system earlier in its existence is because of the ability of power seekers to offer personal lists while remaining under the umbrella of the two major parties. The first section of this chapter examines the basic mechanics of this institutional feature of the pre-2003 electoral system. The second, and longer, section examines how the reforms to the election of the Senate under the 1991 Constitution created a new incentive structure that both amplified electoral list proliferation but also encouraged new party formation. The chapter concludes with an argument that these factors combined to contribute to the electoral reform of 2003 and therefore to the final transformation of the party system in Colombia.

Bargain Shopping and the Sting of the Wasp

Ostensibly, Colombia had a basic closed list–PR system using the Hare quota and largest remainders—very simply a system that one would expect would produce a multiparty system.[2] However, as noted in the prior chapter, the system allowed for intraparty competition in a given district via the offering of multiple lists per district. As such the system that was in place was better described as personal list–PR. In more technical terms, personal list–PR in Colombia shares characteristics with the single nontransferable vote (SNTV), a system in which parties nominate multiple candidates per multimember district and wherein the strategic difficulty is whether the party nominates too many candidates, thus diluting its votes and winning fewer seats than it should have, or whether it does not nominate sufficient candidates, and thus wastes votes that could have been used to win more seats.[3]

So what is the appeal of offering multiple lists in electoral terms? Why would a party or a candidate wish to engage in this behavior? From the perspective of party elites, why dilute control over candidates in this way? As a candidate who can win with one's own list, why not create one's own party? The previous chapter notes several reasons, not the least of which being what was termed the presidential prize of Colombian politics. Additionally the need to have local power networks to go along with the centralized power in the capital meant that there were incentives to have both a local identity (a regional or local set of electoral lists) and a national one (affiliation with a major party within the Congress).

The ability of parties to offer multiple lists per district lent itself to two important phenomena. The first is described below as "bargain shopping" for seats, as the presence of multiple lists from a given party in a specific district more often than not resulted in seats being won for fewer votes than would have been the case had parties been required to offer only one list per district (i.e., at a "bargain price"). The possibility of winning seats at a discounted rate in a largest-remainder system is common but is typically limited to a handful of seats that are often allocated to small parties. However, in the Colombian case, as we shall see, the presence of multiple lists per party meant that the largest parties most benefited from the largest-remainder seat allocations (at least until 2002).

The second phenomenon, which is an outgrowth of the mechanical effect described above, was a specific strategy employed primarily by the PL, which was the purposeful offering of multiple lists with the hope of garnering multiple seats for less than a quota. This strategy was called *Operación Avispa* (or Operation Wasp), and it entailed the notion of victory through multiple little stings rather than one large attack. This strategy, its application by the PL, and its misapplication by other actors will also be examined below.

Seats at Bargain Rates

Let us consider the basics of a Hare quota system with largest remainders. As described in box 5.1, the basic process works like this: take the number of votes cast in a district and divide that total by the number of seats being contested in that district, which provides the quota. So, for example, if there is a district with 100,000 votes and ten seats, the quota would be 10,000 ($V/M = q$, so 100,000/10 = 10,000). Let's consider that the "full price" for a seat. Now, for such a district, consider the following distribution of votes to five party lists:

Party A: 49,000
Party B: 32,000
Party C: 11,000
Party D: 5,000
Party E : 3,000

Using the quota of 10,000 votes, we can easily see that parties A, B, and C can afford to pay full price for seats (four, three, and one, respectively):

Party A: 49,000—spends 40,000 votes for 4 seats, leaving a 9,000 vote remainder
Party B: 32,000—spends 30,000 votes for 3 seats, leaving a 2,000 vote remainder
Party C: 11,000—spends 10,000 votes for 1 seat, leaving a 1,000 vote remainder
Party D: 5,000—cannot afford a quota (full price) seat, keeps all 5,000 votes
Party E : 3,000—cannot afford a quota (full price) seat, keeps all 3,000 votes

However, that allocates only eight of our ten seats; it is time to go bargain-basement shopping by allocating those last two seats via the largest remainders. After having spent the votes needed to acquire the full-price seats, the lists are still left with unspent votes (i.e., the remainders). Of the remaining votes, the parties with the largest unspent pools of votes are parties A and D (i.e., they had the largest remainders). As such, they are able to acquire those seats at a bargain price (Party A had to "pay" only 90% of full price, while Party D got an excellent deal, paying half price for its remaining seat).

Applying these principles of bargain shopping to elections is the key to understanding Colombia's legislative elections from 1974 to 2002 and *especially* elections to the 1991–2002 Senate. In a normal list-PR system with largest remainders, the parties submit only one list per office, and therefore power seekers have to decide if they are better off with a large party or forming their own party. The advantage of belonging to a large party is that a given list will win a fair number of seats. Of course, if one joined

Party A in the example above and was sixth on the list, one did not get to go to parliament. However, the stricture of one list per district means that each party can get a maximum of one "bargain" per district, with all other seats on a multiple-seats-winning list having come at full price.

Now, everyone likes a good deal—after all, who wants to pay full price when one can get a discount? It ends up that a key effect of allowing multiple lists under the quota system with largest remainders is that it creates a large number of bargain seats. For example, if we take the illustration from above and have Party A submit six lists instead of one, the following possible scenario emerges:

Party A: 10,000 (1 quota seat)
Party A: 8,000 (1 largest remainder seat)
Party A: 7,900 (1 largest remainder seat)
Party A: 7,800 (1 largest remainder seat)
Party A: 7,700 (1 largest remainder scat)
Party A: 7,600 (1 largest remainder seat)
Party B: 32,000 (3 quota seats)
Party C: 11,000 (1 quota seat)
Party D: 5,000
Party E : 3,000

Here, the results are the same as in the scenario above for parties B and C, which win three and one full-quota seats respectively. However, instead of Party A winning four quota seats and a largest-remainder seat, it wins one quota seat and *five* largest-remainder seats, and Party D wins precisely nothing. Indeed, if Party B figures out the process, it can likely offer two lists and steal Party C's one seat. It should also be noted that the ability of Party A to offer all those lists creates a more disproportional outcome than in the original scenario. Under the single-list scenario, Party A had 49 percent of the vote and 50 percent of the seats. Under the multilist scenario it still had 49 percent of the vote but instead won 60 percent of the seats.

The upshot of this is that it gives larger parties the ability not only to offer a lot of candidates for office but to do so on multiple lists, so that they have the advantages commensurate with size (name recognition, resources, affiliations with major presidential candidates, and the ability to form legislative majorities) along with the one key advantage that small parties have in a largest-remainder system (the ability for electoral lists to eke out a seat with a remainder rather than a full quota). In the Colombian context this was an especially appealing mode of operation, as it allowed (as noted in the previous chapter) for local leaders to cultivate their own personal electoral followings and clientele networks while still adhering to one of the traditional parties.

Table 6.1 goes beyond the hypothetical and clearly illustrates that there is a long tradition of bargain shopping (far more largest-remainder winners than full-quota winners) when it comes to Colombian congressional elections in the post-Front period. This trend is clearly amplified under the rules of the 1991 Constitution. It should be kept in mind that until 1991 there was a strong two-party system in Colombia, so most of the bargain seats were going to the PL and PC, not to small parties.

If Colombia had, like other list-PR countries, allowed only one list per party per district, then the expectation would have been for substantially higher numbers of quota seats and much, much lower numbers of largest-remainder seats. Essentially, in any given district the PL and PC could have

Table 6.1

Quota vs. Largest-Remainder Seats in the Colombian Congress, 1974–2002

	QS	LRS	Total seats
	Chamber		
1974	108 (54.27%)	91 (45.73%)	199
1978	82 (41.21%)	117 (58.79%)	199
1982	44 (22.11%)	155 (77.89%)	199
1986	56 (28.14%)	143 (71.86%)	199
1990	52 (26.13%)	147 (73.87%)	199
1991	15 (9.32%)	146 (90.68%)	161
1994	4 (2.45%)	159 (97.55%)	163
1998	4 (2.48%)	157 (97.52%)	161
2002	7 (4.24%)	158 (95.76%)	165
	Senate		
1974	48 (42.86%)	64 (57.14%)	112
1978	35 (31.25%)	77 (68.75%)	112
1982	34 (29.82%)	80 (70.18%)	114
1986	25 (21.93%)	89 (78.07%)	114
1990	30 (26.32%)	84 (73.68%)	114
1991	42 (41.18%)	60 (58.82%)	102
1994	14 (13.73%)	88 (86.27%)	102
1998	8 (7.84%)	94 (92.16%)	102
2002	12 (11.76%)	90 (88.24%)	102

Source: Registraduría and author's calculations.

won a maximum of one LRS each, no more than whatever other small parties could have mustered through that mechanism. While it is impossible to know what the exact numbers would have been, if we take the Senate from 1991 onward and combine all the votes for the various parties in hypothetical unified lists, we find that from 1991 to 2002 there would have been an average of 73.25 QS and 28.75 LRS. A better estimate is to look at the 2006 elections, which did require one list per party: applying the Hare quota, we would have had 87 QS and 12 LRS—essentially the mirror opposite of what the system produced under personal list–PR from 1994 to 2002.

List Proliferation and the Wasps' Swarm

It has been noted in previous chapters that the offering of multiple lists by a specific party in a given contest was practiced on occasion in Colombia as far back as the *voto incompleto* electoral regime in the early twentieth century, and that the practice became common under the rules of the National Front. Certainly much of the motivation behind the lists was simply to allow, as has been noted, regional and subregional party bosses to have control over their own clientele networks. And much of the list proliferation that led to the large numbers of largest-remainder seats, as noted in table 6.1, simply grew organically out of the prevailing institutional parameters. Indeed, much of the list proliferation in question was the result of a lack of party discipline and the lack of any legal ability for the parties to assert full control over their labels.[4] However, it is also true that the leaders of the two traditional parties never sought control of their labels, even back when they arguably could have done so during the National Front. Instead it was quite clear that party leaders preferred to have more seats and less control than the other way around. The particularistic nature of Colombia's traditional parties was such that feeding clientele networks was more important than pursuing a public policy program. In such a system, numbers of seats trumped any kind of philosophical cohesion. As was noted in the previous chapter, the combined goals of controlling the presidency and having access to the national budget created a self-reinforcing relationship. On the one hand, political entrepreneurs needed to be part of the larger collectives; on the other hand, the traditional parties and the party elites needed members to have a chance at capturing legislative majorities more than they needed (or wanted) party discipline. Such motivation specifically explains the continued adherence of many political entrepreneurs to the PL while those within the PC started going their own way, given that the PC's chances of winning legislative majorities were clearly small.

Under such conditions, multiple lists per district were very much the norm for the entire 1974–2002 period. For example, if we look at the Senate during this period, the reliance on multiple lists is quite clear. Table 6.2 shows that the large number of lists offered over time by the traditional parties (the numbers grow if third parties are included) versus the number of lists that they would have been able to offer under a standard one list per party system. These one-list numbers, in the right-hand column, are simply the number of Senate districts in the given election multiplied by two.[5]

It is worth noting that in the last two Senate elections under the National Front, the PL and PC, taken together, offered 142 lists for 106 seats in 1966 and 205 lists for 118 seats in 1970.[6] Thus, the post-NF period demonstrates some diminution in the numbers of lists offered by the two parties. Of course, during the Front any third party (like ANAPO) had to offer lists within the two traditional collectives—and often offered lists under both traditional party labels.

The serious proliferation of lists starts when we hit late 1990, with the National Constituent Assembly elections in December. It is clear that the PL leadership, specifically the former president Alfonso López Michelsen, saw that the party could maximize its political clout via strategic list proliferation as the NCA was going to be elected from one national district of seventy seats.[7] As district magnitude increases, the strategy of bargain shopping for seats via largest remainder becomes even more profitable. With such a structure in place, it was decided that the PL would offer numerous lists for the NCA, unleashing a swarming electoral attack rather than a concentrated one. This tactic, the aforementioned *operación avispa*, was meant to win via numerous small stings. Clearly PL leaders decided that the party's fragmented nature was best served by this approach, which maximized the efficacy of Liberal votes. There is a long tradition of resentment within the PL when it comes to list construction, which in the past was referred to as the *tiranía del bolígrafo* (tyranny of the fountain pen), because elites constructing the lists have a great deal of authority, since candidate placement on a closed list can determine that candidate's likely political fate.[8] Given the resistance to centralized list construction, yet the desire to maintain a unified party, list proliferation made strategic sense.

The application of the *avispa* strategy was quite successful in the December 1990 NCA elections and underscores the notion of "bargain shopping" as proffered above, especially if we compare the PL's behavior and fortunes to that of the AD/M-19 in the same elections. In the race to capture a portion of the seventy seats up for election, the PL offered thirty-six

Table 6.2

Lists and the Senate, 1974–2002

	PL	PC	Total PL + PC lists	PL + PC lists under a one list per party system
1974	67	54	121	44
1978	92	61	153	44
1982	102	72	174	46
1986	73	67	140	46
1990	107	57	164	46
1991	90	25	115	2
1994	134	39	173	2
1998	147	25	172	2
2002	148	30	178	2

Note: The Congress originally elected for the 1990–1994 term was dissolved by the NCA with the promulgation of the 1991 Constitution. A new Congress was elected for the 1991–1994 period on October 27, 1991.

lists and the AD/M-19 offered one (for comparative purposes the PC, running as the PSC, offered two[9]). The total number of lists offered was 116, with twenty-nine winning seats.

The AD/M-19 list won the most votes of any list in the election with 992,613 (the next largest total being Álvaro Gómez's MSN list with 574,411), and the most won by any PL list was Horacio Serpa's 138,662. However, the PL won the most seats with twenty-two versus the AD/M-19's nineteen.[10] The combined vote for the winning PL lists was 860,122, and the PL won eight seats via full quota and fourteen by largest remainder.[11] The AD/M-19, by contrast, won eighteen full-quota seats and one largest-remainder seat. As such, the PL underpaid for its seats vis-à-vis the AD/M-19. The PL went on (as did other parties) to utilize the *avispa* approach in post-1991 elections. Given that by 1994 the parties had legal control of their labels, and had to grant the right to use them on ballots, it is fair to say that the strategy of list proliferation was quite conscious at that point.[12] The combination of conscious and unconscious application of the *avispa* stratagem was especially important with the advent of the new rules for the election of the Senate under the 1991 Constitution. The next section deals with the Senate during the 1991–2002 period and the way list proliferation clearly encouraged evolution of the party system.

The Senate: 1991–2002

Prior to the 2003 move to require one list per party, the most significant post–National Front electoral reform was the transformation of the Senate from a body elected from multimember districts based on the departments to one elected in a single national electoral district. This change took the system from one based on twenty-three separate districts with an average district magnitude of 4.96 to one with a district magnitude of 100.[13] Taagepera and Shugart call district magnitude "the decisive factor" and note that "when a proportional representation formula is used, the larger the [district magnitude], the more proportional the system" (1989, 112). What this means in practical terms is that smaller parties have a better chance of winning representation. Indeed, with a district magnitude of 100, a party needed only 1 percent of the vote to win a full-quota seat, and less for a largest-remainder seat. In other words, a large district magnitude increases the chances of bargain prices for seats as discussed above.

Table 6.1 clearly shows that, under the new rules, the number of LRS winners substantially increased, especially after parties adapted to the new rules starting in 1994. Table 6.3 provides another measure of the cost issue in regard to seats under the new rules. Given the low number of QS winners during this period, it is clear that an incentive existed for power seekers to either form their own small parties or engage in *avispa*-like list proliferation. Again: why even try to pay full price when seats were on sale (so to speak)?

Beyond the issue of discounted seat prices, such a system also created the potential for power seekers to create power bases other than departmental clientele networks. This new situation was especially useful for new political

Table 6.3

Quotas, Average Winning Largest Remainders, and Winning Largest-Remainder Range, Senate Elections, 1991–2002

	Valid votes[a]	Quota	Average LR (% of quota)	Highest LR (% of quota)	Lowest LR (% of quota)
1991	5,241,938	52,419	33,742 (64%)	51,654 (99%)	21,064 (40%)
1994	5,170,300	51,703	32,062 (62%)	51,177 (99%)	21,861 (42%)
1998	8,683,680	86,837	50,345 (58%)	79,127 (91%)	37,249 (43%)
2002	9,143,577	91,435	59,529 (65%)	88,570 (97%)	40,460 (44%)

[a] Valid votes equals votes for candidate and ballots marked "en blanco" (literally "blank" but essentially meaning "none of the above"—actual blank ballots are not included in the count).

Table 6.4

Trends in Partisan Competition in the Colombian Senate, 1991–2002

	Number of parties offering lists	*Total number of lists*	*Number of parties with multiple lists*	*Percentage of parties with multiple lists*	*Winners needing more than home district support (NH seats)*
1991	20	143	5	25.00%	44%
1994	24	251	9	37.50%	43%
1998	78	318	20	25.64%	60%
2002	80	322	26	32.50%	56%

parties, as it allowed for them to draw votes from all corners of the country, as well as to exploit the fact that even if they were not from vote-rich urban areas, they could draw votes from those locales, which traditionally had been friendly to third parties (especially the Federal District of Bogotá). The shift from territorial-based districts to a single national district was a key alteration of the power basis of the previous electoral system, as previously the only way to build a power base was through regional strength (primarily clientele networks and political alliances built from various municipalities up to the department and then to the capital). Just as the diminution of the presidential prize took some of the appeal away from the traditional parties, so too the reduction of the importance of territorial power centers changed the power calculus engaged in by power seekers.

As a result, power seekers were faced with three key sets of options under these new institutional parameters: stay with an old party or form a new party, offer a few lists or multiple lists, and adopt a regional approach or a national one. The rules in question led to changes in all three variables; not only did the numbers of parties and lists increase, but also the winners of seats began, over the 1991–2002 period, to need votes outside the home district of the list's head. Table 6.4 illustrates all three trends, which will be examined in detail below.

Going with the Old or the New?

The first, most basic question for power seekers under the new rules became whether they believed that they were better off under an existing party label or under a new one. As has been noted in prior chapters, there were long-term bonds to the traditional party labels that had deep significance to Colombian politicians and citizens since the mid–nineteenth century that often made abandoning those labels difficult. Yet by the late 1980s it was becoming clear that many power seekers, especially those affiliated with the PC, were willing to strike out in new directions. The new Senate rules further encouraged such behavior—in terms of both existing actors and also new ones.

It is empirically clear that the rules instituted by the new constitution inspired new parties. In 1990 the effective number of parliamentary parties in the Senate was 2.24, which jumped to 3.1 in 1991. By 2002 that number was 9.19. The raw number of parties holding seats in 1990 was eleven, and in 1991 it was twenty. The 2002 figure was forty-seven. In 1991 twenty parties offered candidates for the Senate, and in 2002 eighty did so.[14]

Three different types of parties existed in this period: the traditional parties (the PL and the PC), nontraditional parties (truly new actors, such as the AD/M-19 or evangelical parties like the Christian Union [UC] or the National Christian Party [PNC]), and quasi-traditional parties (groups like the FP or the MSN, which used new labels but which drew on traditional power bases). These distinctions are useful, as they play into the issues of label discussed in the previous chapter and allow us to delineate among two different types of new behavior, that is, truly new parties versus parties with new labels but old sources of support. This is especially useful given the propensity of many observers of Colombian party politics to want to force all actors into the Liberal or Conservative categories even when they use new labels.

Nevertheless, as has already been argued, any choice made concerning what label to use is a strategic one. Politicians seeking office do not wake up one morning and capriciously decide to change the way that they will present themselves to the public. Such moves are made because the given politician perceives an advantage to the move in question. When looking at the actual choices being made by power seekers in this context, it is fair to say that many of the new labels did not represent truly new political actors or new ideological space. As such, to treat groups like the aforementioned MSN, NFD, or MNC as truly "new" or "nontraditional" parties would be incorrect. However, to treat them as nothing more than (in this case) Conservatives (as some have done) is to miss the rather key fact that they chose new labels. Of course, to blithely consider them new actors operating wholly outside traditional politics is also incorrect. To escape such a rigid dichotomy, we can trichotomize the system as having traditional, quasi-traditional, and nontraditional elements.

Along these lines, the new electoral conditions also serve to underscore the argument made in the previous chapter: party label matters. Indeed,

Table 6.5

Top Vote-Getters (Multiseat Winners), Senate Elections, 1991–2002

List leader	Official label	Votes	Seats
	2002		
Ramos	Equipo Colombia	227,506	3
Navarro	Fuerza Independiente	211,457	2
Vargas Lleras	Colombia Siempre	208,587	2
	1998		
Betancourt P.	Oxígeno Liberal	158,184	2
Valencia Cossio	FP-PC	134,727	2
Moreno de Caro	Defensa Ciudadana	127,248	2
	1994		
Char	PL	84,322	2
Valencia Cossio	FP-PC	79,553	2
Espinosa F.	PL	74,172	2
	1991		
Grabe	AD/M-19	454,467	9
Pastrana	NFD	436,562	8
Gómez H.	MSN	234,358	5
Montoya	PL	103,609	2
Londono C.	PL	96,061	2
Henriquez G.	PL	93,158	2
Char A.	PL	84,392	2
Turbay Q.	PL	80,365	2
Rueda G.	PL	78,245	2

the national electoral district for the Senate helped make plain that candidates were quite willing to adopt nontraditional labels and that voters were more than willing to vote for candidates running under those labels. In looking at lists winning multiple seats since the establishment of the single national district for the Senate in 1991 (table 6.5), it is noteworthy that the trend is decidedly against the traditional parties and in favor of candidates using new labels, whether it is the quasi-traditional example of Luis Alberto Ramos or the nontraditional example of Antonio Navarro, the former guerrilla commander of the M-19.

Even from just a strategic perspective that discounts the sincerity of the dropping of the Conservative and Liberal nomenclature, there is something significant to the fact that candidates have chosen to adopt different labels, and that the voters have been willing to vote for said candidates in high numbers.

Some commentary and further examples are of use here. It is noteworthy that several of these cases represent former members of the PC and PL going their own way, labelwise. Ingrid Betancourt of the Liberal Oxygen list in 1998 had been a member of the Chamber of Representatives as a Liberal in 1994. She later ran in the 2000 presidential contest as a nontraditional candidate (although her candidacy was cut short when she was kidnapped by the FARC). Carlos Moreno de Caro was a Conservative prior to his 1998 bid for the Senate, as was Luis Alberto Ramos. Each, however, made the conscious choice to run under a new label, with significant success, especially considering the highly fractionalized vote in Colombian Senate elections.

List Proliferation

While new party formation was a clear result of the new rules, so too did those rules lead to even greater list proliferation. Table 6.4 illustrates both facts, as more actual parties offered lists and more of them offered multiple lists over time.

When it came to list formation, parties had to decide if they were better served by pooling their votes under a single list or dispersing them to multiple lists. As has already been demonstrated, winning via remainder is the best option in terms of maximizing one's seats in regard to votes. Logically, therefore, the best strategy is to offer enough lists to garner all of one's seats by largest remainder, spending the fewest possible votes per seat by dispersing them across various lists and hence treating Colombia's largest-remainder system as one of SNTV. If the right number of lists were offered, a party could maximize the effectiveness of its total vote by winning as many seats as possible with as few votes as possible. If done properly, the party in question would avoid wasting votes on quota seats or even high vote remainders. It is basic economic logic. The problem, of course, is that if a party miscalculates and offers too many lists, it then runs the risk of overly dispersed, and therefore wasted, votes and loss of seats.

When we look at the general numbers, it is clear that power seekers understood these choices. We see an increase in the numbers of lists, the numbers of unique party labels, and the numbers of LRS winners. Looking back to table 6.4, we see ratios of lists to seats of 1.40 in 1991, 2.46 in 1994, 3.12 in 1998, and 3.16 in 2002. Given the number of uniquely labeled parties in each of those elections, there should have been only twenty lists in 1991, twenty-four in 1994, seventy-eight in 1998, and eighty in 2002 (had Colombian law required limiting each party to only one list). That would have given us ratios of 0.20 lists per seat in 1991, 0.24 in 1994, 0.76 in 1998, and 0.78 in 2002. By contrast, Israeli Knesset elections, which also employ a single national electoral district and a system for election similar to Colombia's, saw an average of 24.6 lists for 120 seats for the 1992–2006 period (or an average ratio of 0.21 lists per seat).[15]

When looking at the phenomenon of list proliferation and "bargain shopping" as described above, we need to look at the way in which this process was engaged by various political actors and the degree to which the strategy was successful or not. Below we will look at the continuation of *operación avispa* by the Liberals in the Senate, the attempts of the PC to find a way to survive under the new rules, the self-immolation of the AD/M-19, as well as the strategic errors committed by various third parties as they sought to match the PL's stinging wasps.

The PL

The Liberals approached the rules governing the election of the Senate under the 1991 Constitution with the same basic strategy that was taken for the National Constituent Assembly elections: offering substantial numbers of electoral lists. Table 6.6 summarizes the number of lists offered, the quota and largest-remainder seats won, and what the party would have garnered under a hypothetical single list.

In terms of maintaining majority control of the Senate, the many-list strategy worked quite effectively in 1991 and 1994, and it fell only two seats shy of holding the majority in 1998 in terms of pure PL lists (if one counts

Table 6.6

The PL and the Senate, 1991–2002

	Lists	Winning lists	Votes for winning lists	Wasted votes	QS	LRS	Total	Hypo. QS	Hypo. LRS	Hypo. total
1991	90	50	2,263,349	226,298	15	41	56	47	1	48
1994	134	54	1,909,856	731,653	6	50	56	51	0	51
1998	147	48	2,667,306	1,229,966	3	45	48	44	1	45
2002	148	29	1,693,908	1,016,691	1	28	29	29	1	30

several coalitional lists, then an absolute majority for the party is maintained—but since we are discussing electoral strategies, and legislative caucuses, only straight PL lists are counted in the discussion).[16] At a minimum it is clear from the number of LR seats won that the party was underpaying for its seats. However, it should be noted that the PL increasingly wasted a staggering number of votes. In other words, while the party was correct that the *avispa* strategy would win it more seats than a single-list approach (as the hypothetical numbers show until 2002), the unfettered nature of list creation meant that the party substantially overnominated candidates. A more coordinated approach could have led to successful exploitation of a significant number of the wasted votes. The 2002 election, however, demonstrated that the multilist approach was not a guarantee of seat maximization. In that contest, had the PL offered only one list it would have actually won one more seat than it otherwise did (ceteris paribus).

The Partido Conservador and Political Learning

The Conservative Party (PC) has had seemingly minority status since the cessation of power sharing in 1974. As such, many partisans who might associate with the PC have seen the advantage of forming their own legal parties, such as the National Conservative Movement (MNC), the National Salvation Movement (MSN), and the New Democratic Force (NFD). This has resulted in fewer lists, and seats, for the mainline PC. The party's initial reaction to a nationwide electoral district in the NCA elections was to offer two lists (using the label "Social Conservative Party" [PSC] in a short-lived public relations move[17]), with several of the conservative splinters offering their own lists (indeed, the MSN did better than did the PSC in the 1990 NCA election). This poor showing in the election led to the party being shut out of the leadership of the Constituent Assembly, which was headed by a three-part presidency populated by the top three seat-winning parties. This humiliation of one of the two traditional parties in Colombian history caused a clear shift in strategy and the adoption of a moderate "*avispa*-ization" of the party when, less than a year after two lists were seen as insufficient, the party offered twenty-five lists for the Senate elections (see table 6.7).

While it is clear that the PC simply lacked the electoral might needed to directly rival the PL during this period, it did manage to draw itself out of the abyss, which was the NCA elections, back to being the second-largest seat winner in the Senate starting in 1994. This was accomplished partly through offering multiple lists. Indeed, the PC clearly learned something

Table 6.7

The PC and the Senate, 1991–2002

	Lists	Winning lists	Votes for winning lists	Wasted votes	QS	LRS	Total	Hypo. QS	Hypo. LRS	Hypo. total
1991	25	9	346,748	160,753	3	6	9	9	1	10
1994	39	20	700,969	278,128	2	18	20	18	1	19
1998	29	15	756,640	243,392	1	14	15	11	1	12
2002	25	13	758,561	126,702	1	12	13	9	1	10

from the PL by offering more lists in 1994 than it did in 1991. It also managed to win more LR seats over time and thereby better maximized the efficacy of its votes. From 1994 to 2002 its multiple lists outperformed a hypothetical single list.

The Alianza Democrática/Movimiento del 19 de Abril and Miscalculation

The AD/M-19 dramatically burst onto the electoral scene in the 1990 National Constituent Assembly elections with a single list that won nineteen seats—the most won by any list and the second most by any party. This strategy was continued in the 1991 Senate elections, where the party won nine seats, the same as the mainline Conservative Party. However, self-destruction followed in 1994 when the party fragmented, offered twelve lists, won zero seats, and essentially disappeared from Colombian politics. Part of AD/M-19's problem was the dominance of the traditional parties, and it was the victim of high expectations followed up by lack of results, but mainly it was the victim of an utterly disastrous electoral strategy.

In her political autobiography, Vera Grabe (AD/M-19 senator and head of the 1991 list) describes the fragmentation of the party in advance of the 1994 elections. The initial hope of the party was that its leader and list headliner in the Constituent Assembly elections, Antonio Navarro Wolff, would head the list. Once he decided to withdraw from the congressional election in favor of a presidential bid, the party fragmented, with various individuals heading their own lists instead (Grabe 2000, 441–442). The party ended up offering twelve lists, wining a total of 140,819 votes but obtaining no seats. Had the AD/M-19 leadership been able to field a unified list, and had such a list received the same number of votes, the party would have garnered three seats (two QS and one LRS).

Based on the average winning largest remainder in 1994 (which was 32,062 votes), four lists might have been able to garner four seats, and indeed, given that the lowest winning largest remainder was 21,861 votes, there was at least a theoretical chance that the proper mix of lists and campaigning strategy could have resulted in as many as six seats. While it is obvious that one cannot be certain that a different list combination would have necessarily garnered the same votes as were won in the actual elections, these calculations easily demonstrate a simple fact: the decision to offer twelve lists was, as Boudon (2001) put it in the subtitle of his article on AD/M-19, "a case study in new-party self-destruction."

Lack of unity led to the devastation of the party, which had seemed poised in 1990/91 to emerge as a viable long-term third party in Colombian politics. Indeed, in the 1990 National Constituent Assembly elections and the 1991 Senate elections, the AD/M-19 was looking far healthier than the mainline Conservatives. After the debacle of 1994, the party continued to exist only as one of many microparties in the Colombian electoral landscape.

Navarro, along with a few other early AD/M-19 politicians (most notably Gustavo Petro and Samuel Moreno), went on to political success after the debacle in 1994. Navarro has been the most prominent of that group, despite his poor showing in the 1994 presidential elections (he came in a distant third, with 3.7% of the vote). From there he was elected mayor of Pasto (a city near the border with Ecuador) and in 2002 headed a Senate list that garnered two seats. All these political activities were undertaken sans the AD/M-19 label. Navarro went on to become part of the Alternate Democratic Pole and competed in its 2006 presidential primary. He lost that bid to Carlos Gaviria but went on to become part of the party's leadership.

Other Third Party Activity

When looking at the strategic choices of the parties, it is clear that the Liberal Party was the model of success that others wanted to emulate (at least until 2002). As it was the majority party, such imitation is certainly to be expected, although it is clear that many of the parties that pursued the LP strategies failed to understand their consequences. It is one thing to recognize that largest-remainder winning requires fewer votes than quota-seat winning and that, therefore, multiple lists might garner a party more seats than a single list might win with the same votes; it is quite another to successfully pursue that strategy, especially when one is from a small party to begin with. One clear advantage that the PL had was that it could afford to waste votes, especially when it was winning the lion's share thereof. Once parties are in the medium-to-low end of the vote total spectrum, however, errors can become quite costly. As noted above, there has been a marked increase in new party labels as multiple actors seek a seat in the Senate. A great number of these are single-list parties that either win a largest-remainder seat or win too few votes to matter. However, a number of the moderate-size third parties have attempted the multiple-list strategy, typically to ill effect.

When parties sought to use a multilist strategy, they faced the possibility of making one of two main errors: either overnomination or undernomination. In other words, if a party offered too many lists, it could deny itself seats, either by winning fewer than it otherwise could have won or by winning none at all. If a party offered multiple lists, the vote for that party might be spread out among those lists in such a way that no single list would have enough votes to win even one seat, even if the party as a whole had won enough total votes to win a seat; or, one list may win, but diffusion among additional lists may deny the party seats that its vote totals otherwise would have garnered. Undernomination is also possible, as a party could have entered only one list and won enough votes that, had they been dispersed over two lists, would have resulted in two largest-remainder seats, but instead the party obtained only one quota seat. Knowing the optimal number of lists to offer is the crucial issue, and one does not know for certain what that number is until after the vote has taken place; hence deciding on the right number of lists requires some degree of guesswork.

As table 6.4 details, the number of parties offering multiple lists grew each election from 1991 to 2002. Clearly many parties were attempting to replicate, in part at least, the PL's multilist strategy, but also much of the multilist mania was a result of poor party discipline (a hallmark of Colombian parties), as the AD/M-19 example above notes. As the number of multilist parties increased, so too did the number of multilist losers (i.e., parties that offered multiple lists and yet did not win a single seat). In 1991 no multilist party failed to garner a seat (but only five parties offered multiple lists in that election). However, in 1994 two parties that offered multiple lists failed to achieve representation in the Senate. The number jumped to seven in 1998 and was at six in 2002. Given that these two elections had the most multilist parties and the most multilist losers, we will focus our analysis on those two cycles.

In 1998 there were several key examples of overnomination by medium-to-small parties. Of the seven multilist losers, four likely would have won a seat with a single list, and a fifth comes within shouting distance of the lowest largest remainder when the votes from its two lists are combined.

Several other parties recognized the usefulness of pursuing LR seats over quota seats, but overnominated. Three parties—the Citizens' Movement (CM), the Popular Civic Convergence (MPCC), and the NFD—each won a single LR seat with a multilist strategy. However, in each case the party wasted a substantial number of votes by overnomination (i.e., offering too many lists). The initial question for parties such as this is whether a single-list or a multiple-list approach is best. If a multiple-list strategy is warranted, the question then becomes how many lists? In the case of the three parties in question, a single-list strategy would likely have still have garnered only a single quota seat with large, but insufficient, remainders. Thus a multiple-list strategy was warranted. Yet, in all three cases, the parties offered too many lists to adequately take advantage of the votes won, as each had enough wasted votes for an additional LRS.[18] Had they offered fewer lists, each might have been able to win more than one LR seat.

In 2002 there were six multilist losers, but only one of them, the Communal and Community Movement of Colombia (MCCC), had a shot at winning a seat based on vote totals across lists. The MCCC offered six lists, which combined for 56,089 votes, far more than the minimum LR winner in 2002 of 40,460. The remaining parties that offered multiple lists and yet won no seats did not have sufficient votes even across their lists to win a seat.

The 2002 elections also contained numerous examples of overnomination, such as Radical Change (CR), which offered ten lists, won 222,484 votes, and yet garnered only two seats. Now, had the party offered a single list, it likely would still have won only two seats, so a multilist strategy made sense.[19] However, ten lists were far too many and resulted in 104,481 wasted votes (46.96% of the party's total vote). Depending on how the votes fell, four lists could have won four largest-remainder seats for the CR in 2002. In looking at where the CR lists won their votes, it is clear that at least part of the mistake the party made was to try to target lists at specific departments, rather than to focus on a national strategy (all the lists, winners and losers, tended to draw votes primarily from one department).

Undernomination errors were committed as well, although they were rarer given the propensity of even the smallest parties to offer numerous lists. However, one of the top vote-getters, Navarro's Independent Force (FI), could have won as many as five LR seats with a multilist approach, but in fact it won only two quota seats with its single list.

On the other hand, not all parties made large strategic errors. The Movement for Popular Integration (MIPOL) offered five lists and won four LR seats. A unified MIPOL list would have won only three seats.

The Single-List Scenario

If we look at Senate elections from 1991 to 2002, what would have happened, ceteris paribus, had the parties been required to offer only one list? The main change, as one would expect, is that the vast majority of seats end up being won via full quotas, not by largest remainders. Such a circumstance disadvantages the larger parties and helps the smaller ones. As noted in table 6.6, the Liberals would have lost seats in all but the 2002 election under such a scenario. Further, since a single-list requirement would have taken away much of the bargain-shopping capabilities of the large parties, the small parties would have found it easy to win cheaper seats. Again turning to a hypothetical recasting of the 1991, 1994, and 1998 votes into a system requiring a single list, we find that the lowest LRS winner would have been 8,937 (1991), 19,640 (1994), 25,387 (1998), and 37,104 (2002) rather than the actual lowest LRS winners of 21,064 (1991), 21,861 (1994), 37,249 (1998), and 40,460 (2002). So, not only did the multiple-list system allow the large parties to bargain-shop, but in so doing it raised the price of the bargains.

A single-list requirement would also have garnered seats for parties that failed to obtain representation in each of the cycles in question. In 1991, for example, three losing parties would have each been represented in the Senate under a single-list scenario. Likewise, four, eleven, and three parties would have been represented in the 1994, 1998, and 2002 Senates, respectively, under that scenario.

Of course, as the 2006 elections indicate, the requirement to offer a single list changes the calculation of power seekers. Further, the D'Hondt method of seat distribution does not benefit the bargain-shopping party the way the largest-remainder system used from 1991 to 2002 did.

Home Sweet Home or Looking for Help?

Having examined the issue of labels and lists, we are left with the final factor that the post-1991 Senate presented: the potential for power seekers to build a national constituency rather than being limited to a localized one. As has been noted, prior to 1991 the Senate was elected from department-based multimember electoral districts, but the 1991 Constitution altered that situation to create two nationally based districts: a main one of one hundred seats and a special district made up of two seats for indigenous persons. Not only, as noted, does the move have clear effects on the potential strategies that power seekers might employ in their quest for office, but the move also changes the basic power relationship between Senate candidates and other office seekers in the Colombian context.

Historically, the Colombian Senate is significant for reasons beyond its legislative duties: the office of senator has been the elected position most important over time in the development of regional political bosses within the traditional parties. While the electoral prize of prizes has always been the presidency, the foundation of regional electoral strength has been built through the Senate. "Regional" should be understood to mean department-based electoral districts, with the given power of a specific leader deriving from specific municipalities within that department.

The traditional parties in each region of Colombia have typically been dominated by a particular electoral baron (or by competing barons) rather than by a political party per se. Hence there would normally have been a member of the PC in charge of conservative votes in a given department (or even a subregion in that department) and the same for a specific member of the PL. The boss was typically a senator (or senators) from a given region. The lack of centralized control over candidate selection had long meant that local bosses constructed their own electoral lists for the senate as well as down-ballot offices—until the advent of the state-produced ballot (appendix 1 illustrates and explains this shift).

Under the new rules, local electoral elites could still attempt to maintain power within a given department, insofar as this was possible, by offering a personal list and simply continuing to seek votes only locally. However, the ability of such lists to dominate the votes in a given department was disrupted considerably starting in 1991, given that voters had a radical increase in choices with that election. Further, candidates could also choose to pursue strategies aimed at garnering votes on a broader basis than the pre-1991 electoral boundaries. Still, given the bargain-shopping potential under the new system noted above, it remained easy to win a seat with primarily local votes. Specifically, the increase in the number of LRS winners meant that fewer votes were needed for a win, and therefore it became easier to win sufficient votes within one's own local sphere of influence to obtain a seat (or seats) and thereby continue to play the old electoral-baron game. Of course, the ability to play power broker was diminished by the advent of state-produced ballots. And as the number of candidates for the Senate increased, each candidate became more buried in a blizzard of lists. Even as some actors continued to pursue old-school approaches to seeking Senate seats, the at-large district provided ample chances to win seats without regard to specific political geography.

The question then becomes, how many seats were garnered by "home district sufficient" (HDS) winners and how many "needed help" (NH) to win? That is, how many seats in the Senate were won under the new rules by a list winning enough votes within the Senator's home department (i.e., continuing the pattern), and how many required votes from outside the home district (i.e., taking advantage of the new parameters)? Had the new rules required a single list per party, such a discussion would be moot; however with personal lists, parties/candidates had different options as to how they might go about acquiring the votes needed to win a seat.

In the analysis that follows, seats are classified as HDS if the lists that won them had sufficient votes within their home departments (or the Federal District) to have won the seat without any other votes. The basic delimiter is the lowest winning largest remainder for the given election (for the numbers, see table 6.3). Seats are classified as NH if the *only* way for the list to have won a given seat was to pool votes from more than one department. In other words, if the list received fewer votes than the smallest winning largest remainder within its electoral bailiwick and yet still won a seat, it is classified as NH.[20]

By way of illustration, we can look at two examples from the 2002 elections, one a near ideal-type HDS list and another a near ideal-type NH list. A clear example of a home district sufficient list would be that of Victor Renán Barco (PL) of the Department of Caldas. Barco's tenure in the Senate dates back to the National Front and continued into 2006. In 2002 Barco's list won 68,295 votes, which won him one largest-remainder seat. Of the votes that Barco won, 92.92 percent came from Caldas, or 63,458 votes, which was far more than the average LR winner in 2002 of 59,539, let alone the lowest LR winner (40,460). On the other end of the spectrum was Luis Carlos Avellaneda Tarazona of the Democratic Unity Party, who constructed a victory from across the country (the area with the largest contribution to his win was in Bogotá, which contributed only 14.98 percent of the total vote for his list). Barco represents old-style "electoral baron" politics, while Avellaneda represents the full utilization of the post-1991 rules.[21]

Table 6.8 details the HDS versus NH breakdown for the elections in question, examining not only the overall pattern but also the degree to which different types of candidates (traditional vs. quasi- and nontraditional, and incumbents vs. challengers) acquired their support from within home districts or needed additional votes from beyond their home to win.

We see that at the onset of the rules, the majority of seats were coming from home district sufficient seats and that the traditional parties

Table 6.8

HDS vs. NH Seats, 1991–2002 Senate

	1991	*1994*	*1998*	*2002*
	All Parties			
HDS	56 (56.00%)	57 (57.00%)	40 (40.0%)	44 (44.00%)
NH	44 (44.00%)	43 (43.00%)	60 (60.0%)	56 (56.00%)
	Traditional Parties: PL			
HDS	41 (73.21%)	32 (57.14%)	21 (43.75%)	12 (41.38%)
NH	15 (26.79%)	24 (42.86%)	27 (56.25%)	17 (58.62%)
	Traditional Parties: PC			
HDS	6 (66.67%)	16 (80.00%)	9 (60.00%)	6 (46.15%)
NH	3 (33.33%)	4 (20.00%)	6 (40.00%)	7 (53.85%)
	Quasi- and Nontraditional Parties			
HDS	9 (25.71%)	9 (37.50%)	10 (27.03%)	27 (47.37%)
NH	26 (74.39%)	15 (62.50%)	27 (72.97%)	30 (52.63%)
	Incumbents			
HDS	30 (71.43%)	31 (68.89%)	23 (40.35%)	18 (46.15%)
NH	12 (28.57%)	14 (31.11%)	34 (59.65%)	21 (53.85%)
	Challengers			
HDS	26 (44.83%)	26 (47.27%)	17 (39.53%)	26 (42.62%)
NH	32 (55.17%)	29 (52.73%)	26 (60.47%)	35 (57.38%)

and incumbents (made up primarily of members of traditional parties) were more prone to being able to win within their own territorial bailiwick than quasi/nontraditional candidates and challengers. Of course, the effects of the new national district are immediate, insofar as from the get-go almost half of the seats require votes from outside a given list head's home district.

When looking at the traditional parties, there are some noteworthy observations to make. First, the PL's majority status in 1991 and 1994 required a substantial number of seats to be won with votes from outside single districts—a particularly noteworthy finding, given that the PL has been a nigh-permanent majority in both houses of Congress and that if any party should have the capacity to take advantage of old-style vote gathering, it would be the Liberals. Indeed, given the PL's *avispa* strategy, it became quite necessary to have a large number of lists not headed by local electoral bosses. So while the PL was able to continue to dominate Colombia electoral politics for over a decade under the new electoral rules, it did so by adopting behaviors that eroded old-style politics. This, in turn, helped contribute to the evolution of the party system.

Second, we see that the PC continued to be more oriented toward home district seats until 1998. This fact illustrated that the PC had already fractionalized by 1991, and those candidates who saw the advantage of new electoral strategies had already fled the mainline Conservatives and adopted quasi-traditional methods of seeking office (e.g., the NFD, MSN, National Conservative Movement, etc.). Since the PC was already in minority status, there was little for these groups to lose by going it on their own. These numbers confirm that largely only the old-style Conservatives (in terms of generating power from localities) have stayed in the party. Interestingly, as the PC moved to winning LR seats via multiple lists, so too did it start to rely more on non–home district seats.

Third, and most significant, is that as the new rules set in, more seats were won outside the traditional departmental spheres, creating new relationships between parties/candidates and voters. Also such circumstances meant that power seekers did not need to follow the well-trod pathways to power of the past and could instead embark on the quest for a Senate seat without necessarily having connections to existing parties, party elites, or clientele networks.

Conclusions: New Rules and New Behaviors

The 1991 reforms brought about a series of new behaviors that began changing the party system as early as the 1990 elections to select the National Constituent Assembly. Not only did those elections show party adaptation to changing rules (the PL's *avispa* strategy), but it also showed that voters were willing to amass substantial support behind new electoral actors (the AD/M-19) and to deny votes to previously entrenched traditional actors (the PC).

While the 1991 Constitution did not bring about the much-ballyhooed "participatory democracy" often discussed at the time, it did change many of the basic parameters of the electoral system. As was argued in the previous chapter, it altered the significance of the presidency as an electoral prize and also provided new means to access executive power at the local level. It also provided new ways to access the legislature, as was argued extensively above. The combination of these factors meant an important shift in Colombian politics, away from the two traditional collectives acting as the primary repositories of all electoral influence, and toward a situation in which power seekers could achieve their goals of political influence in a way that afforded more autonomy than had been the case in the pre-1991 era.

The 1991 changes to the institutional parameters of Colombian democracy created a new set of opportunities for those seeking influence over the state. As a result, the behaviors of power seekers were altered. The changes to the election of the Senate are of special significance, as they encouraged the most alterations in terms of political party behavior. The combination of the existing elements of personal list–PR with the single, national election district led to a period of increased experimentation within the party system. This led to more lists and more labels, and more choices for the electorate. However, given the absolute numbers in question, the scope of available choices expanded to the point of being overwhelming for the given voter, since the ballot was a bewildering display of small boxes filled with faces, names, and party labels that required four letter-size pages to contain them (and each year the boxes on the pages had to be smaller to get them all to fit—see appendix 1).

The system, however, could not make the next step until those institutional changes eroded the power and influence of the Liberal Party, the last mainstay of the prior system. The 1991 era started with a Liberal in the Casa de Nariño, Cesar Gaviria (1990–1994); as the promulgation of the constitution led to dissolution of the Congress, it did not require a new presidential election, and the first presidential contest under the new rules led to a Liberal winner, Ernesto Samper (1994–1998).

Thus the political realities of roughly the first decade under the new constitution saw a continuation of one key factor of Colombian political life: the political dominance of the Partido Liberal. The Liberals lost the 1998 presidential election to Andrés Pastrana, true, but the party expected to lose the presidency once in a while, and besides, counting coalitional lists and other partisan allies, the Liberals maintained their dominance of the Congress.[22] However, 2002 brought a new political reality: the PL lost its majority status in the Congress for the first time since it had to share the legislature with the Conservatives during the National Front, and to add insult to injury (or, indeed, just more injury), it lost the presidency for the second consecutive election. The PL thus not only lost the ability to block reform; it also was in a position where reform could work to its advantage.

This all led to the adoption of Legislative Act No. 1 of 2003, which transformed the electoral system in a dramatic way by eliminating the personal list system and allocating legislative seats via the D'Hondt method rather than by the Hare quota with largest remainders. It can be argued that the effects of the 1991–2002 period made it possible for this next step to be undertaken.

The wild party fragmentation that was taking place under personal list–PR, and the fact that even the PL had mismanaged the *avispa*-swarm strategy by 2002, no doubt helped the adoption of the long-sought-after (in academic circles, anyway) single-list requirement. The fact that old strategies and behaviors were failing, such as the inability of traditional party elites to control lists via department-based strategies and especially given that even the PL was starting to lose coherence, set the stage for serious electoral reform (especially when coupled with the fact, as argued in the prior chapter, that the presidency was not as easily captured by the PL as had been the case).

By 2002 two key things had happened that allowed electoral reform to have a serious chance at success. First, new constituencies were emerging (e.g., the pro-Uribe faction) that held political sway that was not based solely in the hands of traditional party elites, and second, the PL had lost is capacity to dominate legislative elections.

The likelihood is that the new party configuration, under the new rules and incentives, is moving to a real multiparty system. While the parties that have formed primarily in support of Uribe may fade, it would seem that the PDA represents a true longtime viable actor and that the PL and PC will persist.

Of course, the most pressing issue for Colombian politicians is the inability of the state to deal with the problems of ongoing political violence, a topic that will be discussed in the next chapter. However, while overt optimism is difficult to muster given Colombia's track record, the fact of the matter is that there is at least some room for hope that the new electoral conditions could serve a dual purpose in remedying at least some of Colombia's woes.

First, the new configuration of rules and parties may encourage heretofore alienated power seekers and voters to participate in the system. Second, the presence of new actors may make it easier for the state to deal with armed groups that have been unable to reach rapprochement with the more traditional politicians who have dominated Colombian political life.

CHAPTER 7

The Pernicious Nature of Colombian Political Violence

The lives of most Colombians born after the Second World War . . . have been spent under the sign of violence.
—Gonzalo Sánchez G. (in Bergquist et al., 2001, 1)

HAVING EXAMINED THE question of institutional development and its influence on parties and elections, it is necessary to turn to a major contextual issue: the ongoing violence. More than anything else, Colombia's intransigent violence impedes the development of true liberal democracy in Colombia, and therefore any discussion of the evolution of Colombia's democracy requires an understanding of at least the basics of the internal conflict. We have already noted (in chapter 2) a number of key indicators regarding the violence, and it is clear that the state's inability to fully assert control over its territory is a long-term challenge that remains unresolved.

The main goal of this chapter is to provide a means by which to appropriately identify the various facets of the violence so as to give the student of Colombia a better understanding of the complex relationships involved. The press accounts (and even many academic ones) oversimplify the situation. Even the treatment here is far from comprehensive; the material covered is sufficiently vast to require multiple tomes to adequately address (and, indeed, violence is the most studied issue in Colombia).[1] The issue will be approached by first laying out the basics of Colombian violence in terms of its key history and actors, and then by discussing how the violence affects the issue of democratic development. Ultimately it is impossible to comprehensively deal with these topics here, but it is possible to give some guideposts to the confusing alphabet soup of the various groups fighting (or no longer fighting) as well as to provide something of an operative history of recent issues (especially from the 1980s onward).

The first section of this chapter sketches the basic facts needed for a discussion of the political impact of the violence. The second section examines the intersection between the violence and electoral politics, whether it is the goal of integrating armed groups into civil-political life or it is the pernicious effects of drug money and violence on the politicians and parties. The chapter concludes with an evaluation of the current state of these issues.

Context

As has been noted, violence has permeated Colombia from independence onward. Indeed, Colombia is a land wherein many scholars are often described as "violentologists" (*violentologos*)—that is, persons who study the internal violence. Further, the connection between politics and violence is unmistakable. As table 3.1 details, most nineteenth-century constitutional change took place as the result of political violence. Moving to the twentieth and twenty-first centuries, we see similar patterns. *La Violencia* and the Rojas coup led to the National Front; attempts to address guerrilla violence inspired the move to write the 1991 Constitution; and violence (whether guerrilla, narco, or paramilitary) formed a motivation for constitutional reform, both failed and successful, in the first Uribe administration (2002–2006). As such, it is a topic that is impossible to ignore.[2]

Basic History

The violence is multifaceted and therefore difficult to capture in a concise description. Part of it is a continuation of a seemingly endemic part of Colombian history, while other aspects have clear ties to the broader global political context, some of which are primarily criminal in nature. The complexity in question is frequently oversimplified in the press (especially in the United States) by describing the situation as a "decades-long civil war" or some similar formulation. This formulation is problematic for two basic reasons. First, the term *civil war* is not wholly appropriate, and second the time frame is an oversimplification.

In regard to the question of what to call the Colombian conflict, the term *civil war* is too clear-cut. As García-Peña notes: "Unlike classic 'civil wars,' where nations are split in two along regional lines, as in the U.S. Civil War, or along ideological ones, as in the Spanish Civil War, the Colombian War is a much more fragmented conflict, intertwined with organized crime and narco-trafficking, where the armed political actors—of the insurgent left, the right-wing paramilitaries, and the state itself—have precarious legitimacy" (2007, 116).

In other words, to call the conflict a "civil war" (let alone a decades-long one) assumes a number of facts that are not operative. For one thing, even given the long-term presence of a number of the actors (to be discussed in detail below), the protagonists have shifted over time. At different moments the guerrillas have been the main threat, at others the drug mafias, at yet others the right-wing paramilitaries. To make matters yet more difficult, at any given moment different guerrilla groups, mafia organizations, or para-militaries have been the primary threats from their respective camps. To wit, at different points the M-19 was the most threatening guerrilla group to the Colombian state, while at others it has been the FARC. Likewise different drug cartels (e.g., Medellín, Cali, Norte de Valle) and paramilitary groups have been the preeminent actor within their particular category of violent actor. An additional thread of complexity is that the different types of groups are not mutually exclusive. For example, illegal drugs tend to be a shared thread that weaves through all the categories in question.

Another way that the notion of "civil war" is inappropriate in the Co-lombia case is that the term suggests that there is a substantial likelihood of more than one side ultimately winning control. However, despite the state's inability to defeat various violent actors, leading to a seemingly endless violence, the notion that any of those actors could overthrow the state is beyond dubious. Indeed, not even all those who have taken up arms are interested in governance, per se, since the criminal element of the violence fights not to govern but to be left alone by those who do. In sum, the very fragmentation, in both type and motivation, of the groups fighting makes the designation of "civil war" problematic, and the fact that there is no real contest for ultimate control of Colombia precludes the useful deployment of the term.

Even beyond the question of what to call the Colombian conflict, as-signing a clear time frame to widespread violence in Colombia is likewise not as simple as it might first appear. When the mass media tag the mid-1960s as the start of a multidecade conflict, they are basically taking the rough founding dates of communist guerrilla groups (the ELN in 1964 and the FARC in 1966) and simply counting from there, which is essentially as-signing a time frame that treats the fight as an artifact of the Cold War.

There are multiple problems with that formulation, not the least of which being that the FARC's origins actually stretch back into the 1940s and that many scholars see *La Violencia* as spilling into the mid-1960s.[3] As such, if we are simply talking about ongoing, widespread violence, one could argue that there has been no real cessation of violence since as early as 1946 to the present time. In fact, Dix in his 1987 book essentially argued that there has been an unending violence with different stages from 1946 until the time of his writing (38). Given the parameters used by Dix, we could extend that thinking to the present time and the foreseeable future.

However, there are several issues to disentangle here. First, while the period of 1902 (the end of the War of a Thousand Days) to 1946 was mostly peaceful, it was not devoid of political violence. Second, it is useful to disaggregate *La Violencia* from the general violence in question, as it was a specific era wherein the fighting was between Liberals and Conservatives. Third, even when we wish to speak of later fighting, there are multiple components to consider: various guerrilla groups versus the state, drug traffickers versus the state, paramilitaries versus guerrillas, and paramilitaries versus the state. As such, none of this is a straightforward issue of one armed camp versus another in a clearly defined span of time.

In terms of the beginnings of *La Violencia*, it is best to start with April 9, 1948, and the assassination of Jorge Eliécer Gaitán (and the resultant urban riot known as the *Bogotazo*) as the starting of the interparty violence given the ominous designation of "The Violence." While it is true that there was political violence in 1945 and 1946 that presaged what was to come, the truly intense fighting did not start until after Gaitán was killed. From there some scholars argue that this conflict lasted until differing points in time ranging from 1953 to 1966.[4] Safford and Palacios state (correctly, I would argue) that the "greatest destructive force was released between 1948 and 1953," with the military dictatorship of Rojas being able to reign in some of the fighting. I would therefore set the basic interval for *La Violencia* proper to be from 1948 to 1958 (i.e., from Gaitán's death to the start of the National Front). Even if all fighting did not cease by 1958, the agreement to enter into the National Front was the official end of hostilities between the parties, making it a good date to peg as the end of *La Violencia*. Regardless of the exact end date, we are talking here of a period of violence that left anywhere from 80,000 to 400,000 Colombians dead at the hands of their fellow citizens (although typically the number that is most cited is 200,000).[5]

The 1960s did see the advent of a new form of counterstate challenge: revolutionary communist groups of various stripes, although, as noted above, some of the foundations of these groups stretch back to the previous conflict, creating some continuity from the 1940s onward. From the early to mid-1960s until the 1980s the conflict was essentially one of the state versus various revolutionary groups. However, drug traffickers started to operate in the 1970s and became major players in the 1980s, and soon thereafter came the advent of right-wing paramilitaries. While it is true that "self-defense" groups had existed prior to this point in time, they did not become a major element of Colombia's violence until the 1980s and especially the 1990s.

It should not be ignored, either, that the violence in Colombia, while very much linked to multifaceted elements of domestic politics, has also intersected three major components of the United States' foreign policy: the Cold War, the War on Drugs, and the Global War on Terror.[6] The Cold

War context was the one in which Marxist guerrillas emerged in Colombia and wherein the Colombian state developed its own national security doctrine in response. It was also the circumstance in which the United States first saw the need to provide aid to Colombia. If the Cold War brought U.S. attention to Colombia, the War on Drugs made the United States and Colombia key partners, leading Colombia to be a major recipient of U.S. foreign aid. From there the events of September 11, 2001, transformed the Bush administration's views of armed groups and led to the reclassification of Colombian belligerents as "terrorists" and therefore to an even broader U.S. role in Colombia's internal violence (see Taylor 2005a and 2005b).

It should also be noted that there has been an evolving peace process (really a series of processes) since the Betancur administration (1982–1986) in which numerous groups have been involved. While there is some discussion below of demobilized groups and attempts at moving from armed to unarmed political life, the nature and history of the peace process is not a topic that will be dealt with here in great detail.[7]

Dramatis Personae

In terms of the history relevant to democratic development, it is important to understand the basics of the insurgencies of the Left, the importance of drug trafficking, and the rise of paramilitarism. This is not an attempt to deal with every group ever to take up arms in Colombia since the 1960s, but rather to focus on those which further an understanding of the current state of Colombian politics.

Guerrilla Groups

Already noted above is the fact that there have been a number of significant guerrilla groups operating in Colombia for many decades. The ones that have had long-term significance have been the National Liberation Army (ELN), the Revolutionary Armed Forces of Colombia (FARC), the Popular Liberation Army (EPL), and the Movement of the 19th of April (M-19). Also worthy of mention are the Quintín Lame Movement (MQL) and the Revolutionary Workers' Party (PRT). Numerous other groups have also operated (and some continue to operate) in Colombia since the 1960s.[8] So, which are the groups of consequence to our discussion?

The FARC (known officially since 1982 as the FARC-EP, "EP" [*ejército popular*] meaning "Army of the People") is the most famous (or infamous, depending on one's point of view) of the active guerrilla groups in

Colombia. As has already been noted, it has its origins in *La Violencia* and Liberals at arms as well as the Communist Party of that era (Dix 1967, 280, and Safford and Palacios 2002, 355–357). So while the FARC's formal origins postdate the Cuban Revolution of 1959, it should not be viewed as a specifically Cuban-inspired movement. Indeed, the early origins of the group reach as far back as the 1920s and "peasant agitation" initiated by the Communist Party (Safford and Palacios 2002, 355). The group has been led by Pedro Antonio Marín—better known by his nom de guerre, Manuel Marulanda Vélez, and his nickname, Tirofijo ("Sureshot")—since before its official founding.[9]

By the middle of the 2000–2010 decade the FARC was estimated to have a fighting force of approximately 17,000–20,000 and an annual income of roughly $900 million (as of 1999), which it secures via links to the drug trade and to kidnapping (Bagley 2005, 29–30; Ramírez et al. 2005, 110).[10] The FARC has been involved in numerous negotiations with the government over the years, ultimately to no avail.[11] The most recent round was during the Pastrana administration (1998–2002), when the government ceded a Switzerland-size chunk of the state to the FARC as a demilitarized zone for the purposes of using it as a base for negotiations. This strategy ended when the administration lost patience with the FARC over several high-profile political kidnappings.

Given that the FARC has fought over a very long period of time, it is fair to say that it has also spanned three distinct eras in its conflict with the state. During the Cold War period the FARC was seeking a revolutionary overthrow of the Colombian state and was viewed by the Colombian government (and its U.S. ally) as part of the global struggle between East and West. However, sometime in the 1980s the FARC began to dabble in the drug trade, and by the 1990s it was firmly involved. At that point it became part not only of the Cold War but also of the War on Drugs being waged by both the Colombian government and the United States. Its historical relevance was again altered after September 11, 2001, as the FARC was on the U.S. State Department's list of international terrorist groups.[12] As such, it became a target as well in what the George W. Bush administration (2001–2009) has dubbed the "Global War on Terror."

The inclusion of the FARC (and other armed groups in Colombia) in this conflict is not a mere rhetorical or symbolic gesture. The U.S. government had long maintained that the guerrilla war and the drug wars were two different issues, and therefore it would provide funding for the latter but not the former. While the FARC's involvement in the drug trade was already beginning to erode the notion that it was simply a revolutionary guerrilla group, the shifting in official U.S. government perception of the FARC and like groups into the "terrorist" column allowed for a policy review of funding destined for Colombia. Washington's classification of the FARC as a terrorist group resulted in an important shift in U.S. views on security policy and funding for Colombia, to wit, the view that the U.S. approach to Colombia ought to be a "unified campaign" against foreign terrorist groups in the country, not one aimed only at drug trafficking (Ramírez et al. 2005, 110; Taylor 2005b).

The ELN is more a throwback to the Cold War era and the quest for Marxist revolution, although it, too, has been classified as a terrorist organization by the United States, the European Union, and the Colombian state. Unlike the FARC, the ELN appears to not be intertwined with the drug trade, but it does engage in criminal activities for profit, specifically kidnapping and extortion. The ELN has been involved in on-again, off-again peace talks with the government for some years, and in mid-2007 the talks were ongoing in Havana, Cuba, with a tentative cease-fire agreed on between the two parties. The estimated size of the ELN is between four thousand (Hagen 2002, 24) and five thousand troops (Bagley 2005, 33).

The EPL is the third-largest active guerrilla group in Colombia, although what exists now is a remnant of a larger entity that laid down its arms in exchange for participation in the 1991 National Constituent Assembly. Approximately three thousand members of the EPL gave up armed struggle, and the group transformed itself into the political party Hope, Peace and Liberty (which retained the acronym EPL in Spanish: Esperanza, Paz y Libertad).

Three nonactive guerrilla groups are in need of mention: the MQL, the PRT, and the M-19. All three demobilized, and all three participated in the NCA, the latter two demobilizing specifically for that purpose.

The M-19 is the most important of the three, and for a while in the late 1970s and early 1980s was the most significant of the guerrilla groups operating in Colombia. Unlike the previously mentioned groups, which were primarily or wholly oriented toward rural action, the M-19 was Colombia's first mainly urban-oriented guerrilla group. Further, the M-19, while leftist in orientation, was not Marxist in the same vein as the FARC, ELN, and EPL. Rather, the group had an orientation that sought to reclaim the nation and its symbols for the people of Colombia (such as the sword of Bolívar, the theft of which was its first major act).

The M-19 also intersects the overall theme of our discussion about electoral democracy in a special way, as its name and basic origin are linked to the electoral process, and it eventually entered that process as a new political party (as noted above). The M-19 was founded primarily in opposition to the alleged electoral fraud of April 19, 1970, when the ex-dictator, and ANAPO candidate, Gustavo Rojas Pinilla was denied the presidency so that the last National Front candidate, Misael Pastrana of the PC, could move into the Casa de Nariño. As such, the M-19 is the group that best fits the exclusion thesis concerning the National Front (i.e., the hypothesis that the exclusionary nature of the Front led directly to the taking up of arms). It is noteworthy, however, that the M-19 was not made up wholly of disaffected members of ANAPO but was a combination of persons who had been ejected from the FARC and the Communist Party and socialist-oriented elements of ANAPO (Pizarro 1992, 182).

The group was clearly the most public relations–conscious of the insurgents and was able to pull off a number of high-profile actions that embarrassed the Colombian government (the aforementioned theft of Bolívar's sword, the seizure of the Dominican Embassy, and the theft of arms from a military arms depot,[13] among others). The most audacious, and ultimately disastrous, of its actions was the seizure of the Palace of Justice in 1985 along with most of the Colombian Supreme Court. The end result of that adventure was a military assault of the palace that resulted in the death of many high-level leaders of the M-19, along with most of the Colombian Supreme Court. While the group did survive the Palace of Justice fiasco, it was severely hobbled and by 1989 accepted a negotiated settlement with the government and converted itself to a political party.

The MQL and PRT require mention as well. The MQL is interesting because it was the only fighting group to be overtly organized around the issue of the rights of indigenous persons. More noteworthy for the purposes of this inquiry is the fact that the group, along with the PRT, was willing to demobilize in return for participation in the National Constituent Assembly. Both received nonvoting seats in the assembly in exchange for their rejection of armed politics. The MQL was quite small, numbering around 150 at the time of its demobilization (Safford and Palacios 2002, 359). Neither group was especially important in terms of the overall constellation of armed actors.

Drug Traffickers

While specific individuals and groups within the overall category of drug traffickers can (and will) be discussed, it is important to start any consideration of this topic with an understanding that the very presence of the illicit drug industry in Colombia profoundly shapes the basic contours of

Colombian politics and certainly defines substantial portions of the ongoing violence.

The tendrils of the illicit drug industry have penetrated and intertwined themselves into numerous parts of the body politic in a way that touches and affects every actor in the system one way or another. In other words, when dealing with the illegal drug industry it is incorrect to refer to drug dealers, traffickers, or cartels as if they are a discrete set of actors contained in their own domains. The aforementioned tendrils are everywhere. For example, it is clear that the FARC has used drug-related activities to fund much of its efforts since the early 1980s and especially since the end of the Cold War.[14] Not only is the contemporary paramilitary movement often funded by drug-related activities as well, but the current iteration of right-wing "self defense" groups grew directly out of drug cartel activity in the 1980s (as will be further discussed below). So, at a minimum, it is clear that the size and capacity of belligerents in this conflict are directly linked to the drug industry.

Beyond the nonstate actors, consider the Colombian state itself. Certainly the increase in the need for the Colombian state to be ever-oriented toward questions of violence would be lessened if there was no drug trade. And while the paramilitaries may be primarily the result of the drug trade, there is also the unpleasant fact that the state has been linked to these groups as well. Beyond that, the primary interest that the United States government has in Colombia is the promotion of the War on Drugs (which has, as noted above, been linked by the Bush administration with the Global War on Terror). The billions of dollars spent and the personnel deployed to Colombia would never have been allocated had it not been for the drug issue. There is also the general issue of corruption that drug monies encourage. In light of such issues, it is impossible to understand Colombian politics since the mid-1980s without taking into account this topic.

Further, the very nature of antinarcotics policies has the effect of escalating the overall level of fighting. Consider, for example, the factors involved in the following scenario. Drug cultivation is attacked via aerial spraying by the state. Drug producers then seek to move activities to areas of Colombian territory where the state has less presence and influence. Such areas would already likely be marked by violence and the presence of counterstate actors. The presence of drugs makes the state even more intent on asserting control, which means more military activity. Meanwhile, the presence of drugs means the counterstate actors have more of an incentive to protect the territory, meaning more willingness to fight state-directed violence with more violence. Further, the drugs themselves provide the cash needed to fund the fighting. Beyond that, local peasants, who already are estranged from the state and the national economy, realize that they can more easily feed their families by growing coca leaf or working to harvest it. As a result the local citizenry are more allied with the counterstate actors than with the state (especially since state aircraft frequency fly over to dump herbicide on coca plants, hitting food crops as well). Through such feedbacks, the presence of drugs further destabilizes an already unstable region of the country.

Before dealing with specific groups, it is important to first address precisely what is meant by "the drug industry." By that term I mean the cultivation (as all the relevant drugs are derived from plants), processing, and trafficking of illicit substances and any linked behaviors and businesses. The main product in question is cocaine, but we also are dealing here with marijuana and heroin. Indeed, the basic tale, in terms of product, is that Colombia became a key source for marijuana starting in the 1960s and expanded into being home base for the management of the cocaine industry starting in the 1970s (but did not become the main cultivator state of coca leaf until the 1990s). Along the way, opium poppy cultivation also was introduced, making Colombia the largest supplier of heroin to the United States as well. According to the 2007 *World Drug Report* Colombia accounted for roughly half of all coca cultivation and 62 percent of cocaine production in 2006 (206–205).[15] Figure 7.1 shows the hectares under cultivation of coca bushes for the Andean region and the amount cultivated in Colombia. The sharp increases in cultivation in Colombia took place as counternarcotics efforts drove cultivation out of Peru and Bolivia, a classic manifestation of the "balloon effect" (i.e., if you squeeze the air out of one part of a balloon, the balloon simply bulges out in another location—the same is true about the cultivation of illicit crops like coca leaf).

From the early 1990s until 2004, Colombia was the major cultivator of opium poppy in the Western Hemisphere, but eradication efforts appear to have reduced cultivation to the point that Mexico is now the chief cultivator state in this hemisphere, although the hectares under cultivation there pale in comparison with Afghanistan and Myanmar (UNODC 2007b, 40). Marijuana cultivation is currently a minor part of the drug puzzle at this point in time.[16]

The drug industry has existed through several distinct phases over time. Camacho and López capture the basic evolution of the drug industry in Colombia in the title of their 2007 essay "From Smugglers to Drug Lords to *Traquetos.*"[17] In other words, the drug business in Colombia started in the context of basic smuggling, reaching back as far as the 1920s, and went

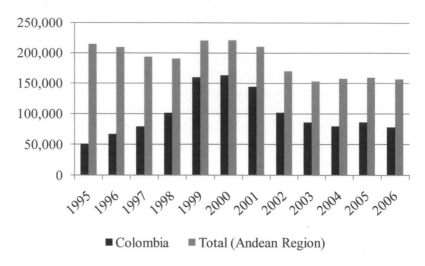

Figure 7.1. Hectares of Coca under Cultivation, 1995–2006. *Source:* UNODC 2007b:7.

through an evolution that took it to the era of the big-time drug lords and then to the current situation with smaller operators who use localized violence to control their business.

The explosion in mainly (although not exclusively) North American demand for powder cocaine in the 1970s drove the evolution of smugglers into drug lords—the image of Colombia most prevalent in U.S. popular culture.[18] During this era Colombia was really the locus of the managerial and production nexus of the cocaine industry, not the cultivation hub. This was the era of the large drug cartels, when Colombian drug lords controlled upward of 80 percent of the Andean cocaine market to the tune of an estimated $2–4 billion in annual revenue (Bagley 1989, 154).

While there were somewhere around ten large drug lords from the 1970s into the 1990s, the prototypical example of this phenomenon is, no doubt, Pablo Escobar, don of the Medellín Cartel. The Escobar era (the early 1980s until his death in a shoot-out in 1993) was one in which the Colombian state first decided to actively confront the business of drug smuggling (partly at the behest of the Reagan administration), and it is also the era during which the drug lords, especially Escobar, pushed back.

Escobar and his allies directly challenged the Colombian state in a manner that no other drug kingpin ever had or has since. Not only did he initially try to use his vast wealth to move from the shadows to some level of acceptance, but when he was unable to do so, he was more than willing to use violence to attempt to get the state to leave him and his business alone.[19]

Assassinations were a key tactic of Escobar and his ilk. Early high-profile examples were the assassination of Justice Minister Rodrigo Lara Bonilla in 1984 and the gunning down of *El Espectador* editor Guillermo Cano Isaza on December 17, 1986.[20] As Bagley notes: "Between 1981 and 1986 over 50 judges, including a dozen Supreme Court Justices, were murdered, and any judge who handled a drug case was bombarded with death threats if he refused to be bribed" (1988). In 1987 fifty-seven judges and twenty-four journalists were killed. The reach of the cartels was demonstrated to be international in scope when there was an attempt on former justice minister Enrique Parejo Gonzales in 1987 while he was serving in Budapest, Hungary, as Colombia's ambassador to that country (Kline 1999, 46). Some of the highest-profile political killing took place in the early portions of the 1990 presidential campaign with the gunning down of the presumptive Liberal nominee for president Luis Carlos Galán at a campaign rally outside Bogotá in 1989. The cartel also took responsibility for the assassination of M-19 candidate Carlos Pizarro.

However, the targeting of public officials and journalists was not the only weapon that the drug barons were willing to deploy. As the Colombian government ratcheted up its attacks on the cartels, the major drug barons sought to avoid extradition to the United States. They adopted the name "The Extradictables" (*Los Extraditables*) and waged a terror campaign against the civilian population in an attempt to persuade the Colombian state to block the sending of arrested drug chieftains to the United States for prosecution. The Extraditables used car bombs and even the destruction of an Avianca flight in the air between Bogotá and Medellín on November 27, 1989, to make their point.[21] In a roughly six-week period between August and October of 1989 "they had carried out nearly 200 bombing attacks nationwide against government offices, banks, businesses, newspapers, hotels, supermarkets, and even schools. At least 10 people were killed and 160 wounded or maimed" (Bagley 1989, 157–158). Escobar's groups also engaged in urban terrorism in early 1993 during the period that he was a fugitive from the law.

The Cali Cartel, which inherited the bulk of the cocaine business with the death of Escobar, took a more corruption-oriented strategy, rather than engaging in violence. Those tactics involved, among other things, sizable contributions to the Ernesto Samper campaign in 1994, which eventually led to the imprisonment of Samper's campaign manager (and later defense minister) Fernando Botero Zea on charges of illegal enrichment. The scandal also led to the "8,000 Process," which investigated Samper's role in receiving the contributions (Samper was exonerated by a 111–43 vote of the Chamber in June of 1996).

However, the days of a major drug organization controlling 80 percent or more of the drug business in Colombia are over; they ended when the Samper administration dismantled the Cali Cartel in the mid-1990s. This is not to say that the drug business was diminished in the 1990s but rather to point out that it has been dispersed into the hands of multiple smaller groups since that time. If the previous era was one of cartels, the post–Cali Cartel era was one of *cartelitos* (or "little cartels"). While it is clear that the dismantling of the Medellín and Cali cartels were successes of Colombian (and U.S.) counternarcotics policies, it is also true that their defeat did not have a significant effect on the availability or price of cocaine on the streets of the United States or elsewhere. Indeed, the defeat of the two monsters of cocaine well illustrate what Bertram, Blachman, Sharpe, and Andreas (1996) refer to as the "Hydra Effect," named after a multiheaded mythical creature that would grow several new heads each time one of its existing heads was chopped off. The influence of the drug industry over Colombian violence and politics continues unabated, even if the form has changed over time.

The Paramilitaries

The generic notion of a paramilitary organization can range from militarized elements of police forces (such as SWAT units) to citizen militias organized to act as auxiliary units to standing militaries to independent (and often illegal) private militias who adopt military-style organization for any number of reasons. Over time in Colombia there have been multiple types of paramilitary organizations. For their legal standing, we can go back to the 1960s and the notion of self-defense against leftist insurgents as a result of Decree No. 3398 of December 24, 1965, and later Law 48 of 1968, both of which allowed for the formation of civilian militias to fight alongside the Colombian military in counterinsurgency actions.[22] Law 48 was revoked in 1989,[23] but the notion of civilian self-defense was revived in 1994 with the creation of another iteration of civilian self-defense, the Special Services of Vigilance and Private Security (also known by the name Convivir).[24] It is important to note, as this brief summary indicates, that there is a long history in Colombia of such groups, and that there is even some legal basis for their operation over time.

On balance the legally organized groups also tend to self-identify (or have been historically identified) as "self-defense" organizations (a term that has been used at least as far back as the *La Violencia* era). The evocation, especially in recent years, of the concept of "self-defense" has often had political implications as groups have sought to mask their violent actions as simply ones born of self-protection. Indeed, the paramilitary groups of the 1990s and onward have frequently described themselves as simply an armed response to counter the left-wing violence of the FARC and ELN.

However, the concept of paramilitarism in Colombia, like so much else in the discussion of the violence, is not as straightforward as it may appear. For example, the U.S. press often portrays these groups as simply a right-wing reaction to leftist insurgents. Such a characterization contains some accurate elements but is a gross oversimplification. We are not seeing here right-wing analogues to existing left-wing guerrilla groups. Nor are we talking about simple cattle ranchers protecting their land (another common description in the press). While it is likely that some self-defense of cattle ranches has taken place, many of the ranches in question are actually part of the holdings of drug traffickers, and that which needs protection is not cattle.

In the broadest sense of the term, a paramilitary group in the Colombian context could mean any number of things: an armed civilian group that is seeking to protect itself from other violent actors, an armed gang seeking to protect drug cultivation or production turf, a right-wing group organized to combat the FARC or other guerrilla groups, or a death squad affiliated in some nebulous way to the state or some other actor within the conflict. And, also typical to the Colombian case, we are likely talking about some combination thereof.

On balance, by the time we get to the mid- to late 1990s, the term *paramilitaries* (or just *paras*) essentially means the United Self-Defense Forces of Colombia (the AUC—Autodefensas Unidas de Colombia). The AUC is a national umbrella organization that united numerous paramilitary groups in 1997; by the time of the start of its peace process with the government in 2002 it numbered between fifteen thousand and twenty thousand militants (Arnson 2005, 1). The paramilitary phenomenon, although it has been growing in Colombia since the early 1980s (and reflects behaviors going back decades before that[25]), is the newest element in an already difficult situation. The *paras* started to be a major national factor in the late 1980s and early 1990s and have only recently been a serious focus of academic study. If one looks at the literature on Colombia written from the early 1990s and earlier, one might not find any reference to the term *paramilitary* let alone a discussion of the generalized phenomenon of these groups as a key factor in the ongoing Colombian conflict. A key issue with paramilitary groups is that they represent, in some cases, an alternative attempt at security in the face of the state's failure to provide order. However, they are also a manifestation of vigilantism, and therefore of the state's partial loss of control of its own territory.

The current manifestation of paramilitarism grew out of the confluence of the drug industry at the height of the drug lord era, the guerrilla conflict, and the willingness of the state to engage in shadowy practices as it pursued the previous two groups. From here we can look at the way a violent conflict between the cartels and the M-19 led to the birth of more organized violence to make an already difficult situation even worse.

As the cocaine industry was growing in the late 1970s, the M-19 leaders saw an opportunity to make some quick money to pay for their revolutionary dreams and decided that kidnapping cartel figures was an easy way to make a lot of money in a hurry.[26] The key case that set into motion a remarkable sequence of events was the kidnapping in November of 1981 of Martha Nieves Ochoa, whose family was prominently involved in the drug trade. The response of the drug lords was not to pay the ransom but rather to respond in a way that would get not only the M-19's attention but that of other actors in the conflict. A meeting was called by Escobar, and he and his associates created a solution to the kidnapping problem.

That solution was a group whose name signaled its purpose: Death to Kidnappers (MAS—*Muerte a Secuestradores*).[27] The group announced its arrival on the scene by air-dropping leaflets onto sporting events in December of 1981 and made its presence known to the M-19 through the abduction, torture, and murder of its members. The confrontation eventually led to a truce between the Medellín Cartel and the M-19 as well as the return of Ms. Ochoa to her family. With that matter concluded, MAS adopted a more generalized mission and "became an ultrarightist armed force whose main task was protecting traffickers' land . . . [and] became the basis for the creation of the powerful Colombian paramilitary movement" (Camacho and López 2007, 75). It is worth noting that Fidel and Carlos Castaño, two of the most important paramilitary leaders of the 1980s, 1990s, and (for Carlos) the decade after 2000, worked with MAS for a time.[28]

If MAS had hinted at a new, violent way to attack the guerrillas, then some disaffected members of MAS, Carlos Castaño included, would go on to show how that violence could be directed at the cartels. In 1992 a series of events led to the formation by Castaño and some associates of a new group: People Persecuted by Pablo Escobar (Los PEPES, *Perseguidos por Pablo Escobar*).[29] The PEPES launched a reign of terror against Escobar and his associates and aided, ultimately, in his death at the hands of Colombian security forces on December 2, 1993.

Both MAS and the PEPES presented a new, brutal variation on the old theme of Colombian violence, and both were at least tacitly approved of by elements of the state. Allegations regarding state complicity in paramilitary actions include anything from direct support and planning by military officers to turning a blind eye to atrocities committed by paramilitary units that are seen to further the state's war against the guerrillas.[30] Certainly there have been numerous examples of links between members of state institutions and paramilitary groups, from military personnel being arrested for complicity with the paramilitaries to links to politicians (the *parapolítica* scandal to be discussed below).

The tale of the Castaño brothers hardly ends with the PEPES (which dissolved after the death of Escobar). Rather, Fidel had been involved, contemporaneously with the existence of MAS, with his own group of thugs to protect his land and interests. They were called the *tangüeros* (named for a Castaño ranch, Las Tangas) and were used to spread fear among locals who were suspected of aiding guerrillas (the Castaños' father had been kidnapped and murdered by the FARC when Fidel refused to pay the ransom they demanded).[31] It was also at this time that Fidel sent Carlos to Tel Aviv, Israel, to receive antiterror training from a private security firm and that the brothers would forge their ties to Escobar and MAS (Kirk 2004, 151–152).

The *tangüeros* evolved first into the Self-Defense Units of Córdoba and Urabá (ACCU) and eventually into the AUC. This history is significant because it does mark a new period in the ongoing violence and demonstrates a key example of a new type of applied violence, one that highlights the influence of the drug industry on the conflict but that also provided a model for the state to exploit. The damage being done by paramilitaries became so great that by late 2002 the government had engaged the paramilitaries in peace talks.[32]

Without a doubt, the increased significance of the drug trade and the increase in *para* activity took Colombian violence to new levels. Indeed, figure 2.1 shows the murder rate in Colombia dramatically trending upward just as the drug lords and state start to go at one another, and rising even more as paramilitary groups increase their activities.

When Electoral Politics Meets the Violence

While it is clear that high levels of violence make governance, let alone democratic governance, difficult, how should we fit the above-described circumstances into the overall question of democratic development in Colombia? Generically it is clear that the violence is a political matter because, at a minimum, the vast majority of Colombian citizens would like to see the violence ended, and the only institution able to even attempt to work toward that end is the state itself. Thus, the fabric of Colombia's public policy has to do with the violence. Certainly it has been a major campaign issue at the presidential level for some time, and nothing shapes Colombia's foreign policy more than the question of drugs, which is inherently part of the violence issue.

Rather than look at the violence in terms of public policy, however, the goal here is to examine how the violence has specifically affected democratic development. To do so, this section will look at the question of integrating belligerents into nonviolent politics (both successes and failures) and the manner in which the violence corrupts democracy (physical harm, drug money, and the example of the *parapolítica* scandal).

Integration: Successes, Failures, and the Future

A key goal of the peace process has been the integration of belligerents into civil society. We have already mentioned the most significant example of success at integrating guerrilla groups into civil politics: the cases of the M-19, EPL, MQL, and PRT. To some degree that past experience may have some influence over the ongoing peace talks with the ELN and perhaps even the AUC.

The most successful demobilization in Colombian history to date has been that of the M-19 and its move into electoral politics. Of course, the degree to which the case of the M-19 provides a model for negotiated settlements is questionable, given that by the time its members agreed to lay down their arms in 1990 their war-waging capabilities had been substantially diminished, first by the Palace of Justice fiasco in 1985, and then by the attacks by MAS. Those incidences, especially the Palace of Justice situation, led to a radical degradation of the group's leadership. Further, the M-19 was always more of a political group than truly an armed insurgency. As such, the combination of the group's basic nature and its diminished fighting capacity made for a unique situation in terms of a negotiated peace.

Further, the usefulness of the EPL, MQL, and PRT as models for political integration is questionable for two reasons. First is their size (especially the latter two), as they were quite small, making demobilization and integration less daunting than, say, dealing with the FARC. More important, however, is the unique circumstances under which they laid down their arms: the context of the writing of a new constitution. That situation provided a specific carrot that could be offered: seats in the NCA and a voice in the shaping of new political rules.

When one tries to apply these experiences to how deals might be worked out with the FARC and ELN, one has to specifically consider the case of the Patriot Union (UP—Union Patriótica). The UP was a leftist political party that was formally founded on November 16, 1985, at its first National Congress, although the party emerged from the 1984 peace talks between the FARC and the Betancur administration. Those talks resulted in the La Uribe accords and a cease-fire that existed from 1984 to 1987. The UP was originally conceived as the civilian political wing of the FARC, although the two formally broke ties in 1987.

The UP competed in the 1986 election, winning five seats in the Senate (two outright and three with coalition partners) and nine in the Chamber (three outright, six via coalition). It also won fourteen deputies in departmental assemblies and 351 seats on municipal councils. Its 1986 presidential candidate, Jaime Pardo Leal, won 4.6 percent of the national vote (328,752 total votes).

However, the entry of this new party into civil life was hardly smooth. Between the 1986 elections and the 1988 elections (for local offices and the first for mayors), "more than 500 militants and leaders" were killed, including the aforementioned Pardo and "two senators, two representatives, five deputies, 45 councillors and four mayors" (Santana n.d., 2).[33] Despite the violence, the UP participated in the 1988 elections and went on to win 15 mayoralties outright, and collaborated in the election of 105 others.

The UP continued to offer candidates, but the attacks also continued, and the death toll mounted. To read the history of the UP through journalistic and other accounts is to see a gruesome tally grow with each subsequent article. In 1987 the number killed was 450, by 1988 it was 550, by 1993 the death toll was 1,163, and a 1994 estimate put it at 2,341. By 2004 the number was at least 3,300, with other estimates going from 3,500 to 4,000. In short, it was, as the UP and others have called it, a "political genocide" (e.g., Cepeda C. 2006, García-Peña 2007, fn6).[34]

A telling example of the party's status a little more than four years after it entered official political life in Colombia is the label the UP used in the 1990 lists that it ran for the NCA: "Lista Unica por Derecho de la Vida," which means "Unified List for the Right to Life." Those accustomed to the political vernacular of the United States might immediately assume that this was an antiabortion slate. However, the right to life in this case was literally the right of the UP politicians and their allies to physical survival.

The UP lingered into the 1990s, including the election in 1994 of Manuel Cepeda Vargas (officially as a candidate of the Colombian Communist Party), who was assassinated in Bogotá on August 9, 1994, less than six months after being elected. The party's legal status was eventually revoked by the National Electoral Council owing to lack of votes (in accordance with Law 130 of 1994).

Unlike the arguments about political exclusion in the National Front, there is no argument here: the slaughter of UP members was clearly a case of elements of the Colombian state and society seeking to refuse, in brutal fashion, access to political power by members of the organized Left. The fact that right-wing paramilitaries linked to the military were involved in many of the deaths of the UP (exact numbers are impossible to come by) simply underscores the distrust that many on the left (armed and otherwise) feel toward the government and offers of peace and reintegration. Further, one can see how the experience of the UP leads to substantial resentments and complications as the Uribe administration negotiates peace with the AUC. Indeed, the situation with the UP links up to several of the already discussed elements of the violence of the 1980s onward. Bagley (1988, 84) links at least five hundred deaths of UP members specifically to MAS between 1985 and 1988, and members of the police and military were linked to MAS by reports compiled by the Colombian government.[35]

The latest attempt at integrating violent actors into the system is the Uribe administration's peace negotiations with the AUC. The AUC declared a unilateral cease-fire in December of 2002, which met a precondition for talks laid down by the newly elected president. That led to a pact, the Santa Fé de Ralito Accord, signed on July 15, 2003, which was to lead to the demobilization of the AUC by 2005.[36] A key aspect of the pact was that paramilitary leaders who surrendered would serve minimal sentences if they cooperated with authorities. The agreement also spared them from extradition to the United States. The process was furthered by the passage of the Justice and Peace Law on June 21, 2005, which granted a series of concessions to paramilitary members and leaders in exchange for disarmament. While the Uribe administration points to demobilized units and a decline in the death rate, critics of the law have been legion, both inside and outside Colombia.[37]

As of mid-2007 the process was ongoing, with a reported thirty-one thousand paramilitary fighters having demobilized, although the degree to which the AUC was truly shut down remains an open question. The process hit a snag in July of 2007 when the Colombian Supreme Court ruled that the acts of the paramilitaries were not seditious in nature but rather undertaken for personal gain. The ruling called into doubt the ability of the Uribe administration to provide special treatments for demobilized members of the AUC. The exact resolution of that issue remains to be seen, although the administration will pursue a legislative course of action.

The fact that paramilitary groups have been responsible for much of the increased violence of the 1980s and 1990s (and have specifically been linked to such actions as the murders of UP members) makes any peace process with them controversial. The aforementioned Supreme Court ruling and its delineation of crimes of political sedition versus personal gain illustrate part of the problem, to wit, how should Colombian law and society view the *paras*? Are they simply right-wing versions of the FARC, or are they something else? As García-Peña notes: "Many in the NGO community and on the democratic left in Colombia find it difficult to use the term "peace process" to refer to talks with the paramilitaries. To have a peace process, there had to first be a war. But there is very little evidence of any serious attempt by the Colombian government . . . to wage war against paramilitary groups" (2005, 64).

In other words, if the paramilitaries are not truly counterstate belligerents and, indeed, have worked with the state (even if unofficially), then to what degree can a political settlement exist? Exactly what would the political disagreement with the state be? In this vein, García-Peña asks how a peace process should be construed—is it a negotiation aimed at resolving political differences between two belligerents (the state and an armed group) or is it a submission to justice for punishment of specific acts? If it is the former, the AUC presents logical problems, if anything because it has never been an antistate belligerent but has rather directed its violence at left-wing insurgents.[38]

Corrupting Democracy

A major issue associated with the violence is the degree to which its presence can compromise and damage the basic fabric of democracy itself. This can manifest in a variety of ways including threats and violence against politicians for the purpose of influencing their behavior. Also, given the high profits gained from the drug industry, the corrupting influence of money cannot be ignored in this context, an issue that was underscored in the Samper administration. Finally, ties between violent, extralegal actors and politicians (whether elected or appointed) create a great deal of difficulty for the quality of democracy, as the *parapolítica* scandal illustrates.

Certainly kidnapping or death have been long-term risks for any who would enter Colombian politics, a fact underscored by the death of eleven departmental legislators on June 18, 2007. The eleven lawmakers from Valle del Cauca had been kidnapped by the FARC five years prior to their deaths and were killed either by the FARC or as a result of cross fire during a rescue attempt, depending on whether one accepts the government's version of the story or the FARC's (Forero 2007). The politicians in question had been kidnapped from the Departmental Assembly building in Cali on April 11, 2002 (Human Rights Watch 2002).

Indeed, as of this writing there were still a number of prominent politicians being held by the FARC, including 2002 presidential candidate Ingrid Betancourt, Alan Jara Uzola (former governor of Meta), and the following (now former because of the length of their captivity) legislators: Senators Luis Eladio Pérez Bonilla and Jorge Gechen Turbay and Representatives Consuelo González de Perdomo, Orlando Beltrán Cuellar, and Oscar Tulio Lizcano. Further, between 2002 and 2003 (leading up to the 2003 local elections), eighteen mayors were taken hostage and sixty-three were assassinated between 1998 and 2003 (El Tiempo 2003a). Of course, such activities result in a lot of citizens deciding to eschew electoral politics. As Orlando Flores, mayor of Libano who decided to leave politics, stated, "I love my town, but whoever chooses politics is a dead man" (Van Dongen 2003). Indeed, in 2002 the FARC issued a "resign or die" order to judges, mayors, and local legislators. In the 2003 electoral cycle, twenty-six mayoral/council candidates were assassinated (El Tiempo 2003c) and forty-eight quit their campaigns owing to the threat of violence (El Tiempo 2003b). Clearly, a career in politics is not necessarily the safest choice one can make in Colombia. There can therefore be little doubt that many otherwise qualified persons have eschewed politics, which is a detriment to a healthy democracy.

Another threat is the fact that drug money has the ability to penetrate the system, not only in terms of bribes, but also in terms of campaign contributions. Generically there is the problem, especially for lower-level politicians and appointees, of the offer of *plata o plomo*, which literally means "silver or lead" but in practical terms means "take a bribe or we'll kill you and/or members of your family." The latter was a favorite tool of the Medellín Cartel, while the Cali Cartel tended to prefer the *plata* part of the formulation, which leads us to the specific case of the Samper campaign discussed above.[39] Of course, Samper is hardly the only politician ever accused of taking drug money for campaigns. In the same electoral cycle (1994), twelve legislators were jailed for accepting money from the Cali Cartel (Lee and Thoumi 1999, 71).

At the end of the day it is impossible to know if Samper's move against the Cali Cartel was the result of true Machiavellian calculus (i.e., take the cartel's money and then use the state against it anyway) or of U.S. and domestic pressure as the only way to save himself from the situation.[40] Regardless, one does have to wonder as to the degree to which the entire affair would be an encouragement to traffickers to use campaign contributions as a major tool to forestall state action against their business operations.

Thoumi argues that the exact effect on policy is debatable. As he notes: "On one hand, many drug traffickers . . . were jailed or killed. . . . On the other hand, most traffickers avoided extradition, and many have continued to run their businesses from jail" (2002, 112). In light of this, he argues (as do Lee and Thoumi 1999, 76) that unlike a bribe to a judge, which is a direct quid pro quo activity, campaign contributions have a more diffused effect that may, or may not, ultimately effect policy (just like, as Lee and Thoumi note, corporate contributions to U.S. campaigns). This is not to argue that one ought to dismiss the role of drug money in campaigns but rather to suggest that it is difficult to fully measure the degree to which such contributions actually directly change what an elected official will do once in office.

At a minimum, the Samper situation had grave consequences for U.S.-Colombian relations. The Samper years were easily the lowest point in bilateral relations between the two countries since the United States helped Panama achieve independence in 1903.[41] The U.S. government not only decertified Colombia's effort in the drug war; it also revoked Samper's visa. The scandal also damaged confidence in the government within Colombia. Certainly the notion that political campaigns in Colombia are funded, even in part, by drug money fuels the notion that Colombia is a "narco-democracy" and detracts from the perceived legitimacy of the system. Certainly even the possibility that mafiosi can influence politicians or campaigns in Colombia via bribes and illegal contributions raises questions about the quality of democracy. Further, the obscene amounts of money available to actors involved in the drug trade means that bribery can also affect basic security policy.[42] One could also argue that the legitimacy afforded to the Medellín Cartel, as well as the treatment of the AUC, whose funding comes from drug trafficking, demonstrates that illicit wealth can lead to a power position in the Colombian context. As Lee and Thoumi note in regard to the interaction of the state with the Medellín Cartel, "In no other country has a government negotiated with criminals so openly and for such an extended period" (1999, 69).

Perhaps the most serious direct effect of the violence on the realm of electoral democracy has been the unfolding (and, as of this writing, far from resolved) *parapolítica* (i.e., parapolitics) scandal wherein politicians (both elected and appointed) have been demonstrated to have had illegal ties to paramilitary organizations, including using intimidation in campaigns to dissuade politicians not aligned with paramilitary groups from running at all. While such ties have long been alleged, an investigation within the Supreme Court began in late 2005 as a result of accusations made by the ex–auditor general and leader of the PDA, Clara López Obregón, regarding illegal clandestine ties between paramilitary groups and elected officials. The initial investigation led to the detention of two senators (Álvaro García and Jairo Merlano) and one representative (Eric Julio Morris), all from pro-Uribe parties.

Information for the investigations of *para*-connected politicians came from a laptop computer belonging to paramilitary leader Rodrígo Tovar (aka Jorge 40). These connections were made even more dramatic with the revelation by Senator Miguel De la Espriella (PCD) that he had signed, along with forty other politicians, a loyalty pledge with the AUC in 2001. This agreement, called the Pact of Ralito (not to be confused with the similarly named accord between the AUC and the government), called for a way forward on issues such as security and peace and specifically called for "the refounding of the state" and a "new social pact" (Gutiérrez R. 2007). This agreement has frequently been referred to in the Colombian press as the "pact with the Devil." It provided evidence to suggest that when the AUC's Salvatore Mancuso stated in 2002 that the paramilitaries controlled over a third of the Congress he was not engaging, as was assumed by some, in braggadocio. These revelations led to further investigations of the signatories of the pact.

A clear example of *para* politics would be the 2003 governor's race in the Department of Magdalena, which is on the Caribbean coast. In that race the office was uncontested, with challengers to the eventual winner, Trino Luna Correa of the PL, quitting after having been intimidated by paramilitary groups. Luna was later arrested on charges of ties to paramilitary groups. The neighboring Department of Cesar also had an unopposed candidate for governor, Hernando Molina Araújo, also of the PL.[43] Molina was charged with complicity in a massacre and for funneling funds to paramilitary leaders.

Indeed, the Araújo family, longtime political barons of Cesar, have been implicated in the scandal in numerous ways. Molina's uncle, former senator and agriculture minister Álvaro Araújo Noguera, and a cousin, Senator Álvaro Araújo Castro, were also arrested on similar charges in 2007. Other members of the family are under investigation, and Araújo Noguera's daughter, María Consuelo, was Uribe's foreign minister, but she resigned because of the arrests of her family members.

The ongoing investigation into ties between politicians and paramilitaries has resulted in at least sixty politicians being called to the Supreme Court to give testimony and the arrest of over twenty politicians (ranging from senators to local legislators).[44] Table 7.1 lists major arrests in the scandal from November 2006 to May 2007, including a number of sitting members of government and the former head of the DAS (the *Departamento Administrativo de Seguridad* or Administrative Department for Security), which is the government's internal intelligence office.

The overall scandal and associated accusations have hit very close to Uribe. Not only are a number of the persons and parties involved pro-Uribe, but there have long been accusations that Uribe himself was too sympathetic toward, if not directly involved with, the paramilitaries. Specifically there have been serious accusations of President Uribe's association with various Convivir during his time as governor of Antioquia. These accusations have been in the public discourse for some time but were also made in the form of a formal presentation by PDA senator Gustavo Petro.[45]

The exact nature of the penetration of the political class by the *paras*, as well as questions such as why these politicians participated and what types of advantages or benefits the *paras* received, is not wholly clear as of this writing. However, there are several key issues here directly relevant to the overall focus of this book. The situation demonstrates the ease by which money and violence can corrupt numerous politicians and therefore the damage in public trust in the system that ensues when such corruption is revealed. Beyond questions of public trust, the infiltration of electoral politics, including the Congress, by paramilitarism raises questions of trust among members of the government. Given the past, especially the history of the UP, there can be little doubt that members of left-leaning parties have reasons to be concerned about their own safety. At a minimum, the atmosphere in the Congress cannot be as conducive to problem solving as one might like or expect in a legislature under these circumstances, especially in regard to the issue of what to do about demobilized paramilitaries.

Looking Ahead

For some, the continuing violence means that discussions of Colombian democracy and elections are hollow and wanting. Indeed, to read the accounts of atrocities perpetrated on civilians for the crime of being in the wrong place at the wrong time is often enough to make one wonder

Table 7.1

Key Parapolítica *Arrested or Warrants Issued, November 2006–May 2007*

Politicians arrested	Party	Office when arrested	Department
Arana Sus, Salvador	Colombia Democrática	Ex-governor, Sucre/ ambass. to Chile	Sucre
Araújo Castro, Álvaro	Alas Equipo Colombia	Senator	Cesar
Araújo Noguera, Álvaro	PL in 1990 (Chamber)	Former senator	Cesar
Caballero Caballero, Jorge Luis	Apertura Liberal	Representative	Magdalena
Campo Escobar, Alfonso Antonio	PC	Representative	Magdalena
De la Espriella, Miguel	Colombia Democrática	Senator	Córdoba
De los Santos Negrete, Jose	PC	Representative	Córdoba
Garcia Romero, Álvaro	Colombia Democrática	Senator	Sucre
García Torres, Rafael		Former DAS info tech specialist	
López Cabrales, Juan Manuel	PL	Senator	Magdalena
Luna Correa, Trino	PL	Governor	Magdalena
Maloof, Dieb Nicolás	Colombia Viva	Senator	Magdalena
Merlano Fernández, Jairo	Cambio Radical	Senator	Sucre
Molina Aráujo, Hernando	PL	Governor	
Montes Alvarez, Reginaldo	Cambio Radical	Senate	Córdoba
Montes Medina, William Alfonso	PC	Senate	Bolívar
Noguera Cote, Jorge		Former head of DAS	
Pimiento Barrera, Mauricio	Partido Social De Unidad Nacional	Senator	Cesar
Pineda, Eleonora	Partido Convergencia Ciudadana	Former representative	Córdoba
Vives Lacouture, Luis Eduardo	Convergencia Ciudadana (MIPOL in 2002)	Senator	Magdalena

whether any talk of democracy in Colombia is warranted. Still, the democracy limps along, wounded though it is from various sources. Without a doubt, it is clear from the preceding discussion that the major problem facing the full development of democracy in Colombia is the ongoing problem with political violence. Perhaps the most disheartening aspect of the discussion is that the main engine that helps to drive violence at this stage of Colombian history, namely, illicit drugs, is unlikely to be stopped anytime soon.

While the situation is quite dire in many aspects, it is also the case that the likelihood of the state collapsing is quite small. The gist of the matter is that one has to recognize the basic stalemate that is, and has been, inherent in the struggle. The state has been unable to militarily defeat the guerrillas and other violent actors, and the guerrillas are incapable of actually fomenting social revolution. And while the paramilitaries create a great deal of violence, they are not seeking overthrow of the government. Their threat is that they will, in fact, seek and gain substantial political influence, and drive the state in a more violent and authoritarian direction.

Some scope for optimism exists, perhaps primarily in the fact that the new institutional order now actually encourages new groups to enter politics, and those rules may actually afford those groups some success. Can, for example, the PDA achieve enough clout in the government to institute new approaches to the violence? And if it does so, will those approaches be efficacious? It is, of course, impossible to say, although such a scenario is one source of optimism. There is also the issue of the institutional strength of the courts, as they have clearly placed themselves into a position to counter many of the Uribe policies in regard to the paramilitaries.

One thing is certain: dire predictions about the direction of the state have been a staple of discussions of Colombia since at least the 1950s. Each difficulty faced has been seen as a possible end of Colombia and its government as we know it, yet the basics have persisted for decades. If one, therefore, was to play the odds, then one should put one's money on a messy continuation of the basic status quo for as far as the eye can see.

CHAPTER 8

The State of Colombia (Evaluations and Conclusions)

The political violence . . . is directly linked to the clarity, transparency and veracity of the electoral system.
—Luis Carlos Galán

THIS CONCLUDING CHAPTER will provide a summary of the key assessments that have been made in this text, a summary of factors to consider in Colombia (including a specific look at the 2006 elections), and a look forward.

Basic Assessment

There are a number of conclusions that this study has reached, specifically about the development of the Colombian party system, the state of Colombian democracy, and the role of institutional change.

Parties Rethought

In regard to an understanding of the Colombian party system, the argument has been made herein that a number of issues that persist in the conventional wisdom regarding Colombia's party system need to be rethought. Specifically, there has been a long-standing thesis that has both romanticized the pre-Rojas party system (especially the 1930s) and exaggerated the exclusionary powers of the National Front's rules. The second issue has been the ongoing misapplication in some quarters of the party labels, specifically the desire to shoehorn candidates into the PC and PL categories.

Let us start with the Front. A foundational notion of the rethinking advocated here is that the National Front did not substantially transform the Colombian party system from a functional form to a dysfunctional one. Further, the rules of the Front were not as restrictive as is commonly argued.

Chapter 4 details the serious empirical problems with the assumptions that are made about the parties (as well as the Colombian polity) in the years before *La Violencia* and the Gómez administration and the coup by Rojas. Yes, there were some progressive reforms passed in the first López Pumarejo administration. However, it is a mistake that cascades into others to assume that one set of social reforms, made by an administration elected sans opposition, equates to an era in which the parties were truly oriented toward programmatic politics on a mass scale, and were therefore more responsive to voters. Simply put, the pre-Front parties were not as impressive as the arguments that make up the conventional wisdom require them to be.

First, a good number of the behaviors of the Colombian parties are consistent over time (elitism, clientelism, fragmentation, and the like). Second, there were other important changes (e.g., urbanization and the expansion of the franchise) between the pre- and post-Front eras that make it analytically difficult to say that the only independent variable of significance was the Front itself. In other words, where comparisons can be made, the pre- and post–National Front parties do not really look all that different. Beyond that the context in which the parties operated in the two eras are sufficiently different as to call into question any arguments that the changes in party behavior are directly or exclusively attributable to the Front's structures.

The key to the conventional wisdom is the exclusion issue. After all, if the state was truly divided up between the two parties, how can we call the system democratic? As has been shown, the fragmentation of the traditional parties and the inability of the state to guarantee that each party list belonged to one of the established parties meant that access to Front-era elections was quite open. The presence of the MRL and especially ANAPO (running both as PL and PC factions, no less) clearly demonstrates that one could win access to the Congress even with the Front's rules in place. The issue was less the ability of groups to access the system than whether the voters wanted to place them in office in the first place. One could argue that the clientelistic nature of the system provided a built-in advantage for the PL and PC; however, that was not a creation of the Front but rather had been an endemic element of Colombian politics since its inception.

As such, the argument here is that flaws in the Colombian parties or in the policy-making capacities of the state are not to be laid at the feet of the Front. The flaws in the parties are long-standing, and the perpetuation of those flaws has long been aided by the institutional structure of the system, specifically the electoral rules and the combination of largest remainders sans any type of threshold coupled with the ability of parties to offer multiple lists. The long-term presence of particularistic parties with regional elites who controlled their own political networks, coupled with those rules, is far more responsible for the behavior of Colombian parties after the Front than the strictures of the Front itself.

Also of issue in the rethinking of the parties is the usage of party labels and the engrained desire on the part of many to try and classify Colombian politics primarily in terms of the PC and PL. The label issue is ultimately pretty straightforward: despite the long-term historical significance of the Conservatives and Liberals, it is a grave analytical mistake to overgeneralize the applicability of those labels. As has been demonstrated, the main metric for behavioral change is the adoption of new labels. As such, the undercounting of labels leads to system change being missed.

If one were classifying nascent parties with old labels in the 1980s and 1990s, one might not have been able to see when the actual changes in the system took place. Overly focusing on traditional labels and forcing actors into those labels means missing subtle changes in the system. The threat of oversimplification continues, as one can see in the press at times a tendency to take pro-Uribe parties and simply call them *uribistas* (which is ultimately a combination of a shorthand and laziness). Further, if one is not careful, one might still be tempted to look at la U and the CR and simply see Conservatives and Liberals, since many of the members of those parties previously served in government under traditional labels.

Institutions Matter

It is by now not a new observation in the literature that institutions matter, but it is an observation that the Colombian case clearly reinforces. It has been demonstrated that institutional change has mattered in Colombia's politics and specifically that as the rules of the game changed, power-seeking actors altered their behaviors in response. The entire discussion is one of rules mattering to the behavior of actors seeking power (and with that pursuit of power often being about obtaining a stake in the shaping of the rules). Whether we look at the nineteenth century's wars over various constitutions or the adaptation of actors to the National Front, the 1991 Constitution, or the 2003 electoral reform, the long-term importance of the rules of the game in Colombia is quite clear. Both the history of the Colombian party system and its current state attest to this fact.

The 1974–1991 era demonstrates how the unitary state, which controlled both the budget and appointments of local executive officers, made capturing the presidency and majorities in Congress so important. Those seeking power understood that to further their particularistic goals they needed to function in large electoral confederations. The existence of the personal list–PR system allowed for the PL in particular to maintain power in Bogotá. The failure of the PC to directly and successfully compete under those rules caused the party to start unraveling toward the end of the time frame in question.

The new constitution in 1991 brought about the national district for the Senate and the chance for substantial "bargain shopping" for seats, which in turn led to greater fragmentation of the parties (a process clearly manifested by 1998). Further, the majority election requirements for electing the president as well as the popular election of governors and mayors changed the value of the presidency, and more fragmentation ensued. The PC dropped out of direct pursuit of the presidency, instead endorsing independent candidates, and the PL learned that its hold on the presidency was not what its leaders thought it was. By 2002 the traditional parties were in shambles, and the stage was set for electoral reforms.

The installation of the D'Hondt method in 2003 led to the reevaluation of the electoral system by power seekers. No longer able to offer multiple lists (and with the new rules making such strategies moot in any event), new, moderate-size parties emerged creating a true multiple party system in Colombia. Further the lesson (and popularity) of Álvaro Uribe demonstrated that access to the Colombian presidency no longer had to run through the traditional parties. Indeed, the unfulfilled aspiration of Horacio Serpa of the PL indicated clearly that the traditional means of accessing the highest office in the land were no long operable.

Electoral versus Liberal Democracy

The discussion herein of the electoral process should underscore the clear significance of the electoral enterprise in Colombia. Elections do matter. Indeed, despite the contentious (to put it kindly) nature of Colombian politics, the electoral process is remarkably sound. Yes, there was the tainted 1970 contest, and there have been allegations of fraud and manipulation at the local level over time (although a lack of systematic problems). Most significant of all is the fact that violence has disrupted, if not led to the cancellation, of elections in portions of the state over time. Yet, despite all that, the electoral system actually functions well and does perform its task of selecting those who will govern Colombia for a specific period of time.

This is not to say that serious challenges to the integrity of the system do not exist; they do. The *parapolítica* scandal and its allegations of localized candidate intimidation are quite serious. On the other hand, the fact that at least some of those involved have been identified, removed from office, and jailed speaks to the fact that such actions are neither the norm nor will they be tolerated by the Colombian state or its society.

After the lengthy discussion of constitutional development from the early goings, plus the centrality of parties and elections (and the absence of the military as a constant meddler in the political), it should be easy to see why it is legitimate to assert that the case is one of electoral democracy. However, the various flaws noted in chapter 2 and the discussion of the violence in chapter 7 also underscore clearly that the Colombian state does not adequately provide security and order for its citizens and that these deficiencies have led to the inability of the citizens of Colombia to fully enjoy the promises of democracy. As such, the assignation of "liberal democracy" is unwarranted at this time.

Key Issues for Ongoing Consideration

What, then, should we pay attention to in Colombia going forward? Obviously the new rules, with only one national election completed, require far more scrutiny. Likewise, the 2006 elections themselves and the new parties that have emerged, along with Uribe himself, require further study. Sadly, the role of drugs and violence also require our ongoing attention.

The Importance of the New Rules

It is difficult to overly stress the importance of the shift to the D'Hondt method for the election of legislatures. This shift alone removed the motivation of large parties like the PL to offer multiple lists for the same office. To make sure that this happened, the new rules also impose a threshold that must be achieved in order to win a seat as well as the legal requirement that parties offer only one list. As a result, many adherents to the PL no longer saw the advantage of sticking with that collective, and sought new political pastures—especially given the party's diminished capacity to acquire the presidential prize.

Of course, it should be remembered that the shift in the process of legislative elections took place in the context of a number of changes to the system that had been put into place in the 1991 Constitution. Those changes had already begun a significant shift in the party system, but that shift was leading to atomization. The insertion of D'Hondt into the mix should lead (as it appears to have done already) to new parties and patterns of behavior but also to a more stable system overall. As such, there is an expectation that

2006 marks the beginning of a new party system for Colombia that will firmly coalesce over the next several cycles.

The Significance of 2006

While the 2006 election has been discussed in the broader context of long-term trends in Colombian electoral history, it bears specific consideration here as we conclude our discussion. The key question is whether the 2006 election indeed represents something new and different, and an examination below confirms what has already been asserted in previous chapters: yes, it does. This section examines the congressional and presidential results from 2006. As was argued in chapter 6, Legislative Act No. 3 of 2003, which instituted D'Hondt, defined an electoral threshold, and limited each party to one list per office, was the most significant piece of electoral reform in Colombian history. The effects on the system were immediate, obvious, and almost certainly long lasting. Now, it is certainly the case that this reform alone was not what transformed the party system, but it was a vital change that brought to fruition the full evolution of the system that started in the early 1990s.

Table 8.1 underscores the changes that have taken place. We no longer have the PL as the clear majority party (which was the case until 2002), nor do we have dozens of microparties (which was the hallmark of the 1991–2002 period). When we look at the Senate results versus the Chamber, we also see that the Senate's national electoral district, now that it restricts parties to one list, is functioning in a way that does capture a representational profile somewhat different from that of the Chamber. For example, the traditional parties (whose strength remains regional clientele networks) did better in the Chamber, which is elected in the department-based districts. The PDA, on the other hand, did better in the Senate elections, where it was able to draw strength nationally.

When examining the historical significance of the 2006 presidential election, there are several key issues to note. The most obvious is that this was the first election after the reform allowing the immediate reelection of the president, a task that Uribe handily accomplished. Further, he is the first president to serve consecutive terms since Rafael Nuñez in 1892, whose reelection was not via popular vote.[1] Second, the 2006 presidential election is the first in which a truly nontraditional party came in second, besting one of the traditional parties.[2] Indeed, the PL came in third, behind an independent and a nontraditional party (see table 8.2). Not only is the PDA a nontraditional party, it is a party of the center-left—which is a portion of the ideological

Table 8.1

The 2006–2010 Congress

Chamber			Senate		
Party	Seats		Party	Seats	
PL	35	(21.08%)	la U	20	(19.61%)
la U	30	(18.07%)	PC	18	(17.65%)
PC	29	(17.47%)	PL	18	(17.65%)
CR	20	(12.05%)	CR	15	(14.71%)
AEC	8	(4.82%)	PDA	10	(9.80%)
CC	8	(4.82%)	CC	7	(6.86%)
PDA	8	(4.82%)	AEC	5	(4.90%)
AL	5	(3.01%)	PCD	3	(2.94%)
IR	4	(2.41%)	MIRA	2	(1.96%)
HNL	2	(1.20%)	CV	2	(1.96%)
MN	2	(1.20%)	ASI	1	(0.98%)
MPU	2	(1.20%)	MAIC	1	(0.98%)
PCD	2	(1.20%)	Total seats =	102	
PPQS	2	(1.20%)			
ASA	1	(0.60%)			
Afro	1	(0.60%)			
POC	1	(0.60%)			
MORAL	1	(0.60%)			
MPP	1	(0.60%)			
MSN	1	(0.60%)			
MIRA	1	(0.60%)			
MNP	1	(0.60%)			
PAS	1	(0.60%)			
Total seats =	166				

spectrum in Colombia that has largely failed to achieve relevance in presidential elections.[3] Third, this election marked a resounding defeat for the Liberal Party, which had not that long ago seen itself as the permanent majority party. The embarrassing defeat of Serpa is especially noteworthy given that his power base in the party is very much grounded in the traditional modes of Colombian politics (regional power bases and clientele networks, as discussed in chapter 4). Serpa's status as three-time loser (1998, 2002, and 2006) indicates either that the PL is irrevocably stuck in the past and has run its course or that the party will have to adapt if it wishes to climb back into the process as a serious contender. The demonstrated ability of the traditional parties to adapt would suggest that the latter is more likely. It is also worth observing that this election marked the fourth in a row that lacked a candidate using the Conservative label on the ballot.[4]

Also of issue here is where these parties came from. In other words, how new is the new? The PDA is clearly the party that is truly nontraditional in its origins and orientation, although elements of its foundation have been operating in Colombia for decades. The PDA emerged from a merger of two nascent left/center-left groups, the PDI (Independent Democratic Pole/*Polo Democrático Independiente*) and the AD (Democratic Alternative/*Alternativa Democrática*). The AD itself was an alliance of numerous political groups from the Colombian left, many of which had been in operation for decades.[5] The PDA represents the most coherent attempt in Colombian history at building a viable political party on the left side of the spectrum. It is also noteworthy that the alliance emerged in significant measure as an alliance in opposition to Uribe's politics.

The Party of National Social Unity (la U) has its origins in PL dissidents seeking to align themselves with the political fortunes of President Uribe. Of the party's founders, eight were PL senators in the 2002–2006 Congress, and two were PL Senate candidates. Four others were senators affiliated with various pro-Liberal microparties. Further, the party's primary founder, Juan Manuel Santos, is a member of a key Liberal family that includes an ex-president.[6]

La U illustrates the type of strategic choice discussed earlier in the text wherein power seekers recognize that old patterns of behavior (in this case,

Table 8.2

2006 Presidential Election Results

Candidate	Party	Votes	Percentage
Álvaro Uribe Vélez	Primero Colombia[a]	7,397,835	62.35%
Carlos Gaviria Díaz	PDA	2,613,157	22.02%
Horacio Serpa Uribe	PL	1,404,235	11.83%
Antanas Mockus Šivickas	ASI	146,583	1.23%
Enrique Parejo González	MRDN	42,652	0.35%
Alvaro Leyva Duran	MNR	18,263	0.15%
Carlos Arturo Rincon Barreto	MCCC	15,388	0.12%

[a] "Primero Colombia" ("Colombia First") was a slogan used on the ballot rather than a party label, in the sense that it was used only for this election by one candidate (not unlike the way Andrés Pastrana used the space for a party label on the 1994 and 1998 presidential ballots).

sticking with the PL) are no long advantageous, because of changes in the prevailing political climate. In this case a combination of institutional changes that diminished the presidential prize and altered the conditions for election to the Senate, coupled with specific political considerations (i.e., the diminishing political fortunes of the PL and the rising star of Álvaro Uribe), led to a strategic choice to defect from the PL to form a new party.

Radical Change presents a more eclectic set of preexisting politicos coming together to form a new party than does la U—although, like la U, CR has origins in PL discontent (its initial leaders were of Liberal lineage), and it is a pro-Uribe party. However, unlike la U, which is made up of PL members who defected from the PL between 2002 and 2006, the CR membership (as based on its current congressional class) represents far more politicians who had already decided to flee from the PL and seek new labels as well as a few from existing third parties. For example, of the fifteen CR senators elected for the 2006–2010 term, eight held elected office in the 2002–2006 Congress, and only two were there under the PL banner. The other six used various other labels, such as Colombia Siempre (two, both of whom had been in the PL prior to 2002), NL (two), MIPOL (one). and the Movimiento Nacional. The CR's 2006 class also included a member of the PNC and the MNC.

Of note, too, is the fact that Senate delegations of la U and CR are both younger, on average, than the delegations of the PC and PL. The average ages of the la U and CR delegation as of election day were 45.19 and 47.5 years of age respectively, while the PL and PC delegations were 51.67 and 53.12.[7]

The Significance of Uribe

Álvaro Uribe is one of the most significant (and popular) presidents in recent Colombian history, if anything because of his independent status and his ability to have engineered reelection for himself. It is worth reemphasizing a key point about Álvaro Uribe: he may have once been a Liberal, but he did not seek the presidency as a Liberal; indeed he beat a Liberal not once but twice. It may be that the press will still call Uribe a "former Liberal," but the emphasis should be on the "former," not the "Liberal." His defeat of Horacio Serpa (twice) is symbolic as well, given that Serpa represents the old ways of Colombian politics, from his career path to the way he achieved the nomination.

It is also of note that the fact that he won the presidency without the PL or PC has meant that other power seekers in Colombia see a new path to the presidential palace, and that has helped foster new party formation.

Some of it will, no doubt, be ephemeral, but by the same token the incentives needed to create and sustain medium-size parties exist now in a way that they never have before. The days of the wasps' sting are done, and with a majority requirement for winning the presidency, it is safe to go into the first round with less than a plurality. As such, a system of parties that can win between the low twenties and midthirties, percentage-wise, is a sustainable situation. This is especially true now that the PL's dominance appears to be utterly broken and the PC has settled in as one of those midtwenties kind of parties (in the Congress, at least).

Uribe's administration will also be irrevocably tied to the politics of the paramilitary groups, a story whose end has yet to be written. At a minimum, Uribe has overseen the seeming demobilization of a very large number of paramilitary fighters. This demobilization appears to have contributed to a diminution (although by no means as large a one as is needed) of the murder rate in Colombia (see figure 2.4). Of course, the long-term justice of the demobilization and its actual efficacy have yet to be determined. Additionally, the ramifications of the *parapolítica* may yet affect his legacy.

The Significance of Violence and Drugs

The inability of the various actors in Colombia to find a way to stop the cycle of violence is clearly the issue that has inhibited and will continue to inhibit the deepening of democracy in Colombia. At the forefront of the problem is the drug issue. The obscene amounts of money that are made annually from the drug trade are so enormous as to defy containment. Further, to date U.S.-Colombian success at containing the cultivation of coca leaf, let alone the production and trafficking of cocaine, has been limited (to put it kindly). The inability to contain this industry will continue, so it is utterly fair to say that one of the key engines of the violence will continue to run unabated for the foreseeable future. As such, any assessment of the health and development of Colombian democracy has to take account of the drug industry's ongoing influence.

Looking to the Future

Whenever it comes times to make statements about Colombia's future, one is tempted to take a dramatic stand, and the truth of the matter is that one could stake out claims for both a bright and optimistic future as well as a grim and bitter one. For example, should one wish to be a wild-eyed optimist, one could try to argue that the reforms will radically transform party politics and lead to a renaissance of policy making as new actors are brought into the process. On the other hand, one could easily look at the murder rate, internal displacement figures, and the like and predict a slide into collapse and ruin. Such extremes are not simply hyperbole deployed for effect. One can go back to the 1990/1991 era, when many in Colombia actually thought that Navarro Wolff of the M-19 was going to be elected president, or to an endless stream of enthusiasm for the "participatory democracy" that the new constitution was going to usher in. Similarly, doom has been predicted for Colombia and its parties for decades. And while the tragedies continue daily for scores of Colombians, there are some reasons for guarded optimism about changes to elements of basic political life, even if the larger problems are likely to continue. At a minimum, the newly realigned party system provides a new set of voices in prominent roles, as we have seen with the PDA and its criticisms of the Uribe administration and its vigilance in regard to the *parapolítica* situation.

The institutional imperatives for particularism have been replaced, and the party system will be less driven by regional bosses seeking primarily that state resources be funneled into their clientele networks. While clientelism and pork-barrel politics will hardly leave Colombia, it is now easier to build a programmatic political party that has a chance at serious congressional representation. Certainly there are now other clear routes to power that do not require traditional clientelism. Such changes are slow to fully take effect, but we have already seen that politicians in the Senate were having to branch outside their departmental strongholds in the last two elections of the prereform era (see table 6.8). For any progress to be made on the larger problems, small steps have to be taken to reshape policy making and especially to better orient the government and its occupants to national problems away from the particularistic approaches of the past. The new rules have some hope of doing just that.

Colombia remains a troubled and in many ways incomplete state, yet it persists. Despite all the great tragedies that are part of daily life for so many Colombians, there is no reason to assume that the state will do anything other than continue. The likelihood that the most significant and major problems facing Colombia, violence and drugs, will be soon solved is rather unlikely. The measuring stick in all these matters going forward is one of management, not of elimination.

Chapter 1 begins with a reference to living in interesting times. As if on cue, 2008 provided quite a bit of excitement in Colombia. Apropos to the book's title there has been much to consider in terms of the general themes of voting and violence. This afterword is aimed at dealing with some of the significant events that occurred after the main manuscript was submitted to the editorial process.

The first section examines the issue of violence as it pertains to the drama surrounding the FARC. The second section is not about elections per se, but the politics surrounding the top elected official in Colombia, Álvaro Uribe.

Violence

As was noted in chapter 7, the FARC was on something of a roll into the mid-2000s. However, as the decade headed into its latter half, the guerrillas' fortunes began to change. The year 2007 held its share of problems for the guerrilla group, and 2008 contained the most serious set of political setbacks in the group's multi-decade history.[1]

Early 2007 saw a couple of high-profile escapes by FARC prisoners, specifically former Development Minister Fernando Araújo Perdomo, who had been held since 2000, and policeman Jhon Frank Pinchao, who had been in captivity for approximately eight and one-half years. Araújo soon returned to government as Uribe's Minister of Foreign Affairs. July of 2007 also saw the accidental killing of eleven department-level legislators that the FARC was holding as hostages (as noted in chapter 7) and the hijacking of a plane by a female rebel who sought to escape life with the FARC (BBC 2007b).

None of these events could be seen as especially debilitating in themselves but, at the very end of 2007, a string of incidents began that would raise questions about the FARC's long-term viability.

We start with what can be called the "Baby Emmanuel" debacle. In December, the FARC was reported to be willing to enter into talks to release three high-profile hostages: Clara Rojas González, a campaign manager to Ingrid Betancourt, her son Emmanuel (allegedly fathered by a member of the FARC) and Consuelo González, a former member of Congress. Negotiations were ongoing with Venezuelan President Hugo Chávez and the FARC for a handoff when a story emerged that the FARC was not holding the child. Instead, it turned out that three-and-one-half-year-old Emmanuel Rojas was actually in foster care in Bogotá. This was something of an embarrassment for the FARC leadership, who clearly hoped that the goodwill generated by the prisoner release might lead to further negotiation for the release of guerrillas held by the government. Instead, they appeared not to know whom they had in custody. Despite the confusion over Emmanuel's whereabouts, the FARC did release Clara Rojas and Consuelo González in January 2008.

These events were followed by massive anti-FARC rallies in early February. According to press estimates, between 500,000 and 2 million people marched in Colombia's capital, with other protests taking place in approximately 100 cities across Colombia and around the world. The marches drew a great deal of public attention, due both to their content and to the fact that they were largely organized via Facebook, the Internet-based social network. All of these setbacks, however, were pinpricks compared to what was to come. February ended with the FARC releasing four high-profile hostages—former members of Congress Gloria Polanco, Luis Eladio Pérez, Orlando Beltrán, and Jorge Gechem[2]—and the beginning of a stunning string of defeats.

In late February, the Colombian military engaged in a strike across the Ecuadoran border against a FARC encampment. One result of that strike was the death of Raúl Reyes (the *nom de guerre* of Luis Édgar Devia Silva),[3] a member of the FARC's governing secretariat. Along with Reyes, sixteen other guerrillas were killed, including Julian Conrado (Guillermo Enrique Torres Cueter), considered by the Colombian government to be a key FARC ideologist. Intelligence also was gathered, including a laptop computer containing a great deal of information on FARC plans and contacts. (This incident ignited an international confrontation with Ecuador, which was joined by Venezuela and Nicaragua in protesting the incursion. Indeed, Venezuela briefly mobilized troops on its border. Tensions were high for several days, until a summit held in the Dominican Republic led to a quelling of the angry rhetoric. Even after the summit, however, Ecuador did not fully restore normal diplomatic relations with Colombia.)

In March, soon after Reyes' death, word arrived that another of the FARC's seven-member secretariat had met his demise: Iván Ríos (Manuel Muñoz Ortiz). Ríos was murdered by one of his own men for the reward offered by the Colombian government. The rebel produced a severed hand as proof of the deed. It was also in March that the founder and leader of the FARC, Pedro Antonio Marín, died of a heart attack. While this information was not released to the Colombian public (and quickly confirmed by the FARC) until May, it marked the third death among the secretariat in a matter of weeks.[4]

While April 2008 was relatively calm, May brought the arrest of three additional FARC commanders (although not of the secretariat level). Santiago (Gustavo Arbeláez Cardona) was captured while visiting a paramour; Karina (Nelly Avila Moreno) and Michin (Abelardo Montes Suárez) surrendered to authorities. Karina had been under the command of Ríos, and had taken over for him after his death. Along with these arrests came press reports of a plot by bodyguards to kill secretariat member El Mono Jojoy (Julio Suárez Rojas[5]) (El Tiempo 2008a).

Just when it seemed that news for the FARC could not get any worse, the Colombian military launched a dramatic and successful mission to retrieve fifteen hostages, including four of the FARC's most high-profile captives: presidential candidate Ingrid Betancourt and three U.S. contractors. Their July rescue led to international embarrassment for the FARC, the loss of the group's most valuable bargaining chips, and also resulted in the capture of two additional FARC members.[6] The fact that the rescue was pulled off without firing a shot added salt to the wounds.[7]

The roughly six-month stretch from February though July of 2008 was clearly the most eventful in the FARC's multi-decade history. It is unclear exactly what the long-term effects will be. The group is now under the command of Alfonso Cano (Guillermo León Sáenz), who is considered to be committed to the FARC's ideological roots and revolutionary cause. Speculation abounds as to whether or not the more profit-oriented elements (i.e., drug traffickers) of the group will come into conflict with the more ideological wing. Further, it should be understood that the FARC operates with a cellular structure, so that different portions of the organization often function without the knowledge or consent of the others. Indeed, the Colombian military exploited this fact in the Betancourt rescue. Meanwhile, the FARC continues to hold a large number of hostages, including politicians, and has committed more kidnappings since the Betancourt rescue.

Press accounts state that the Ministry of Defense believes that there have been as many as 3,000 desertions from the group in the last year or so, placing the number of members at 9,000[8], a level far lower than earlier in the decade (and as cited in chapter 7). But too much focus on the relative decline in numbers misses the fact that the FARC has historically functioned with less than 10,000 fighters. For example, Bushnell (1993, 255) put their number at approximately 4,000 in the mid-1980s, while Safford and Palacios (2002, 362) noted that the group had roughly 3,000 insurgents in 1986, growing to approximately 7,000 in 1995 and around 15,000 in 2000. So, while the current estimates represent a significant diminution in members in the near term, it is worth remembering that the FARC has operated effectively with far fewer troops in the past.

Voting

Not surprisingly, the FARC's very bad year translated into a pretty good one for President Uribe. The rescue of Betancourt saw his approval ratings soar to 86% in July 2008, although they were down to 78% as of September.[9] Uribe's ongoing popularity feeds into the less dramatic but ultimately quite significant issue of whether he will pursue a third term in office. I would assess this as more important than the FARC's fortunes, because the likelihood remains that the FARC will continue their fight, while the health of Colombian democratic development could be harmed if Uribe decides that he is more important than the institutions of the state and decides to try and hold onto power for an additional four years. Such a move would require, as did his 2006 reelection, an amendment to the constitution.

The process in question was started by la U, as it sought to acquire the requisite number of signatures needed to place the Congress on the appropriate path to considering a referendum to amend the constitution. The party gathered what it said was more than 5 million such signatures, of which roughly 4 million were considered valid, far more than enough to send the measure to the Congress (El Tiempo 2008e). From there, debates and votes in both chambers are needed before a referendum can be called which, if successful, would result in a constitutional amendment.

Uribe has a majority coalition in the Congress. However, the question remains as to whether the coalition parties are all amenable to the notion of a third term. Whether we are talking about an old-guard party like the PC or a relatively new actor such as Radical Change, it is unclear whether ambitious politicians in the pro-Uribe bloc have their own plans for candidacy in 2010. The disposition of the PC is unknown, since they have not yet indicated support for the reform (El Tiempo [2008e] calls it a "great mystery"). Indeed, when la U was involved in the gathering of signatures, one member of the PC, Representative Santiago Castro, commented, "[The] Partido de la U is the only party that has committed to the project. The rest of us still have not" (Bronstein 2008).[10]

With roughly two years left in Uribe's second term, it is apparent that some coalition members are calculating the political cost of blocking his chance at a third. In addition to issues of policy and legislation, they also must consider how Uribe's support (or lack thereof) might affect future presidential elections.

Uribe himself has been coy on the subject, not clearly indicating which way he wants to go. Whether this is a sign of actual indecision or a purposeful strategy is unclear, though by September he appeared to be stepping back from the prospect of a third consecutive term. In response to a question about where he thought he would be at the next presidential inauguration (in 2010), Uribe commented that he would likely be playing with his grandson and suggested that Noemí Sanín Posada (Colombia's ambassador to the United Kingdom) might be a good candidate to replace him (El Tiempo 2008d). More definitively, on the very week that the signatures were delivered to Congress, he told students in Bogotá: "I think that for the future of the country it is much better that Colombians continue to internalize Democratic Security than simply having us perpetually occupy the presidency," and "I want to ask the Congress that they would please occupy themselves with reforms to general politics, justice and other themes, not the referendum" (El Tiempo 2008f).[11] He did, however, drop hints that he might take a term off and run for reelection in 2014 (El Tiempo 2008f)—although that also would require constitutional reform, since Article 197 of the Constitution (as amended by Legislative Act Number 2 of 2004) limits presidents to two total terms.[12]

One of the stranger episodes in the reelection saga was the conviction of Representative Yidis Medina[13] for accepting a bribe for her vote to amend the constitution and allow presidents to serve two terms. Because of her conviction, the Supreme Court of Justice raised the question of investigating the legality of the vote, and hence the amendment that allowed reelection. This resulted in Uribe taking to Colombia's airwaves and angrily stating that he would send a reform package to the Congress requesting a re-vote of the 2006 election to confirm its validity (BBC 2008; El Tiempo 2008b). Several days later, he withdrew the suggestion. Uribe's fit of pique over the Yidis situation is part of a broader, and still developing, series of public confrontations between Uribe and the courts.

While there is much drama associated with the notion of a third term for Uribe (in addition to its implications for Colombian democracy), one key question has been typically ignored in the press: what does this situation say about the party system in the Uribe era, especially since the reforms of 2003? The uncertainty highlights the lack of actual party formation by Uribe himself, and raises the further question of which coalition party might produce his successor. Such issues will be of relevance for future studies of Colombia's party system.

Will any of Uribe's allies be able to parlay their support into electoral relevance? At least one prominent associate of the PC, Fabio Valencia Cossio, has a key ministerial position in the Uribe administration. Or, could one of the Santos cousins, Vice President Francísco Santos Calderón or Defense Minister Juan Manuel Santos Calderón, capitalize on the success of the Uribe administration to launch a presidential bid? It is worth noting their roots in a prominent Liberal family and that Juan Manuel is a key founder of la U (as noted in chapter 8). And what about Radical Change and other pro-Uribe parties? At this point, there appear to be several possible candidates, and several party bases from which ambitious politicians within the Uribe administration could launch presidential bids without having to rely on the independent route that Uribe pursued.

One other component of Uribe's legacy has yet to be written, and that concerns his role in the *parapolítica* scandal (discussed in chapter 7). The basic questions—how much did he know and when did he know it—remain unanswered. Also extant are the ongoing clashes between Uribe and the Supreme Court, many of which involve the parapolitics situation.

Moving Forward

Casual observers of Colombian politics might think that recent events foretell a significant departure from Colombia's past, whether it be the defeat of the FARC or the abrogation of democracy by Uribe's ambitions. I am not convinced of either. The events of 2008 have not altered the conclusion reached in chapter 8 of this book. I continue to think that the recent electoral reforms will continue to shape a new party system that will, in turn, have important policy implications. However, neither the setbacks to the FARC nor the maneuverings of the Uribe administration and its allies have altered the fundamentals in Colombia to date.

Cautious optimism remains the best approach, with a realistic understanding that violence in unlikely to vanish as a key element of Colombia's sociopolitical fabric anytime soon, considering the continued presence of the illicit narcotics trade. We need to see how the reforms to the electoral system influence party development, and we very much need to see how Uribe's approach to the violence plays out once he leaves office. One thing is for certain: interesting times will continue in Colombia for the foreseeable future. Our only hope is that the nature of those interesting times will be less violent than they have been, and that the citizens of Colombia can, in the decades to come, focus far more on voting than they currently must focus on violence.

The Evolution of the Ballot in Colombia

Prior to the 1990 presidential elections, the Colombian state did not produce ballots. Instead, parties and other entities would print *papeletas* (or ballot papers), which citizens would place in an envelope and then deposit in the ballot box. These ballot papers might manifest as publications in newspapers (examples below), or they could even be handwritten.[1] From the 1990 presidential elections onward, ballots became state-produced and were called *tarjetones electorales* (literally "election cards"). Each office has a separate *tarjetón*.

Beyond the issue of who produced the ballots, the ballot format served several functions in the Colombian party system. First, it was the perfect vehicle for regional electoral barons to assert control over clientele networks, and second, it made personal lists within parties easy to disseminate. As such it aided in the ability of dissident lists to be offered during the National Front and aided the general list proliferation that took place during the 1974–1990 period.

Figure A.1 contains a mock-up of a party-produced ballot from the 1974 elections (which is the last time that congressional and presidential elections were held concurrently). The mock-up is provided for ease of reading. Figure A.2 is a scan of an actual *papeleta*.

The mock-up represents a series of attached *papeletas* (ballots) as they would have been published in Colombian newspapers prior to 1990. Voters could cut or tear the ballots at each of the dotted lines to separate different offices and mix and match them at will. For example, one might use one portion of a given *papeleta* for president, Senate, and departmental assembly but use different lists for Chamber and municipal council. Anecdotal evidence suggests that such ticket splitting was unusual.

The original ballot had fifteen candidates (and alternates) listed for the Senate, twenty-nine for the Chamber, thirty for departmental assembly, and twenty for municipal council. It should also be noted that for all offices (save president) there are two columns. The first column is for the actual candidates, while the second column is for the *suplentes* or alternates. Theoretically the purpose of the *suplentes* was to have someone to replace the candidate if he or she could not finish the electoral term. In terms of

Listas oficiales

PARTIDO LIBERAL COLOMBIANO
VOTO PARA PRESIDENTE
DE LA REPUBLICA POR
EL DR. NOMBRE APELLIDO APPELLIDO
PERIODO CONSTITUCIONAL 1.974 – 1.978

LISTA OFICIAL DE CANDIDATOS DEL PARTIDO LIBERAL
AL **SENADO DE LA REPUBLICA,** EN LA CIRCUNSCRIPCION
ELECTORAL DE CUNDINAMARCA, PARA EL PERIODO
CONSTITUIONAL 1.974 – 1.978

Principales	Suplentes
CANDIDATO	CANDIDATO
Candidato	Candidato
Candidato	Candidato

LISTA OFICIAL DE CANDIDATOS DEL PARTIDO LIBERAL
A LA **CAMARA DE REPRESENTANTES,** EN LA CIRCUNSCRIPCION
ELECTORAL DE CUNDINAMARCA, PARA EL PERIODO
CONSTITUIONAL 1.974 – 1.978

Principales	Suplentes
CANDIDATO	CANDIDATO
Candidato	Candidato
Candidato	Candidato

LISTA OFICIAL DE CANDIDATOS DEL PARTIDO LIBERAL
A LA **ASAMBLEA DEPARTMENTAL,** EN LA CIRCUNSCRIPCION
ELECTORAL DE CUNDINAMARCA, PARA EL PERIODO
CONSTITUIONAL 1.974 – 1.978

Principales	Suplentes
CANDIDATO	CANDIDATO
Candidato	Candidato
Candidato	Candidato

LISTA OFICIAL DE CANDIDATOS DEL PARTIDO LIBERAL
AL **CONCEJO DE BOGOTA,** PARA EL PERIODO
CONSTITUIONAL 1.974 – 1.978

Principales	Suplentes
CANDIDATO	CANDIDATO
Candidato	Candidato
Candidato	Candidato

Figure A.1. Reproduction of a Pre-1990 *Papeleta*

actual practice it was not unusual for the main officeholder to step down during a significant portion of the term to allow the *suplente* to serve part of the term. In fact, before the practice was banned in the 1991 Constitution, regional party elites often would head a congressional list and that of a departmental assembly or municipal council so as to boost the electoral appeal of the local list, even though the candidate had no intention of actually serving in the office. Instead, the *suplentes* automatically took the local seats.

Figure A.2 is a scan of the actual ballot as published in the Bogotá daily *El Espectador* on April 20, 1974, on page 5c. The actual ballot was approximately 10.5 by 2.5 inches and contained lists for all the offices noted in the previous paragraph. This particular ballot is for the PL faction headed by the Senate candidate for the Department of Cundinamarca, Julio César Turbay Ayala, and thus includes the candidates he supported for local office. Turbay's list was one of five Liberal lists competing in 1974 in Cundinamarca, all of which would have supported the presidential bid of López Michelsen.

Starting in 1978, congressional elections came first with presidential elections being held a few months later. This allowed for the usage of the congressional elections as a quasi primary. The Liberals utilized this mechanism in the 1978 and 1986 electoral cycles.[2] Since the congressional elections came first, *papeletas* could be labeled in terms of which presidential candidate the list supported. As such, instead of having a presidential candidate at the top, as was the case in 1974, a specific congressional list could instead indicate which would-be candidate it supported. In 1978, for example, the contest was between two prominent Liberals, Julio César Turbay Ayala and Carlos Lleras Restrepo, and lists would state which candidate they supported; the congressional list headed by Álvaro Uribe Rueda, for example, contained the message that the list "supported the presidential candidacy of Doctor Julio César Turbay Ayala." The nomination was settled based on whose congressional lists did better in elections. In 1978, Turbay was the victor in terms of both the nomination and also the presidency.

Once the presidential elections were separated from the congressional elections, the *papeletas* for the latter office were quite straightforward. Figure A.3 has an example from the 1986 election, the last presidential contest that used the *papeleta*.

The most famous *papeleta* was the "*septima papeleta*" (the "seventh ballot") that was used in the March 1990 elections. In that contest there were six other possible *papeletas* that could be used for voting: Senate, Chamber, departmental assembly, municipal council, mayor, and the PL presidential

PARTIDO LIBERAL COLOMBIANO
VOTO PARA PRESIDENTE
DE LA REPUBLICA POR
EL DOCTOR ALFONSO LOPEZ MICHELSEN
PERIODO CONSTITUCIONAL 1.974 - 1.978

LISTA OFICIAL DE CANDIDATOS DEL PARTIDO LIBERAL
AL SENADO DE LA REPUBLICA, EN LA CIRCUNSCRIPCION
ELECTORAL DE CUNDINAMARCA, PARA EL PERIODO
CONSTITUCIONAL 1.974 — 1.978

Principales	Suplentes
JULIO CESAR TURBAY AYALA	RAUL VASQUEZ VELEZ
Indalecio Liévano Aguirre	Alfonso Angarita Baracaldo
Germán Zea Hernández	Migdonia Barón Restrepo
Virgilio Barco Vargas	Francisco Gaviria Rincón •
Diego Uribe Vargas	Alicia Cuervo de Barrero
Jaime Posada Díaz	Alfonso Rodríguez González
Enrique Pardo Parra	Jaime Pinzón López
María Elena de Crovo	Eduardo Vanegas
Cecilia Vargas de Reyes	Antonio Bustos Esguerra
Juan Pablo Gómez	Mario Calderón B.
Gregorio Duarte Jiménez	Jorge Cáceres Bejarano
Luis Alberto Blanco Gutiérrez	Manuel Arbeláez Pava
Darío Samper	Tancredo Herrán
Pilar Calderón de De la Mora	Pedro L. Camargo
Bernardo Gaitán Mahecha	José Gutiérrez

LISTA OFICIAL DE CANDIDATOS DEL PARTIDO LIBERAL
A LA CAMARA DE REPRESENTANTES, EN LA CIRCUNSCRIPCION
ELECTORAL DE CUNDINAMARCA, PARA EL PERIODO
CONSTITUCIONAL 1.974 — 1.978

Principales	Suplentes
LUIS VILLAR BORDA	LUZ CASTILLA DE MELO
Fabio Lozano Simonelli	Rafael Corrales Ramírez
Abelardo Forero Benavides	Alberto Orjuela
Consuelo Lleras de Zuleta	Misael Chaves Rey

Figure A.2. Partial Scan of a 1974 *Papeleta*

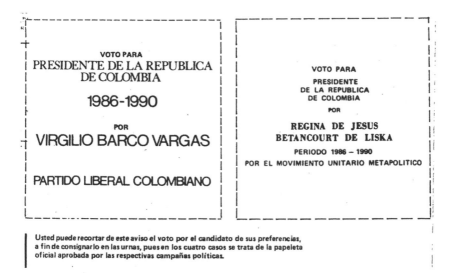

Figure A.3. *Papeletas* from the 1986 Presidential Election

Note: This is a scan of two ballots from the 1986 presidential race as published, along with ballots for Álvaro Gómez and Jaime Pardo Leal, in an advertisement sponsored by Caracol Radio in *El Tiempo* on May 25, 1986.

primary. The seventh ballot was an unofficial ballot that was promoted by student movements and other groups who were seeking a constitutional assembly. The seventh ballot led to an official referendum in the May presidential election that called for the convocation of a National Constituent Assembly. The text of the ballot, as published in newspapers and elsewhere, is contained in a mock-up of the ballot in figure A.4 and has been translated into English by the author.

If anything, the seventh ballot demonstrated what could happen with a determined population, the appropriate political moment, and privately produced ballots (although the legal move to start the use of the *tarjetón* predated this event).

The 1990 presidential election was the first to use the state-produced *tarjetones*. The legal basis of the move from *papeletas* to the state-produced *tarjetones* was Law 62 of 1998. Starting with the 1990 election, the ballot would consist of a black-and-white photo of the candidate, a full-color display of the candidate's party symbol, and the name of the candidate and party. Figure A.5 shows a 1990 ballot. (Note: This ballot was produced before the assassination of M-19 candidate Carlos Pizarro Leongómez. Ballots used on election day had Antonio Navarro Wolff correctly inserted.) The original ballot was eight inches wide and seven and a quarter inches tall.

VOTE FOR COLOMBIA

FOR A NATIONAL CONSTITUENT

ASSEMBLY TO REPRESENT DIRECTLY THE COLOMBIAN

PEOPLE, WITH THE AIM OF REFORMING

THE NATIONAL CONSTITUTION

As an exercise of the sovereignty recognized in the Second Article of the

National Constitution. The electoral authorities will count this vote.

Figure A.4. Mock-up of the *Séptima Papeleta*

Figure A.5. The 1990 Presidential *Tarjéton*
Note: The original is in color.

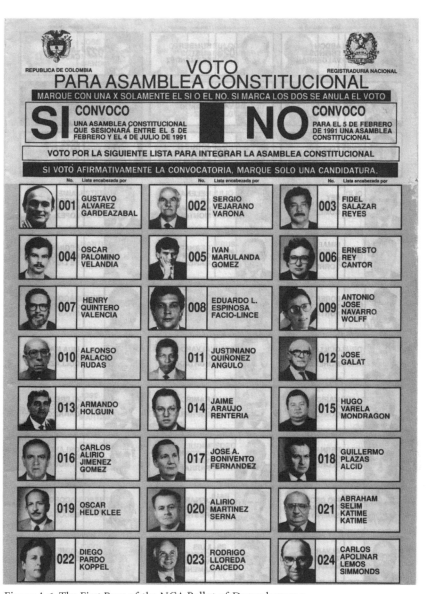

Figure A.6. The First Page of the NCA Ballot of December 1990

Figure A.7. The First Page of the 1991 Senate Ballot
Note: In the original, the header is orange, but the candidates' images are in black and white.

Figure A.8. The 2006 Senate Ballot
Note: The original is in color (the full ballot can be viewed online at *http://www.registraduria* *.gov.co/elec2006/images/tarj_elec_sen_2006.jpg).*

The first legislative election to use state-produced *tarjetones* was the December 1990 NCA election. The black-and-white ballot for this election featured a photo and name for the heads of all the lists, but it did not indicate party affiliation (despite the fact that the Registry did inscribe the lists by party and tallied the votes by party. Figure A.6 shows the first page of this ballot; its size was just shy of a normal 8.5-by-11-inch sheet of paper, and the whole ballot consisted of four pages of candidate lists (two pages printed front and back).

From 1991 onward, all elections for all offices have used state-produced ballots. From 1991 to 2002, said ballots were frequently quite lengthy, owing to the list proliferation discussed in the text. This was especially true for Senate ballots. The Senate ballots had the same basic design as the NCA ballot, although starting with the 1991 election party affiliations were also included. Also starting in 1991 the *tarjetones* were color coded (e.g., orange for the Senate, blue-green for the Chamber, dark green for the assemblies, and so forth). Figure A.7 shows the first page of the 1991 Senate ballot.

The Senate ballots clearly illustrate the effects of list proliferation on the physical act of voting. In 1991 the ballot was two pages, printed front and back with four columns of lists for voters to wade through. By 1998 it became necessary to have the ballot unfold to reveal four pages of lists, of five columns and thirteen rows each. The foldout ballots continued in 1998 and 2002 with smaller boxes and more columns and rows. Candidates had to advertise which number they were on the ballot so that voters could find their preferred list.

The 2006 ballot (figure A.8) provides a visual representation of how the electoral reforms changed the Colombian electoral system, with Senate ballots going from a crowded, confusing format to a simple one. Starting in 2006, parties could choose to have their list open or closed. The extra boxes with numbers in them are for lists that allowed voters to express their rank-order preferences in terms of the candidates on the list of a given party.

Notes on Electoral Data

Obtaining complete and accurate electoral data is not always as easy as one would like it to be. So as to provide as much explanation for the data used here as possible, as well as to provide some guidance for those interested in researching these matters on their own, a few words about electoral data and Colombia are shared. There are a few issues to address in terms of data sources as well as some of the exigencies of Colombian politics that are worth discussing. These notes should also help to explain a few of the choices made in the analysis (or to explain what may appear to be inconsistencies or errors for those who like to go inside the numbers). A few of the items discussed below will hopefully help some future researchers to avoid some of the headaches that I have encountered in the past.

Sources

With the exception of some of the National Front elections (those in 1960, 1962, and 1964), all data concerning legislative elections came directly from Colombia's National Civil Registry (the Registraduría Nacional del Estado Civil). As noted in the text, the 1960–1964 information came from Dix (1967). Data from the 1957 plebiscite and the 1958 elections came from a book published by the Registry titled *3,000,000 de Colombianos Cedulados: Informe del Registraduría del Estado Civil* that was published in December of 1958. The second half of the books contains the electoral data from those contests. For the National Front presidential elections, summary data from the appendix B of Bushnell (1993) were used.

During the National Front era to 1994, the Registry published printed volumes with complete electoral results after each election (usually titled *Estadisticas Electorales* along with the year in question). The exact presentation of the data varied over time, and some information (like numbers of inscribed lists, or the quotas by department) was not always included and therefore had to be teased out of the information provided.

Starting in 1998 the data were produced in an electronic format, first on CD-ROM and later on the Web. The Registry began publishing to the Web with the 2002 election and at that time also posted data from 1998. The

Registry's Web site is http://*www.registraduria.gov.co* (it should be noted that Colombian government sites will not load if one leaves off the "www" from the URL). In the first several years of the site's existence, access was often spotty. However, in recent years there have been no substantial outages of service. It would appear that the Registry will keep an archive of electoral data from 1998 onward available online, although this is not guaranteed (and the 1998 data are not as complete as are those for subsequent years).

Final versions of the electoral results have to be certified by the National Electoral Council, which issues formal resolutions containing the certified results. The CNE also has a Web site, http://*www.cne.gov.co/*. The CNE has not done as good a job as the Registry in keeping an archive of past activities.

It should be noted that results published in the press are almost always based on preliminary counts, not the final tallies, and that sometimes scholarly work is based on those numbers, not the final certified results. This fact will account for some discrepancies that might be found between journalistic (and even some academic) accounts and the numbers used here.

The Problem with 1997/1998

Researchers interested in the 1997 local elections and the 1998 national elections should know that that information was not published in book form but was instead the first set of elections to be covered in electronic format by the Registry. This was initially done via CD-ROM (*Elecciones 97–98*[1]).

The software included on the CD was quite limited for research purposes, and required extracting the raw data files and decoding them (a labor-intensive proposition). If one simply consulted the software on the disk, there were some errors, such as assigning zero votes to lists 717 (Jaime Dussan Calderon of the party Education, Work, and Social Change) and 718 (Luis Eduardo Vives LaCouture of the Liberal Party), which were especially glaring, given that both these candidates won seats in the 1998 elections (information that could be gleaned only from other data on the disk, as well as from other sources). Further, the data on the CD do not contain the finalized totals for that election. Resolution 218 of 1998 as issued by the National Electoral Council of Colombia contained the final vote totals for the 1998 senatorial elections, and those numbers are different from the totals on the CD.[2] This was further confirmed when the Registry posted the 1998 congressional election data to its Web site the week of March 11, 2002.

An additional failing of the CD is that it includes no information on the number of lists that competed for the indigenous seats, nor does it indicate the preliminary quotas used to assign the seats.

2002 Chamber Data

If one looks at the list of seats elected for the Chamber of Representatives as listed on the Registry's Web site (*http://www.registraduria.gov.co/elecciones 2002/e/ccamara.htm?1*), one would see that the header notes that there are 166 seats available in the Chamber for that election. However, if one adds the seats listed, there are only 165. The error is replicated, in part, on the page containing the tallies for the special seats (*http://www.registraduria.gov.co/ elecciones2002/e/vcamespo.htm?1*), which states that there are five seats to assign. However, only four seats are noted as having been assigned.

There are 161 regular seats in the Chamber, based on the populations of the departments. The constitution provides for special seats to increase the representation of groups in the society that otherwise might not be represented. This started with two set-aside seats for blacks in 1994. Later this would be expanded to include a seat for indigenous persons and for Colombians living abroad, so that the grand total of seats in 2002 was 165 (161 + 4 special seats). An additional seat for "political minorities" was added for the 2006 election, raising the total to 166.

2006 Chamber Data

Depending on where one looks, one will find reporting errors for the 2006 allocation of seats as well. If one looks at the official press release from the Registry (Bulletin Number 10 of June 14, 2006), which has the final results for the congressional elections, one should note that in the final table in the document ("Elected Representatives by Party") there are two errors. First, the table lists the number of seats dispersed in the departmental districts as 162. That number should be 161. The table leaves off one of the special districts used in 2006, the set-aside seat for indigenous persons.

The other error (which allows for the column to sum to a 162 subtotal) is that Radical Change is listed in the table as having 21 seats, when in fact the party won only 20 (which is confirmed if one looks at the departmental breakdown of seats won in the very same press release where one will find that CR's list in the Department of Quindio is listed twice, giving both the party and the department one more seat than either should have).

Table A.1

Set-Aside Seats for the 2006 Chamber

Type of seat	Winner	Party
Comunidades Negras	Maria Isabel Urrutia Ocoró	Alianza Social Afrocolombiana
Comunidades Negras	Silfredo Morales Altamar	Afrounincca
Comunidades indígenas	Orsinia Patricia Polanco Jusayú	PDA
Colombianos en el exterior	Manuel José Vives Henriquez	La U
Minorias políticas	Rodrigo Romero Hernandez	Partido Opción Centro

In generating the final tallies for the Chamber, it should be noted that the official press release simply identifies the set-aside seats by the group they represent, rather than by party label. However, the party label is significant here, as it affects the final tallies, specifically in that la U and the PDA both gain a seat. Thus, many of the tallies published may undercount both parties if this classification issue is not noted.

For clarity's sake, table A.1 lists the set-aside seats, their winners, and the party labels.

Problems with Labels

One problem that occurs with some of the election results is that the Registry often lists nontraditional candidates as "other," and coalitional lists as simply "coalition." This makes classification of the lists more difficult, as it requires consulting the ballots or other sources to determine the exact label that the list ran under.

The Problem with Alternates

Another issue that should be noted is that there has long been a practice in Colombia of allowing alternates to serve portions of a given term (the exact practice is discussed in appendix 1). This practice can create problems when one is trying to determine the content of the Congress at a given moment in time, as the actual roster changes quite a bit over the course of a four-year term. This should be noted by students of Colombia, because if one encounters a list of senators or representatives from the middle of a term, one might discover that the roster differs greatly from the list of candidates voted into office on election day. Also, there have been cases where the party label of the alternate is not the same as the one given on the original list. It is therefore possible for the partisan breakdown of a Congress to shift as a result of alternates taking over a given seat. This is an observation based on noting shifts over time between 1998 and 2002 when comparing an online Senate roster to the original electoral results, and the phenomenon has not been subject to systematic study.

NOTES

Chapter 1. An Introduction to Colombia

1. Specifically we see a relative lack of interest shown in the case by political scientists since the advent of serious study of Latin America (indeed, of the developing world in general in the 1960s). The specifics of this lack of interest as manifested in the literature will be examined below.

2. Displacement figures from CODHES (*www.codhes.org*); kidnapping figures for 1995 from U.S. Citizenship and Immigration Services (available online at www *.uscis.gov/graphics/services/asylum/ric/documentation/COL00001.htm*) and for 1996–2005 from Departamento Nacional de Planeación (available online at www.*dnp .gov.co/paginas_detalle.aspx?idp=562*); murder figures for 2000–2004 from *Forensis 2004*, 51, and for 2005 from *Forensis 2005*, 2 (both available via the Instituto Nacional de Medicina Legal y Ciencias Forenses, www.*medicinale gal.gov.co*). Emigration number from Bérubé 2005.

3. Colombia was behind Mexico, Venezuela, and Brazil. Statistics are available via the U.S. Census Bureau online at http://*www.census.gov/foreign-trade/balance /c3010.html*.

4. At the time of writing, the agreement had not been ratified by either country's legislature.

5. The FARC, ELN, and AUC were all designated as foreign terrorist organizations by the U.S. government prior to the attacks of September 11, 2001. The FARC and ELN were both originally so designated on October 8, 1997, with redesignation taking place on October 8, 1999, and November 5, 2001. The AUC was originally placed on the list on September 10, 2001. See Cronin et al. 2004 for more details. In regard to the basic question of the war on terror and Latin America, see Weeks 2006, especially table 1 on page 63, which notes that a major determining factor for defining terrorists in the region is drug trafficking. For more on the question of Colombia specifically and the war on terror, see Taylor 2005a and 2005b.

6. Both quotations come from Adam Isacson, "Washington's 'New War' in Colombia: The War on Drugs Meets the War on Terror," *NACLA Report on the Americas* 36, 5 (March/April 2003): 13.

7. To be fair, there was a chapter on Colombia (Wilde 1978) in Linz and Stepan's *Breakdown of Democratic Regimes: Latin America*. Of course, that work was focused on the breakdown of democracy in Colombia in the 1950s.

8. Such a minimal definition captures the fact that parties can offer candidates for office yet not win enough votes to gain office. Again, the fundamental theoretical assumption is that power seekers enter electoral competition to gain access to, or to influence, the government. It is possible under this definition that political

parties might compete knowing that they will lose but, nevertheless, trying to influence the debate in a given election, or to bring attention to an issue that might affect governmental debate after the election.

Chapter 2. Colombian Democracy

1. Hartlyn (1988, 2) noted the "qualified" nature of Colombia's democracy and provided a list of modifiers similar to the one I provide below, although the list here is much longer—demonstrating that attempts to define Colombia's democracy have not especially improved in the roughly two decades between Hartlyn's work and this one.

2. It should be noted that Dahl was looking at the National Front era.

3. Most famously, perhaps, by Joe Toft, who ran the Drug Enforcement Administration in Bogotá and who, on his way out of office in September 1994, told Colombian national TV that Colombia was "a narco-democracy" (Gutkin 1994).

4. See Dahl 1971, chap. 1.

5. The exact date for when Mexico made its transition away from pseudodemocracy can be debated. The 2000 election was the most dramatic, as it was the first to see the PRI lose the presidency. One could go back to the 1994 presidential election which, as a result of the fraud in 1988, had substantial international scrutiny. The PRI's loss of control of the Chamber of Deputies in 1997 could also be chosen.

6. Freedom House uses a similar definition: "1) A competitive, multiparty political system; 2) Universal adult suffrage for all citizens (with exceptions for restrictions that states may legitimately place on citizens as sanctions for criminal offenses); 3) Regularly contested elections conducted in conditions of ballot secrecy, reasonable ballot security, and in the absence of massive voter fraud that yields results that are unrepresentative of the public will; 4) Significant public access of major political parties to the electorate through the media and through generally open political campaigning" (Freedom House 2005, available online at http://www.freedomhouse.org/template.cfm?page=351&ana_page=292&year =2005).

7. See Bushnell 1993, app. B.

8. The Clinton administration suspected President Ernesto Samper of ties to drug cartels, and even went so far as to block Samper's ability to visit the United States by revoking his visa. See Crandall 2002 for a discussion of U.S.-Colombian relations during this period.

9. There was an attempted coup against President Alfonozo López Pumajero in 1936, and another in his second term in 1944. These are mentioned by Fishel (2000, 52) and briefly discussed by Dix (1967, 297–298). A sense of the significance of the

events can be obtained by noting that two excellent recent political histories of Colombia (Bushnell 1993; Safford and Palacios 2002) make no mention of the events in question.

10. Dix (1967, 295) omits 1866 from his list. Safford and Palacios (2002, 386–389) list all the chief executives of Colombia from independence and indicate which were removed by coup or came to power by coup. The coup of 1900 is discussed by Bergquist (1978, 151–152, 176). Dix (1967, 295) describes the event as deposing "a decrepit president in the midst of a civil war and replac[ing] him with the vice–president."

11. Valencia Tovar would go on to run for the presidency in 1978, winning 65,961 votes (1.3%). Landazábal was assassinated in a drive-by shooting on May 12, 1998, while on a morning walk near his home.

12. A list of defense ministers from 1821 to the present can be found online at the Defense Ministry's Web site: http://*alpha.mindefensa.gov.co/index.php?page =194& id=376&actual=http://www.mindefensa.gov.co/nuevoweb/ministerio/Min_ Historia.html*.

13. See, for example, J. Giraldo 1996 and 1999; Human Rights Watch 2000, 2001, and 2005. This topic is also revisited in chapter 7.

14. For discussions of civil-military relations in Colombia see Ruhl 1981; Fishel 2000; and Watson 2005.

15. Translation mine.

16. See Dugas 2003, 1133, in regard to examples of the court striking down orders by Uribe in 2002.

17. This paragraph draws heavily on Dugas 2003, 1132. The Constitutional Court's ruling in the matter was Sentencia No C-551/03.

18. Chapter 3 discusses the decrees that led to the National Constituent Assembly.

19. In the region, Colombia is the only major country that does not have some form of obligatory voting. Indeed, the only other country in the region not to have some form of obligatory vote is Nicaragua (which is not construed as a "major" case by any measure). For details see Transparencia 2005 and Payne and Mateo 2006. Of course, as García and Hoskin note, the patterns of turnout in these states appear to be historically consistent, with or without the obligatory vote. Of the countries with the obligatory vote, many have no sanctions associated with failure to vote (see Payne and Mateo 2006, 269).

20. For a narrative version of the UP's story, see Dudley 2004 and Kirk 2003. The extermination of the UP is discussed in more detail in chapter 7.

21. General information on Freedom House can be found at www.*freedom house.org*.

22. A complete discussion of Freedom House's system and method is available at http://*www.freedomhouse.org/research/freeworld/2005/methodology.htm*.

Chapter 3. Cartas de Batalla

1. Valencia adds two to that list: the Organic Decree of 1828 that gave Bolívar dictatorial powers and the 1861 Union Pact, which functioned as a provisional constitution until the promulgation of the 1863 model (1987, 119 and 137).

2. As per the declaration made at the congress held in Angostura, Venezuela (known today as Ciudad Bolívar) in 1819, which declared on December 17, 1819, the Fundamental Law of the Republic of Colombia, also known as the Fundamental Law of Angostura (Valencia 1987, 112). It is typical to refer to 1819–1830 version of Colombia as "Gran" or "Great" Colombia to distinguish it from the smaller Colombia of later years (Bushnell 1993, 50).

3. Uribe (1986, 8) also notes individual constitutions in Tunja (1811), Cartagena (1811), Antioquia (1812), and Mariquita (1815).

4. The 1863 Constitution was the most decentralized of the postindependence charters. The nine states of the United States of Colombia (Antioquia, Bolívar, Boyacá, Cauca, Cundinamarca, Magdalena, Panamá, Santander, and Tolima) were considered sovereign and coequal in terms of electing the president (each state having one vote). Further, the states were free to form independent institutions such as militias and post offices. See Bushnell 1993, 122–125; and Dix 1967, 296.

5. The 1936 and 1945 versions of the 1886 Constitution can be found in Gibson 1948. Note: the reforms from Legislative Act No. 1 of August 5, 1936, are to be found in the 1945 codification of the constitution, not the 1936 version. For information on the reforms of 1910 see Dix 1967, 79; Bushnell 1993, 161–162; and especially Bergquist 1978, 252; Gibson 1948, 356; and Valencia 1987, 153–154. In regard to 1936 see Bushnell 1993, 189; and Valencia 1987, 155–158. For the 1945 reforms see Gibson 1948, 401–405; and Valencia 1987, 158–159.

6. This was the first Colombian election with universal adult (male and female) suffrage.

7. It took four pacts to secure the deal: the Pact of Benidorm, the March Pact, the Pact of Sitges, and the Pact of San Carlos. See Kline 1995, 47–48.

8. Laureano Gómez was the president who had been deposed by Rojas. Also worthy of note: the Ospina faction had been working with the Rojas government, which made negotiations even more complicated.

9. The original intention was for alternation to last for twelve years, but negotiations over who would be the first post-Rojas president bogged down because of conflicts between the Gómez and Ospina factions of the PC. As a result, the first slot was given to the PL, and the total number of terms to be alternated was extended from three to four (Dix 1967, 135–136).

10. Adapted from Dix 1967, 134.

11. See chapter 2 for a more thorough discussion of the theoretical and definitional issues surrounding democracy.

12. Rojas had returned to Colombia in 1958 after a brief exile. He stood trial in the Senate in 1959 and was found guilty of "engaging in contraband in cattle and collusion in some minor cases" (Safford and Palacios 2002, 329). His political rights were permanently revoked, but that sentence was later overturned by the Supreme Court (ibid.). Bushnell (1993, 228) also has a brief discussion of Rojas' unexpected return to Colombia in October 1958—little more than a year after his ouster.

13. This division within the Conservatives dated to the early 1950s and linked each group to two former presidents: Mariano Ospina Pérez and Laureano Gómez and his son Álvaro. The Ospina faction was also known as the Unionistas and the Gómez faction as the Laureanistas or Lauro-Alvaristas or Alvaristas (and additionally, the Doctrinarios or Independientes (Dix 1980b, 134).

14. See the Consejo Nacional Electoral's Web site (*http://www.cne.gov.co/partidos/generalidades.htm*), where parties are considered permanent and capable of being assigned specific political tasks as a group that movements cannot undertake.

15. See Dix 1967, 257–269, for a complete discussion of the MRL—its origins, evolution, and activities.

16. Indeed, they polled as follows from 1958 to 1970 (elections every two years): 42%, 44%, 45%, 49%, 44%, 47%, and 49%.

17. For example in Nariño and Sucre—see Semana 1995 for a detailed discussion.

18. Both of whom were active in the party in the 1960s, serving in the Congress. For a discussion of the inner workings of ANAPO during the early period see Dix 1980b, 152–156.

19. Moreno was an AD/M-19 senator from 1991 to 1994. Samuel's brother Iván was elected to the Senate for the 2006–2010 period under the PDA label.

20. For the full text of the 1968 reform, see Presidencia de la República 1969, 581–610. For a discussion of the reform, see Hartlyn 1988, 97–102; Latorre 1986, 53–98; and Pécaut 1989, 49–52.

21. See Uribe 1986, 137, for the original text. Translation mine.

22. For a synopsis of this attempt, see Kline 1999, 156–158.

23. There were 4,991,887 yes votes and 226,451 no votes. Consejo Nacional Electoral 1991, 93.

24. That is, votes/seats = the quota, with seats going first to lists with full quotas and then being distributed to lists with the largest remainders—the system, in place in Colombia for legislative elections until 2006, will be discussed in full in chapter 6.

25. The PC was temporarily known as the PSC (Partido Social Conservador) in the late 1980s early 1990s.

26. Indeed, of the 903,984 total votes cast for PL lists, only 860,122 went to winning lists; 43,862 votes went to PL lists that did not win a seat.

27. Not that the running of multiple lists was a new phenomenon. However, the usage of this tactic in this context—and going forward under the new rules for electing the Senate—was a greater aid to the PL than to any other party.

Chapter 4. Rethinking the Traditional Parties

1. A comparable case might be Uruguay's Blanco and Colorado Parties.

2. This is discussed at length below.

3. In other words, when compared with the rest of Latin America, or even with the emerging democracies of the United States and Europe at the time, Colombia's politics could be broadly understood as being "democratic" in the nineteenth century in particular and even in the twentieth. Of course, some provisos are necessary, such as the already mentioned late move to universal suffrage.

4. Both individuals were generals in the wars for independence (Bolívar, of course, being the Great Liberator). Bolívar was the first president of Gran Colombia, and Santander the vice president. Santander was the second elected president of Gran Colombia (from 1830 to 1832 there were several nonelected presidents between Bolívar's exit from power and Santander's ascension). Both men have departments named after them in Colombia—indeed, Santander has two: Norte de Santander and Santander. Bolívar has but the lone department but wins the overall geographical competition by having the country of Bolivia named after him, as well as the recently rechristened (in 1999) Bolivarian Republic of Venezuela.

5. For a discussion of party origins see, for example, Archer 1995, 171; El Tiempo 1992; Kline 1980; Partido Conservador Colombiano 2006; Partido Liberal Colombiano 2006; and Safford and Palacios 2002, 198.

6. Bushnell 1992, 13–14, identifies nine such "rebellions" including two (1854 and 1900) that were intraparty (Liberal vs. Liberal and Conservative vs. Conservative, respectively). These were: 1839–1841 (the War of the Supremes), 1851, 1854, 1859–1862, 1867, 1885, 1895, 1899–1902 (the War of a Thousand Days), and 1900. Safford and Palacios 2002, 238, add 1876 to the mix.

7. For examples of the discussion of the role of elites in Colombia's traditional parties, see Archer 1990, 13–15; Bagley 1984, 126–127; Dix 1967, 11, 42, and 72; Dix 1987, 89, 91, and 97; Dugas 2000, 81; Hartlyn 1988, 27; Hoskin 1990; and Scarpetta 1991.

8. For examples of the focus on clientelism, see Archer 1990; Cárdenas, Junguito, and Pachón 2006, 9; Diaz 1986; Dix 1987, 93; Hartlyn 1988, 171; Hoskin 1990, 152–153; Leal 1990, 32; Leal and Dávila 1991; Nielson and Shugart 1999; Kline 1983, 76, 94; and Peeler 1976, 203.

9. See Cepeda 1986, 88–91, for a description of the *papeleta* and how it functioned.

10. The specific functioning of the *papeleta* as opposed to the *tarjetón* (along with examples) is detailed in the appendix 1.

11. I interviewed a former mayor of a municipality in the Department of Caldas who noted that to get funding for the paving of a main road into town he was faced with finding a way to raise money locally through donations or trying to get the money from the national budget.

12. For examples of the discussion of abstentionism, see Bagley 1984, 126; Cepeda and González 1976, 25; Peeler 1976, 219; Pinzón de Lewin and Rothlisberger 1991, 134+; Ruhl 1978, 34, 39–41; Ungar 2003, 122–125; and Wilde 1982, 32.

13. For example: "The current effort to enact political party reform is rooted in the notion that the traditional Colombian parties and the party system itself are in crisis. For the past two decades, there has been widespread acceptance of this thesis among Colombian social scientists" (Dugas 2001, 4).

14. The references to Colombia being in a general state of crisis are legion. A few examples include Bagley 1984, 144; Bergquist, Peñaranda, and Sánchez 1992; García and Hoskin 2003; González 1993, 16; Guerrero 1999; Hartzell and Marín 1993, 77; Hoskin, Masías, and García 2003, 21; Kalmanovitz 1990; Leal 1989a; Leal 1989b; Leal 1990; Leal 1996; LeGrand 2003; Medellín 1999, 413–414; Murillo and Torres 1991; Murillo, Ungar, Fajardo, and Peña 1993, 41; Orejuela 1993, 110; Pécaut 1989, 367; Peeler 1976; Pizarro 1996, 229–233; Rodríguez and García 2001; Scarpetta 1991, 162; Shugart, Morean, and Fajaro 2007; and Valencia 2003.

15. This is a question that has been raised before: see Hoskin and Pinzón de Lewin 1989, 199; Hoskin 1993, 152; and Taylor 1996, 69–71. In particular Hoskin (1993, 152) notes that it appears that crisis is "an integral component of Colombian politics" and that the concept itself is "ambiguous" and of "limited analytical utility." A rare example of the direct questioning of the idea that the parties are in crisis can be found in Dávila 2000.

16. A partial list would include Dugas 1993a, 16; Dugas 2000, 81; Dugas 2001, 4; F. Giraldo 2003, 25–36; González 1993, 20; Hoskin 1990; Hoskin and Pinzón de Lewin 1989; Hoyos and Bonilla 2005; Leal 1987; Murillo 1999, 49; Peeler 1976; Pizarro 1996, 208, 217, 227–229; Rangel 1989; Restrepo 1992; Roll 2002, 56; Ruhl 1978; Sánchez D. 1993; and Sánchez T. 1993.

17. To be fair, Fluharty devoted an entire chapter (17) to the ongoing presence of party-based opposition, especially in terms of Liberals, into 1955 and 1956. Still, his concluding chapter did not foresee a significant resurgence of the traditional parties. Rather, he saw the Rojas dictatorship as the manifestation of the will of the masses in opposition to the elite's parties: "Rojas has turned the clock forward on social achievement for the masses. He has given them status, and a sense of their importance" (1957, 316). "It is a step forward for all the people, one step more into the background for the supremacy of oligarchies" (317).

18. A representative list would include Bagley 1984; Delgado 1993; Dugas 1993a, 2000, and 2001; F. Giraldo 2003; Hoyos and Bonilla 2005; Leal 1973, 1987, 1989a,

1989b, 1990, and 1996; Murillo and Sánchez 1993; Murillo, Ungar, Fajardo, and Peña 1993; Orejuela 1993; Restrepo 1992; Roll 2002; and Scarpetta 1991.

19. Translation mine.

20. Bagley 1984, 144; Leal 1973, 133; Leal 1989a, 151; Hoyos and Bonilla 2005, 116; and Orejuela 1993, 111 (among others) make similar arguments.

21. The word *democracy* is used here in a conditional sense. Further, it should be noted that the breakdown of democratic processes began in the Laureano Gómez administration (1950–1953), before the Rojas coup.

22. Law 31 of 1929 established the usage of the Hare quota with largest remainders. Chapter 5 will discuss the specifics of the evolution of the electoral system.

23. Payne, however, indicates that there was congressional competition in 1949 (1968, 202).

24. Leal (1973) is an especially good example of this. Hoskin (1995, 7, and 1980, 107–109) also deals with the question of how the Front changed the parties and looks back to the 1930s. Hoskin and Swanson specifically identify the 1930s as a key period of ideological conflict (1973, 322).

25. Population statistics are available online at http://www.populstat.info. Urban/rural numbers courtesy of Hanratty and Meditz 1990, appendix A, available online at http://lcweb2.loc.gov/frd/cs/colombia/co_appen.html#table4.

26. See Flórez and Bonilla (1991), who call the changes to Colombia from the 1930s to the 1980s an era of "demographic transition without precedent."

27. See Bushnell 1993, 244; and Safford and Palacios 2002, 355–356.

28. At the time he was likely fighting as part of anti-Conservative Liberal activity. Marín's father was killed by Conservatives during *La Violencia*.

29. My thanks to Matthew Søberg Shugart for the observation (private correspondence).

30. Such numbers are small compared with where the system would be during the Front and after, but they demonstrate that the PL and PC were capable of exploiting the loopholes in the electoral system that allowed multiple lists per district. If the parties were functioning under a strict list-PR system in the period in question, then there would have been only one list per party per district. The issue of list proliferation and strategies associated with it will be discussed at length in chapter 5.

31. López won 938,808 votes versus 3,401 for "others" (Bushnell 1993, 291).

32. The basic shift was away from a system that incentivized a personal vote and instead toward a system that cultivated a party-based vote. The specifics of the relationship between the electoral system and the party system will be dealt with in detail in chapter 5.

33. Given that under the system in question the president appointed governors and mayors, among other officials.

Chapter 5. Parties: Reform and Adaptation

1. See, for example, Duverger 1959 and 1986; Grofman and Lijphart 1986; Lijphart 1990 and 1994; Lijphart and Grofman 1984; Rae 1971; and Taagepera and Shugart 1989.

2. See Strøm 1990 for a discussion of the different types of motivations that a political party might have. Strøm rightly notes that, for any given party, there are likely to be multiple motivations that drive action.

3. For an overview see Delgado 2002 in the section titled "Cinco tipos de voto y de escrutino," available online at http://*www.observatorioelectoral.org/biblioteca/?-bookID=15&page=9.*

4. For more on the issue of the electoral rules leading up to the War of a Thousand Days, see Bergquist 1978, 60, 77–79, 114, 121–122.

5. For a discussion of the *voto incompleto* see Baron 1915, 3–17; Eastman 1982, 226–227; and Mazzuca and Robinson 2006. It is worth noting that the term *incomplete vote* is not standard in the electoral studies literature. This system is currently employed in the election of three-fourths of the Mexican Senate (starting in 1996). It is also used for upper house elections in Argentina and Bolivia.

6. Specifically, these changes were part of a broad set of constitutional reforms promulgated on October 31, 1910. The portion of the reform that affected elections can be found in Title XVII, Article 45. The text of the reform can be found online at http://*www.cervantesvirtual.com/servlet/SirveObras/12726101947818273098435/p0000001.htm.*

7. For the full text of the 1968 reform, see Presidencia de la República 1969, 581–610. For the portion specifically pertaining to Article 120, see 595–598.

8. As Bushnell (1993) notes, it was "the first strictly one-party administration since the deposition of Laureano Gómez in 1953" (250).

9. Laakso and Taagepera (1979) built on the Rae fractionalization index ($F = 1 - \Sigma p_i^2$) to create the "effective number of parties" index (N), which measures "the number of hypothetical *equal*-size parties that would have the same total *effect* on fractionalization of the system as have the actual parties of *unequal* size" (4). The formula is $N = 1/\Sigma p_i^2$ and can be used to measure the number of electoral parties (based on votes won) and seats (based on the seats won in the election). The calculation used in table 5.1 is the effective number of parliamentary parties based on the seats won by each party.

10. Note: Only the "pure" PC and PL seats, in the sense that the officeholders ran as candidates of the mainline traditional parties, are counted. If a splinter party using a permutation of the traditional labels won seats (such as New Liberalism or the National Conservative Movement), they were not counted in that measure. The issue of labels and their significance will be further discussed below.

11. A handful of third parties, mostly left leaning, won a smattering of seats in the 1974–1982 period: ANAPO, UNO, FUP, and the Civic Movement. In 1986–1990 the NL arose, as did the UP and the MNC as well as a number of coalitional and regional lists.

12. In 1986 the PL was one seat away from a "pure" PL majority, but given that there were several coalitional lists with the PL (not to mention the NL seats), there was no doubt which party was in control of the legislature.

13. The number of seats (out of 199) controlled by third parties in the Chamber were are follows for the 1974–1990 period: 20 in 1974, 5 in 1978, 2 in 1982, 21 in 1986, and 18 in 1990 (some of the seats counted as "third parties" were won by coalitional lists that might have included traditional party labels. In terms of the Senate (112 seats in 1974 and 1978 and 114 seats thereafter) the totals were as follows: 9 in 1974, 1 in 1978, 2 in 1982, 13 in 1986, and 10 in 1990.

14. While it is certainly possible that candidates might run for office for other reasons, such as publicity, the basic rationale is that individuals enter electoral contests for the purpose of winning office, which in turn is for the purpose of influencing public policy outcomes. Thus, we can assume that, on balance, behaviors engaged in by candidates are undertaken for the purpose of increasing the given candidate's odds of winning. Of course, it is worth noting that mistakes can be made—i.e., some choices are bad ones.

15. At the time of writing it is unclear if Paul will run for reelection to the U.S. House of Representatives in 2008.

16. Certainly it is impossible to know what would have happened had Galán not run, but Betancur's margin of victory over López was 5.73%, and Galán won 10.92%.

17. In 1991 his Fuerza Progresista list came in a respectable twenty-seventh in the country, but his coalitional FP-PC lists in 1994 and 1998 came in second in vote totals. In all cases the lion's share of the votes came from his home department of Antioquia.

18. The official filing papers for Pastrana's 1994 race expressly state that the name of his "party or political movement" was "ANDRES PRESIDENTE."

19. The ballots in 1994 and 1998 included pictures of the candidates for president and vice president, the party's name, and its logo. Also note: the accent over the *e* in Andrés is not present on either of the printed ballots, so I left it off here as well.

20. In fact, in 1988 the party was known as the Partido Social Conservador—a temporary name change that was engineered by Pastrana's father.

21. Dugas does not expressly detail which seats he included in the 29; these are extrapolations I have made.

22. Dugas (2000) uses similar counting rules for other years in the Senate (83) and the Chamber (82). Other examples of conflation of the PC-linked parties can

be found in the Political Database of the Americas (online at http://*pdba.georgetown* *.edu/Elecdata/Col/legis70_98.html*) and Muñoz (2003, 218), which does a similar accounting for the 1994 congress. Ghilodes (1993, 47) conflates New Liberalism with the Liberal Party and the National Salvation Movement with the Conservative Party, as do McDonald and Ruhl 1989, 85. Archer 1995, 192–193 (which does include footnotes breaking out some of the different labels) has a similar treatment of presidential and congressional results. Even the Senate Web site (as was available on March 5, 2002) grouped seats not by unique party label but by "Liberal," "Conservative," "Christian," "Indigenous," "Green," and "Other," although for the Senate elected for the 2006–2010 period the seats are clearly delineated online by unique party label.

23. El Tiempo 2007, "Murió el senador liberal Luis Guillermo Vélez, por una falla cardiaca," *El Tiempo* (6 de Febrero), accessed online February 6, 2007. An excerpt of the piece can be found online at http://*poliblogger.com/colombia/?p=23 %20@*. Also, *El Tiempo* offers an online archive.

24. The National Electoral Council (CNE) keeps track of the legal status of parties and keeps an updated list online: http://*www.cne.gov.co/partidos/vigentes.htm*.

25. See Archer and Chernick 1989 and Archer and Shugart 1997.

26. All major-party candidates for the presidency had experience in the Congress, and of first-time candidates during the 1974–1990 period only Álvaro Gómez did not serve as a cabinet minister before running. Of the winning candidates in the 1974–1990 period, all had previously served in the cabinet. For more on this topic see Taylor, Botero, and Crisp (2008).

27. See, for example, Archer 1990, 24.

28. The PL share of the Chamber during the period was as follows: 56.8% in 1974, 55.8% in 1978, 57.8% in 1982, 49.2% in 1986, and 60.0% in 1990. For the Senate it was 60.0% in 1974, 55.4% in 1978, 55.3% in 1982, 51.0% in 1986, and 58.0% in 1990. It should be noted that 1986 was the one year that the NL was a significant electoral force.

29. In the 1986 electoral statistics, the National Registry identified the party as separate from the PC, and it was officially listed as the "Movimiento Nacional" in the returns. From 1990 to 2002 the party operated as the MNC and consistently offered lists in multiple districts, winning seats in both chambers during that period (from 1986 to 1994 the party won only one Senate seat, but it garnered eight in 1998 and six in 2002. In the Chamber the party won three seats in 1986 and 1990, six in 1991 and 1994, four in 1998, and only one in 2002.

30. In the next chapter the degree to which the Hare quota in Colombia created a large number of small-remainder winners is discussed in detail.

31. According to the party's history page, Democratic Colombia grew out of a Liberal Party faction run by Uribe and his cousin in Antioquia starting in 1985 that was called the Sector Democrático. The party known as Democratic Colombia was not formally founded until 2003. And while the banner graphic of the party's Web

page prominently displays President Álvaro Uribe Vélez as a founder of the party, Uribe has not actually run for office under the party's label. The party's Web address is http://*colombiademocratica.com/*. The history page is accessible at http://*colombiademocratica.com/index.php?option=com_content&task=view&id=18&Itemid=32.*

32. Radical Change was founded in 1998 by dissident Liberals. It won two Senate seats and seven Chamber seats in 2002. It was also the first party to support Uribe's 2002 presidential bid. In the 2006 contest it won fifteen Senate seats and twenty-two Chamber seats.

Chapter 6. Parties, Rules, and Strategic Choices

1. As of the writing of this passage, we have only one election by which to judge. However, the argument will be made below that we are likely to see a similar configuration of parties in the 2010 elections and onward. Certainly, however, we cannot proclaim the 2006 system as set in stone.

2. Duverger's hypothesis clearly predicts that an electoral system built around multimember districts and proportional representation will lead to a multiparty system, assuming that there are sufficient issue dimensions present in the society. See Duverger 1986, 70; Riker 1986; and Taagepera and Shugart 1989, 50, 142–146.

3. For a specific discussion of SNTV and Colombia see Cox and Shugart 1995 and Shugart, Moreno, and Fajardo 2007. For a more general discussion of SNTV see Lijphart, Lopez, and Sone 1986.

4. Hartlyn (1988, 161), for example, argues that the large number of lists was nothing but the lack of party discipline.

5. This calculation also assumes that the PL and PC were not offering lists for the set-aside indigenous seats under the post-1991 rules.

6. In the first National Front Senate contest in 1958, the PL offered only one list per district, except in Cundinamarca and Valle (with the dissident lists in question winning scant votes—only five in the case of the Valle list). The PC began the era more fragmented, offering three lists per district, save Cundinamarca and Magdalena, where it offered four, and Cauca, where it had only two.

7. It is widely held that the strategy was proposed by President Alfonso López Michelsen. In an interview with the author in 1995, however, López asserted that that explanation was a press construction and that the *avispa* strategy used by the PL in the 1990 NCA elections was specifically employed to keep López from controlling a unified PL list.

8. This concern (and specifically a reference to the *bolígrafo*) came up in an interview I had with a prominent PL senator in 1995. This is also discussed in Shugart, Moreno, and Fajardo (2007, 218).

9. Some authors assign the two lists from the "United for Colombia" movement (Movimiento Unidos por Colombia) with the PSC, taking their total number of lists to four. Here, unique labels are counted as unique parties (as discussed in chapter 5), and hence those lists are counted separately.

10. All electoral data cited in this section are from the National Civil Registry of Colombia as published in 1991. Any calculations based on those numbers were done by the author.

11. Because of the incomplete nature of the records kept by the National Registry, it is impossible to tally all the votes to the thirty-six PL lists. For some reason the Registry's results do not indicate the party affiliation of all the lists when they provide the votes per list even though the Registry data report thirty-six PL lists. The ballot itself is unhelpful, as it contained only a photo of the candidate and the candidate's name. A partial total of six identified lists provides an additional 43,862 votes. All that can be said with certainty beyond the information already provided is that all the unidentified lists won 19,580 or fewer votes and more likely than not won fewer than 10,000 votes each (based on the vote totals of the unlabeled lists in the official Registry data).

12. Law 130 of 1994 created a system by which parties must grant an official endorsement (an *aval*) of a candidate before that candidate can use the party's label and colors. In practice, the PC and PL granted *avales* to almost all comers prior to the 2003 reform.

13. From 1974 to 1978 there were twenty-two department-based districts with an average district magnitude of 5.10. From 1982 to 1990 there were twenty-three department-based districts with an average district magnitude of 4.96. The new constitution also created a second national electoral district with the magnitude of 2 for indigenous communities.

14. See table 5.1 for a rundown of the parties and seats in the Senate, 1974–2006.

15. The Knesset is a unicameral legislature with 120 seats and is elected from a single national district. The main difference from Colombia's system (aside from the lack of personal lists) is the use of the D'Hondt method for allocating seats rather than the Hare quota (although the Hare was used for the second and seventh Knesset elections).

16. List 625 was a coalition of the PL and LIDER, 661 a coalition of the PL and the Civic Convergence, and list 672 was a three-way coalition of the PL with We Are Colombia and the CCN. Further, other winners would end up caucusing with the Liberals once in the Senate.

17. This temporary label change was in effect from 1987 until 1992. The change was the initiative of former president Misael Pastrana and was reevaluated after the 1991 elections.

18. The CM offered eight lists and won 107,860 votes, yet wasted 69,402. Likewise the MPCC offered twenty-one lists, won 104,836 votes, and wasted 66,675, while the NFD offered four lists, won 100,643 votes, and wasted 62,091 of them.

19. Given a quota of 91,435 in 2002, the list would have had a remainder of 39,614, which would likely not have won an LRS, as the lowest LRS winner in 2002 was 40,460.

20. Multiseat winners are classified as follows: Lists that won a single quota seat are classified as HDS even if they did not win all the quota votes within their home district, as long as their district-specific votes were larger than the lowest winning largest remainder in the election. For the rare multiple quota-seat winner, the first seat is classified as HDS even if the whole quota did not come from the home district so long as the home district votes themselves exceeded the number of votes won by the smallest LRS winner. For the second quota seat a full quota is subtracted from the home district votes to account for the first quota seat. If the home district remainder would have been a sufficiently large remainder using the same criterion as above, the seat is classified as HDS; otherwise it is an NH seat. For multiseat-winning lists, the first seat is classified as NH if the home district votes would have been insufficient to win even an LRS. In the actual cases of multiwinner lists for the Senate elections in question, all won at least one HDS seat.

21. Another way to look at the difference between the lists is to use Rae's fractionalization index ($F = 1 - \Sigma p_i^2$, where p_i is the decimal share of votes per department for each list—this is an adaptation of a metric that Rae [1971] used as a means of measuring how concentrated or dispersed a given party system was). The more dispersed the votes, the closer to the value of 1 the index gets; and conversely the more concentrated, the closer to the value of 0. HDS seats should have a low fractionalization, while NH lists should have a high fractionalization. For the examples given, for Barco's 2002 list, $F = 0.14$, and for Avellaneda's, $F = 0.93$.

22. Indeed, the margin of victory for Pastrana in 1998 was only 2.37%, which hardly was considered a major defeat.

Chapter 7. The Pernicious Nature of Colombian Political Violence

1. For overviews of contemporary violence in Colombia see, for example, Berquist, Peñaranda, and Sánchez 2001; Livingstone 2004; and Rojas and Meltzer 2005. For a description of the basic histories of the major (and several minor) guerrilla groups see Pizarro 1992.

2. Indeed, as Medina (2004) notes: "Colombia's civil war may go down in history as one of the best documented and diagnosed civil conflicts in record" (1).

3. Indeed, as Pizarro (1992, 175) notes, there are multiple linkages between the guerrilla violence of the 1960s onward and the events of *La Violencia*.

4. A rundown would include 1953 (Payne 1968, 173), 1958 (Bejarano 2003, 227; Serres 2000, 193), 1964 (Dix 1967, 362; Safford and Palacios 2002, 345), "at least 1965" (Sánchez and Meertens 2001, ix), and 1966 (Berquist, Peñaranda, and Sánchez 1992, xii; Roldán 2002, 1; and Manwaring 2002, 2).

5. Safford and Palacios (2002, 345) provide the range cited in the text. Bushnell (1993, 205) provides the range of 100,000–200,000, as does Dix (1967, 362) (who went with simply 200,000 in 1987, 37). Serres (200, 193) goes with 200,000 as well. Payne (1968, 4) cites the figure of 134,820 for the 1949–1953 period.

6. There is little doubt that the phrase "Global War on Terror" and it various permutations have serious definitional problems. Nonetheless, the phrase is deployed here, as it is one that the U.S. government applied to its broad foreign policy post-9/11. It is also a phrase that has, for good or ill, entered the political lexicon of our times.

7. For a historical overview of the peace process (*el proceso de paz*) see García-Peña (2007). Kline (1999) contains an account of the Barco (1986–1990) and Gaviria (1990–1994) administrations' policies toward guerrillas, narcos, and paramilitaries. Arnson (2007) details the Pastrana (1998–2002) administration's attempt to deal with the FARC and also looks at U.S. involvement. Arnson (2005) provides a basic overview of the Uribe (2002–2006, 2006–2010) administration's attempts at peace talks with the AUC.

8. For example, there is the People's Liberation Army (ERP), a group of former ELN fighters who are estimated to number around 150 (Bagely 2005, 34). Other ELN breakaways include the still active Guevarist Revolutionary Army (ERG) and the demobilized Current of Socialist Renovation (CRS).

9. Marín's status is a question mark, and he has been presumed dead on numerous occasions over the decades. He participated in peace talks with President Pastrana in 2001. In 2004 the BBC reported that Marín was within six months of death from cancer (BBC 2004), but apparently the U.S. government considered Marín to be alive in 2006 and offered a $5 million reward for his capture (Forero 2006). For a profile on Marín, see Cala (2000). The U.S. government's online "wanted" poster can be found here: http://*www.state.gov/p/inl/narc/rewards/63840.htm*. Marín's fate is detailed in the afterword.

10. It is almost certainly not coincidental that the FARC grew from 3,600 combatants in the mid-1980s to as many as 20,000 today—the same period of time that it began to dabble in the drug trade. The FARC is arguably the wealthiest guerrilla group in history. Is should be noted, as well, that this is also the period in which paramilitary actions against peasants thought to be collaborating with the guerrillas has grown, leading to both a pool of recruits for the FARC as well as a need for the FARC to grow its ranks to protect itself from the paramilitaries. Chernick (1998) notes that there is a correlation between paramilitary activity and the growth of the FARC.

11. For a list of peace talks involving the FARC (and other armed groups as well) see García-Peña 2007, 93.

12. See note 5 in chapter 1 for the dates of designation as a foreign terrorist organization.

13. The arms theft was accomplished by digging a 246-foot tunnel from a house near the army base into the building that housed the weapons (Kirk 2004, 104).

14. By "drug-related" is meant anything from levying a per gram tax on the product, to collecting protection money on land, to being directly involved in trafficking. The FARC's initial interest and involvement in the drug trade is frequently pegged to its Seventh National Conference in 1982 (Serres 2000, 204; Labrousse 2005, 177), and the argument is frequently made that the end of the Cold War in particular required that the FARC find new sources of funding (Thoumi 2002, 106).

15. In 2006, both cultivation and production were slightly down in Colombia after years of applying the eradication program that is part of Plan Colombia. However, as is the typical pattern in the ongoing drug war, the decreases in Colombia were more than offset by increases in Peru and Bolivia. According to the UNODC, the overall cultivation of coca leaf during the 2002–2006 period was lower than during the 1995–2001 period (2007b, 7), but the actual potential for cocaine production was up for the 2004–2006 period as compared with 1995–2003. In other words, while eradication plans can be argued to have had some success in reducing the number of hectares under cultivation, the policies have not had an effect on the ability to produce the drug. And, despite efforts to decrease supply, street prices in the United States (adjusted for inflation) are at the historically low end of the spectrum (UNODC 2007b, 228).

16. The 2007 *World Drug Report* does not contain estimates of hectares under cultivation for cannabis, but based on comparative seizure figures, Colombia (with 3% of the world's seizures of cannabis herb) is a minor player compared with Mexico (38%) and the United States (24%) (2007b, 107). Of course, seizure figures do not directly correlate to production, but the huge differences between Mexico and Colombia in terms of seizures give a basic feel for the relative involvement of the two countries in marijuana production. Unlike coca and poppy cultivation, no good estimates of cannabis cultivation are available, and so the UNODC focuses on seizure statistics. Bagely (2005, 22) estimated that in the late 1990s there were roughly 5,000 hectares of cannabis under cultivation and that at that point in time Colombia accounted for roughly 40% of imports into the United States.

17. A *traqueto* is a gunman and connotes connection to the drug industry and illicit enrichment.

18. A quintessential example would be the Tom Clancy novel (and later movie) *Clear and Present Danger* and its main antagonist, the not so subtly named Pablo Escobedo.

19. The most visible, and infamous, example of Escobar's attempt at being accepted as a mainstream power player was his election as an alternate to the Chamber of Representatives in 1982. He was on the list of Antioquia Liberal Jairo Oretga Ramírez, which won 16,650 votes to capture one largest-remainder seat (the lowest winning list and lower LRS winner for the twenty-six seats from Antioquia in that election). The purpose of the alternate (or *suplente*) is to serve if the elected official cannot. However, it is not unusual in Colombia for the elected member to step down at some point in the term to allow the alternate a chance to serve. In Escobar's case he was denied his seat by the Chamber when he sought to take his turn.

20. The Lara Bonilla killing was the point at which "the peaceful-coexistence pact between drug dealers, politicians, and authorities [was] broken" (Ceballos and Cronshaw 2001, 128). In regard to Cano Isaza, his paper had been extremely critical of the drug lords, and Cano himself had written numerous anti-Escobar columns. The violence did not end with Cano's murder, as the family attorney overseeing the murder investigation was also killed and the *El Espectador* offices were bombed more than once, with the most devastating attack coming in early September of 1989, when a truck bomb destroyed a substantial amount of the newspaper's main facility, including its production equipment.

21. The motive for the destruction of the airplane was that there were allegedly police informants onboard (Bushnell 1993, 264).

22. Sánchez and Meertens (2001, 179–180) discuss the organization of citizens for their own self-defense by the military as early at 1961.

23. Chernick (1998) notes that the revocation of the 1965 law was a move by the Supreme Court in response to the growing usage of narco-inspired paramilitary violence against the state. The ruling stated that it was unconstitutional for the military to arm civilians.

24. Ironically, the Spanish word *convivir* means "to live together" or "to coexist."

25. Not only can we go all the way back to *La Violencia* to find some of the same behaviors, but also, as Richani (2000, 40–41) notes, the usage of paramilitaries in conflicts over control of emerald-mining territory can be documented from the early 1970s into the late 1980s. Indeed, Richani demonstrates a seamless connection (via emerald baron Víctor Carranza) between the emerald conflicts and the growth of the paramilitaries of the 1980s and 1990s. See also Kirk (2004, 7, 130–131, and 239) and Dudley (2004, 111 and 192–193), both of whom discuss Carranza's connections to the paramilitaries as well as his role in the attacks on the UP.

26. Kirk (2004, 104–105) details the beginning of this strategy, including the kidnapping of Medellín Cartel cofounder Carlos Lehder (who escaped before a ransom was paid) and that of the children of drug baron Carlos Jader Álvarez.

27. The importance of MAS is discussed, among other places, in Richani 2000, 38–39, and Camacho and López 2007, 75. For more information on the group see Kirk's book, which has a narrative account of its history (2003, 105–130).

28. Fidel disappeared in 1994, likely dying at the hands of guerrillas, although the story is something of a mystery (see Dudley 2002). Later on Carlos also would disappear, in 2004, and the government believes that he was killed by his brother Vicente (who also was part of the AUC leadership) (El País 2006).

29. Some of the "associates" in question included the Cali Cartel, which helped fund the PEPES (Kirk 2004, 157). Further, numerous allegations have been made that the Colombian and U.S. governments worked clandestinely with the PEPES (Kirk 2004, 158; Dudley 2004, 196–197).

30. For a specific example see Chernick 1998, and for a comprehensive study, Human Rights Watch 2000 and 2001.

31. The tactic of using violence against unarmed citizens thought to be aiding the guerrillas would be a hallmark of the behavior of the AUC over time. The Castaños believed that even indirect help of the guerrillas was tantamount to being a member of the FARC or other groups. Hence their men would regularly massacre towns thought to be helping the guerrillas.

32. The Uribe-AUC disarmament will be discussed below.

33. Translated by the author.

34. The figures cited come from the following (in order cited): Collet 1987 and 1988; Cepeda C. 2006; Dermota 1994; Fundación Manuel Cepeda Vargas 2004; García-Peña 2007, fn6; and Schemo 1997.

35. A report by Procurador Carlos Jimenez Goméz in 1983 cited fifty-nine active-duty members of the police and armed forces linked to MAS (Human Rights Watch 1996).

36. The text of the accord can be found online at http://www.altocomision adoparalapaz.gov.co/acuerdos/acuerdos_t/jul_15_03.htm.

37. Senator Jimmy Chammoro (C4), at the passage of the law, stated, "It should be called what it really is, a law of impunity and immunity," and Iván Cepeda, son of the slain senator Manuel Cepeda, said, "This law tried to simulate truth, justice and reparations, but what it really offers is impunity." Further, U.S. senator Richard Lugar (R-IN) expressed concerns that the law left the "mafia-like structures" in the country in place (Forero 2005). A more detailed, point-by-point critique can be found in a Human Rights Watch report (2005, 8–9). The report's title is *Smoke and Mirrors*, which provides a clear idea of the group's view of the process and the Justice and Peace Law itself. Indeed, beyond the specific list cited, the entire report is critical of the entire paramilitary demobilization process.

38. Indeed, part of Carlos Castaño's stated reasons for entering into negotiations with the state was that the government was "demonstrating its capacity and political will" against the left (Forero 2002). Later, when AUC leader Salvatore

Mancuso addressed the Colombia Senate, he "cast his group as an ally of the state in the fight against the rebels" (Forero 2004).

39. For a description of the scandal, see Lee and Thoumi 1999, 74–77; and Tickner 1998, 64–65.

40. Crandall (2002, chap. 4) makes a compelling case that Samper acted against the Cali Cartel as a direct result of U.S. pressure.

41. See Crandall 2001 and 2002 for a detailed discussion of U.S.-Colombian relations during the Samper era.

42. For example, in July of 2007, Defense Minister Juan Manuel Santos made it public information that the FARC and the Norte de Valle Cartel had acquired state security information likely via bribery (BBC 2007a).

43. Initially there were two other candidates (Cristian Moreno Panezo and Abraham Romero Ariza); however, they were intimidated into not running. See *Semana* 2007.

44. For a list of those called, see http://*www.elcolombiano.com.co/Banco Conocimiento/I/ir_a_la_corte_no_es_estar_vinculado/ir_a_la_corte_no_es_estar _vinculado.asp*. And for a list of those arrested (as of April 24, 2007) see http:// *www.cipcol.org/?p=380*.

45. For an overview of the presentation, along with audio and supporting materials, see the PDA's Web site: http://*www.polodemocratico.net/Uribe-autorizo-varias -Convivir-a*.

Chapter 8. The State of Colombia (Evaluations and Conclusions)

1. Beyond simply the issue of immediate reelection, it has been a historical rarity for Colombian presidents to serve even nonconsecutive terms. Only Nuñez (1880–1882, 1884–1892, 1892–1894), Tomás Cipriano Mosquera (1845–1849, 1861–1864, and 1866–1867), and Alfonso López Pumarejo (1934–1938 and 1942–1946) served multiple terms prior to Uribe's reelection. Under the 1886 Constitution, politicians were allowed to serve multiple nonconsecutive terms, but only López managed the feat, although his son (López Michelsen) tried and failed (losing the 1982 election to Belisario Betancur).

2. In 1990, a quasi-traditional party, the MSN, came in second. See chapter 6 for a discussion of traditional versus quasi-traditional versus nontraditional parties.

3. The most successful center-left challenger previously was Navarro Wolff, who won 12.48% of the popular vote in 1990.

4. The PC did endorse Andrés Pastrana in 1994 and 1998, and Uribe in 2006. The last official PC candidate was Rodrigo Lloreda in 1990. The party's 2002 candidate, Juan Camilo Restrepo, withdrew before the election.

5. The AD included the Frente Social y Político, MOIR, Unidad Democrática, the Movimiento Ciudadano, the Movimiento Opción Siete, and the Autoridades Indígenas de Colombia; see PDA 2007.

6. The Santos family owned *El Tiempo*, the nation's leading daily newspaper, which has long been pro-Liberal, until 2007. Further, Eduardo Santos, Juan Manuel's granduncle, was president from 1938 to 1942. *El Tiempo* is currently owned by Spanish conglomerate Grupo Planeta.

7. These figures represent 17 of 20 members of the "la U" delegation, 14 of 15 for CR, 15 of 18 for the PL, and 17 of 18 for the PC.

Afterword

1. The only comparable event is the systemic attacks on the Patriot Union discussed earlier. Really, only the M-19's experience with the Palace of Justice in 1985 tops these events in the annals of Colombia's guerrillas.

2. Polance, Pérez and Beltrán had been held since 2001; Gechem since 2002.

3. In subsequent discussions of FARC leaders, their *noms de guerre* will be used and their real names given in parentheses.

4. The news of Marín's death emerged in an interview with Defense Minister Juan Manuel Santos by the weekly newsmagazine *Semana*. Oddly, the news was not the stated reason for the interview, which was otherwise fairly routine. The interviewer asked Santos if the government knew where Tirofijo was and Santos casually answered "He must be in Hell . . . the one where dead criminals go" (*Semana* 2008). An English translation of the pertinent portions of the interview can be found online at *http://www.cipcol.org/?p=604.*

5. Suárez is also known as Jorge Briceño Suárez.

6. César (Antonio Aguila), and Enrique Gafas (Alexander Fanfán).

7. Press reports indicate that the Colombian military used Red Cross symbols to trick the FARC, leading to criticism. The FARC itself later declared that the captured commander was a "traitor" for allowing himself to be tricked.

8. See, for example, Associated Press 2008. It should be noted that the actual numbers are unclear at this point.

9. These numbers are from Gallup (El Tiempo 2008c).

10. It is noteworthy that Castro's Web site (*http://www.santiagocastro.org/*) shows him campaigning with Uribe for reelection in 2006 and displays a banner at the top which states "en frente con Uribe" (up front with Uribe).

11. Translation by the author.

12. Indeed, a "transitory paragraph" inserted as part of the amendment states that presidents who had held office prior to the reform are limited to only one more term in office. See *//www.secretariasenado.gov.co/leyes/CONS_P91.HTM#197*

13. Medina was a down-list candidate on list 24 of the Santander Chamber ballot in 2002. The list, which won one seat, was headed by Iván Díaz Mateus. At some point Díaz stepped down to allow Medina to assume the seat (a practice noted in the appendices). Medina occupied the number-two slot on Díaz's electoral list.

Díaz went on to win a Senate seat in 2006. He also was arrested in connection with the reelection bribe scandal.

Appendix 1. The Evolution of the Ballot in Colombia

1. Cepeda 1986, 87–92, contains detailed instructions on the voting process using the *papeleta*.

2. For a discussion of this mechanism see Taylor, Botero, and Crisp (2008).

Appendix 2. Notes on Electoral Data

1. My thanks to Brian Crisp and especially Marci Ribetti for their help in my obtaining the CD.

2. My thanks to a personal communication from Luis Fajardo via Matthew Shugart for that information.

REFERENCES

Aguirre, Katherine, Robert Muggah, Jorge A. Restrepo, and Michael Spagat. 2006. "'Colombia's Hydra: The Many Faces of Gun Violence.'" Chapter 9 of the *Small Arms Survey 2006*, copublished with CERAC. Available online at http://www.smallarmssurvey.org/copublications/CH9%20Colombia_English_Web.pdf

Anderson, Charles W. 1982. "Towards a Theory of Latin American Politics." In Howard Wiarda, ed., *Politics and Social Change in Latin America*. Boston: University of Massachusetts Press.

Archer, Ronald P. 1990. "The Transition from Traditional to Broker Clientelism in Colombia: Political Stability and Social Unrest." Working Paper #140, Kellogg Institute.

——. 1995. "Party Strength and Weakness in Colombia's Besieged Democracy." In Scott Mainwaring and Timothy R. Scully, eds., *Building Democratic Institutions: Party Systems in Latin America*. Stanford, Calif.: Stanford University Press.

Archer, Ronald P., and Marc W. Chernick. 1989. "El presidente frente a las instituciones nacionales." In Patricia Vásquez de Urrutia, comp., *La democracia en blanco y negro: Colombia en los años ochenta* (pp. 31–79). Bogotá: Cerec.

Archer, Ronald P., and Matthew Søberg Shugart. 1997. "The Unrealized Potential of Presidential Dominance in Colombia." In Scott Mainwaring and Matthew Søberg Shugart, eds., *Presidentialism and Democracy in Latin America* (pp. 110–159). Cambridge: Cambridge University Press.

Arnson, Cythnia J., ed. 2005. *The Peace Process in Colombia with the Autodefensas Unidas de Colombia-AUC*. Washington, D.C.: Woodrow Wilson International Center for Scholars.

——. 2007. "The Peace Process in Colombia and U.S. Policy." In Christopher Welna and Gustavo Gallón, eds., *Peace, Democracy, and Human Rights in Colombia*. Notre Dame, Ind.: University of Notre Dame Press.

Associated Press. 2008. "Manuel Marulanda, Leader of Colombian Rebel Group, Dies." *International Herald Tribune*. (May 25). Available online at http://www.iht.com/articles/2008/05/25/america/colombia.php

Bachelet, Pablo. 2005. "Mexico Now Top Supplier of US Drugs." *Miami Herald* (July 31).

Bagley, Bruce M. 1984. "Colombia: National Front and Economic Development." In Robert Wesson, ed., *Politics and Economic Development in Latin America*. Stanford, Calif.: Hoover Institution Press.

——. 1988. "Colombia and the War on Drugs." *Foreign Affairs* 67 (Fall): 70–92.

———. 1989. "Dateline Drug Wars: Colombia; The Wrong Strategy." *Foreign Policy* 77 (Winter): 154–171.

———. 2005. "Drug Trafficking, Political Violence, and U.S. Policy in Colombia under the Clinton Administration." In Cristina Rojas and Judy Meltzer, eds., *Elusive Peace: International, National and Local Dimensions of Conflict in Colombia*. New York: Palgrave Macmillan.

Barczak, Monica. 2001. "Representation by Consultation? The Rise of Direct Democracy in Latin America." *Latin American Politics and Society* 43, 3 (Fall): 37–59.

Baron, Felipe. 1915. *La reforma electoral*. Bogotá: Minerva.

BBC. 2004. "Colombia Rebel 'Dying of Cancer.'" *BBC News Online* (February 18). Available online at http://*news.bbc.co.uk/2/hi/americas/3500459.stm*

———. 2007a. "Colombia Admits Army Infiltrated." *BBC News Online* (July 31). Available online at http://*news.bbc.co.uk/2/hi/americas/6923589.stm*

———. 2007b. "FARC Woman Steals Plane to Desert.' *BBC News Online* (September 29). Available online at *http://news.bbc.co.uk/2/hi/americas/7019434.stm*

———. 2008. "Colombia's Uribe Calls for Vote." *BBC News Online* (June 27). Available online at *http://news.bbc.co.uk/2/hi/americas/7476752.stm*

Bejarano, Ana María. 1994. "Recuperear el estado para fortalecer la democracia." *Análisis politico* 22 (May–August): 47–79.

———. 2003. "Protracted Conflict, Multiple Protagonists, and Staggered Negotiations: Colombia, 1982–2002. *Canadian Journal of Latin American and Caribbean Studies* 28, 55–56: 223–247.

Bejarano, Ana María, and Carlos Pizarro. 2002. "From 'Restricted' to 'Besieged': The Changing Nature of the Limits to Democracy in Colombia." Working Paper #296, University of Notre Dame Kellogg Insitute for International Studies. Available online at http://*www.nd.edu/~kellogg/publications/*

Bergquist, Charles W. 1978. *Coffee and Conflict in Colombia, 1886–1910*. Durham, N.C.: Duke University Press.

Bergquist, Charles, Ricardo Peñaranda, and Gonzalo Sánchez, eds. 1992. *Violence in Colombia: The Contemporary Crisis in Historical Perspective*. Wilmington, Del.: Scholarly Resources.

———. 2001. *Violence in Colombia, 1990–2000: Waging War and Negotiating Peace*. Wilmington, Del.: Scholarly Resources.

Berry, R. Albert, Ronald G. Hellman, and Mauricio Solaún, eds. 1980. *Politics of Compromise: Coalition Government in Colombia*. New Brunswick, N.J.: Transaction Books.

Berry, R. Albert, and Mauricio Solaún. 1980. "Notes toward an Interpretation of the National Front." In R. Albert Berry, Ronald G. Hellman, and Mauricio Solaún, eds., *Politics of Compromise: Coalition Government in Colombia*. New Brunswick, N.J.: Transaction Books.

Bertram, Eva, Morris Blachman, Kenneth Sharpe, and Peter Andreas. 1996. *Drug War Politics: The Price of Denial*. Berkeley: University of California Press.

Bérubé, Myriam. 2005. "Colombia: In the Crossfire." *Migration Information Source* (November). Available online at http://*www.migrationinformation.org/Profiles/ display.cfm?ID=344*

Boudon, Lawrence. 2001. "Colombia's M-19 Democratic Alliance: A Case Study in New-Party Self-Destruction." *Latin American Perspectives* 116, 28 (January): 73–92.

Brauer, Jurgen, Alejandro Gómez-Sorzano, and Sankar Sethuraman. 2004. "Decomposing Violence: Political Murder in Colombia, 1946–1999." *European Journal of Political Economy* 20, 2 (June): 447–461.

Bronstein, Hugh. 2008. "Colombian Rightists Want Third Term for Uribe." *Reuters News Online* (July 22). Available online at http://*www.reuters.com/article/bonds News/idUSN2228995920080722*

Bunivić, Mayra, and Andrew R. Morrison. 2000. "Living in a More Violent World." *Foreign Policy* 118 (Spring): 58–72.

Bushnell, David. 1992. "Politics and Violence in Nineteenth-Century Colombia." In Charles Bergquist, Ricardo Peñaranda, and Gonzalo Sánchez, eds., *Violence in Colombia: The Contemporary Crisis in Historical Perspective*. Wilmington, Del.: Scholarly Resources.

———. 1993. *Colombia: A Nation in Spite of Itself*. Berkley: University of California Press.

———. 2004. *Simón Bolívar: Liberation and Disappointment*. New York: Pearson Longman.

Cala, Andrés. 2000. "The Enigmatic Guerrilla: FARC's Manuel Marulanda." *Current History* 99, 634 (February): 56–59.

Camacho Guizao, Alvaro, and Andrés López Restrepo. 2007. "From Smugglers to Drug Lords to *Traquetos*." In Christopher Welna and Gustavo Gallón, eds., *Peace, Democracy, and Human Rights in Colombia*. Notre Dame, Ind.: University of Notre Dame Press.

Cárdenas, Mauricio, Roberto Junguito, and Mónica Pachón. 2006. "Political Institutions and Policy Outcomes in Colombia: The Effects of the 1991 Constitution." Inter-American Development Bank Latin American Research Network, Working Paper #R-508. Available online at http://*www.iadb.org/res/publications /pubfiles/pubR-508.pdf*

Carey, John M., and Matthew Søberg Shugart. 1995. "Incentives to Cultivate a Personal Vote: A Rank Ordering of Electoral Formulas." *Electoral Studies* 14, 4: 417–439.

Carrigan, Ana. 1993. *The Palace of Justice: A Colombian Tragedy*. New York: Four Walls Eight Windows.

Ceballos Melguizo, Ramiro, and Francine Cronshaw. 2001. "The Evolution of Armed Conflict in Medellín: An Analysis of the Major Actors." *Latin American Perspectives* 28, 1 (January): 110–131.

Cepeda, Manuel José. 1985. "Las relaciones entre el presidente y la corte durante la emergencia económica: Un semidios enfrentando a un monstruo." In Manuel José Cepeda, ed., *Estado de sitio y emergencia económica*. Bogotá: Contraloría General de la República.

———. 1986. *Cómo son las elecciones en Colombia: Guia del votante*. Bogotá: FES-COL, Cerec, Cider Uniandes.

———, ed. 1993. *Introducción a la constitución de 1991: Hacia un nuevo constitucionalismo*. Santafé de Bogotá: Presidencia de la República.

Cepeda Castro, Iván. 2006. "Genocidio político: El case de la Unión Patriótica en Colombia." *Revista Cetil* 1, 2 (September): 101–112.

Cepeda Ulloa, Fernando, and Claudia Gonzalez De Lecaros. 1976. *Comportamiento del voto urbano en Colombia: Una aproximación*. Bogota: Departamento de Ciencia Política, Universidad de los Andes.

Chernick, Marc W. 1998. "The Paramilitarization of the War in Colombia." *NACLA Report on the Americas* 31, 5 (March/April).

Collet, Merrill. 1987. "In Colombia, Death Is Routine as Political Violence Soars." *Christian Science Monitor* (October 15). Available online at http://*www.csmonitor* .*com/1987/1015/ovaz.html*

———. 1988. "Battling for Power with Bullets and Ballots." *Christian Science Monitor* (May 16). Available online at http://*www.csmonitor.com/1988/0516/olom3.html*

Collier, David, and Steven Levitsky. 1996. "Democracy 'with Adjectives': Conceptual Innovation in Comparative Research." Working Paper #230, Department of Political Science, University of California, Berkeley.

———. 1997. "Democracy with Adjectives: Conceptual Innovation in Comparative Research." *World Politics* 49, 3 (April): 430–451.

Consejo Nacional Electoral. 1991. *La 7a papeleta*. Bogotá: CNE.

Consultoría para los Derechos Humanos y el Desplazamiento (CODHES). 2005. "Cifras de desplazamiento forzado en Colombia." Available online at http://*www.codhes.org/index.php?option=com_content&task=view&id=3&Itemid=5*

Cox, Gary W., and Matthew Søberg Shugart. 1995. "In the Absences of Vote Pooling: Nomination and Allocation Errors in Colombia." *Electoral Studies* 14, 4: 441–460.

———. 1996. "Strategic Voting under Proportional Representation." *Journal of Law, Economics, & Organization* 12, 2 (October): 299–324.

Crandall, Russell. 2001. "Explicit Narcotization: U.S. Policy toward Colombia during the Samper Administration." *Latin American Politics and Society* 43, 3 (Fall): 95–120.

———. 2002. *Driven by Drugs: U.S. Policy toward Colombia*. Boulder, Colo.: Lynne Rienner Publishers.

Crisp, Brian, and Rachel E. Ingall. 2002. "Institutional Engineering and the Nature of Representation: Mapping the Effects of Electoral Reform in Colombia." *American Journal of Political Science* 46, 4 (October): 733–748.

Cronin, Audrey Kurth, Huda Aden, Adam Frost, and Benjamin Jones. 2004. *Foreign Terrorist Organizations*. Washington, D.C.: Congressional Research Service. Available online at http://www.fas.org/irp/crs/RL32223.pdf

Dahl, Robert. 1971. *Polyarchy: Participation and Opposition*. New Haven, Conn.: Yale University Press.

Dávila Ladrón de Guevara, Andrés. 2000. "Anotaciones sobre la crisis, fragmentación y pulverización de los partidos en Colombia." Paper presented at the 2000 Congress of the Latin American Studies Association.

Delgado, Oscar. 1993. *Modernidad, democracia y partidos político*. Santafé de Bogotá: FIDEC: FESCOL.

———. 2002. *Los sistemas electorales para el congreso en Colombia (1821–2002)*. Available online at http://www.observatorioelectoral.org/biblioteca/?bookID=15

Dermota, Ken. 1994. "The Death of a Colombian Party." *Christian Science Monitor* (May 26). Available online at http://www.csmonitor.com/1994/0526/26061.html

Diamond, Larry. 1999. *Developing Democracy: Toward Consolidation*. Baltimore: Johns Hopkins University Press.

Diaz Uribe, Eduardo. 1980a. "Consociational Democracy: The Case of Colombia." *Comparative Politics* 12:303–321.

———. 1980b. "Political Opposition under the National Front." In Albert R. Berry, Ronald G. Hellman, and Mauricio Solaún, eds., *Politics of Compromise: Coalition Government in Colombia*. New Brunswick, N.J.: Transaction Books.

———. 1986. *El clientelism en Colombia: Un studio exploritorio*. Bogotá: El Áncora Press.

Dix, Robert H. 1967. *Colombia: The Political Dimensions of Change*. New Haven, Conn.: Yale University Press.

———. 1987. *The Politics of Colombia*. New York: Praeger.

———. 1990. "Social Change and Party System Stability in Colombia." *Government and Opposition* 25, 1: 98–114.

Dudley, Steven. 2002. "Dead Man's Bluff." *Washington Post* (November 24), W10. Available online at http://www.washingtonpost.com/ac2/wp-dyn/A11783-2002Nov19?language=printer

———. 2004. *Walking Ghosts: Murder and Guerrilla Politics in Colombia*. New York: Routledge.

Dugas, John. 1993a. "La constitución política de 1991: ¿Un pacto política viable?" In John Dugas, ed., *La constitución de 1991: ¿Un pacto politico viable?* Bogotá: Departmento de Cienceia Política, Universidad de los Andes.

———. 1993b. "El desarrollo de la Asamblea Nacional Constituyente." In John Dugas, ed., *La constitucion de 1991: ¿Un pacto politico viable?* Bogotá: Departmento de Cienceia Política, Universidad de los Andes.

———. 2000. "The Conservative Party and the Crisis of Political Legitimacy in Colombia." In Kevin J. Middlegrook, *Conservative Parties, the Right, and Democracy in Latin America.* Baltimore: Johns Hopkins University Press.

———. 2001. "Sisyphus in the Andes? The Pursuit of Political Party Reform in Colombia." Prepared for delivery at the 2001 meeting of the Latin American Studies Association, Washington, D.C.

———. 2003. "The Emergence of Neopopulism in Colombia? The Case of Álvaro Uribe." *Third World Quarterly* 24, 6: 1117–1136.

Duverger, Maurice. 1959. *Political Parties: Their Organization and Activity in the Modern State.* 2nd English rev. ed. Barbara and Robert North, trans. London: Metheun and Co.

———. 1986. "Duverger's Law: Forty Years Later." In Bernard Grofman and Arend Lijphart, eds., *Electoral Laws and Their Political Consequences.* New York: Agathon Press.

Eastman, Jorge Mario. 1982. Seis reformas estructurales al régimen político: Resultados electorales de 1930 a 1982. In Ministerio de Gobierno, *Colección: "Legislación, doctrina y jurisprudencia."* Bogotá: Impreso en la División de Edición del Departamento Administrativo Nacional de Estadística, DANE.

El País. 2006. "Vicente Castaño habría matado a su hermano." *El País* (August 23). Available online at http://www.elpais.com.co/paisonline/notas/Agosto232006/vicentecas.html

El Tiempo. 1992. "Partidos . . . ¿qué tan partidos?" *El Tiempo* (November 15), 7A.

———. 1997a. "Los barones electorales se defienden." *El Tiempo* (April 2).

———. 1997b. "¿Qué opinan los políticos independientes?" *El Tiempo* (April 2).

———. 1997c. "División liberal enterró la reforma electoral." *El Tiempo* (April 2).

———. 2002. "Ocho candidates tienen chance de ser senadores." *El Tiempo* (March 15).

———. 2003a. "Reportan el asesinato de 25 candidatos a las comicios del 26 de octubre." *El Tiempo* (October 7).

———. 2003b. "198 alcaldes del pais estan amenazados por la guerrilla o los paramilitares." *El Tiempo* (October 13).

———. 2003c. "Alvaro Uribe asegura que las Farc ordenaron asesinar candidatos." *El Tiempo* (October 13).

———. 2007. "Murió el senador liberal Luis Guillermo Vélez, por una falla cardiaca." *El Tiempo* (February 6).

———. 2008a. "Hombres de su círculo de seguridad iban a asesinar al 'Mono Jojoy'." *El Tiempo* (May 11).

———. 2008b. "Referendo para que el pueblo ordene repetir elecciones del 2006 anunció el Presidente." *El Tiempo* (June 27).

———. 2008c. "Pasó la euforia de la operación 'Jaque': popularidad de Uribe bajó aunque levemente." *El Tiempo* (September 2).

———. 2008d. "Guiño a Noemí Sanín hizo el presidente Uribe durante un encuentro con empresarios." *El Tiempo* (September 3).

———. 2008e. "Proyecto de referendo por la reelección de Uribe será presentado mañana en el Congreso." *El Tiempo* (September 8).

———. 2008f. "Reelección por ahora no, pero quizá en 2014, plantea el Presidente Álvaro Uribe." *El Tiempo* (September 11).

Fishel, John T. 2000. "Colombia: Civil-Military Relations in the Midst of War." *Joint Forces Quarterly* (Summer): 51–56. Available online at http://*www.dtic.mil/ doctrine/jel/jfq_pubs/1125.pdf*

Flórez, Carmen Elisa, and Elssy Bonilla. 1991. "The Demographic Transition in Colombia." In Eleonora Masini and Susan Stratigos, eds., *Women, Households and Change*. Tokyo: United Nations University Press. Available online at http://*www .unu.edu/unupress/unupbooks/uu10we/uu10we09.htm#the%20demographic%20 transition%20in%20colombia*

Fluharty, Vernon Lee. 1957. *Dance of the Millions: Military Rule and the Social Revolution in Colombia, 1930–1956*. Pittsburgh: University of Pittsburgh Press.

Forero, Juan. 2002. "Colombian Rightists Declare Cease-Fire as Prelude to Talks." *New York Times* (November 30).

———. 2004. "At Colombia's Congress, Paramilitary Chiefs Talk Peace." *New York Times* (July 29).

———. 2005. "New Colombian Law Grants Concession to Paramilitaries." *New York Times* (June 23). Available online at http://*www.nytimes.com/2005/06/23/ international/americas/23colombia.html?ex=1277179200&en=0763ce99ea/a2140 &ei=5090&partner=rssuserland&emc=rss*

———. 2006. "U.S. Indicts 50 Leaders of Colombian Rebels in Cocaine Trafficking." *New York Times* (March 23). Available online at http://*www.nytimes.com/ 2006/03/23/international/americas/23colombia.html?ex=1300770000&en =c89b3f3d6c9f5350&ei=5090&partner=rssuserland&emc=rss*

———. 2007. "Colombian Leader Says Rebels Killed 11 Civilian Hostages." *Washington Post* (June 29), A15. Available online at http://*www.washingtonpost.com/ wp-dyn/content/article/2007/06/28/AR2007062802490_pf.html*

Freedom House. Various years. *Freedom in the World*. Washington, D.C.: Freedom House. Available online at http://*www.freedomhouse.org/template.cfm? page=15*

Fundación Manuel Cepeda Vargas. 2004. *El genocidio de la Unión Patriótica*. Available online at http://*manuelcepeda.atarraya.org/article.php3?id_article=13*

Fundación para la Libertad de Prensa. 2004. *Estado de la libertad de prensa en Colombia: A pesar de una leve mejoría, la situación sigue siendo grave.* Available online at http://www.flip.org.co/informes/indice_informes.htm

———. 2005. *Libertad de prensa en Colombia—deciembre de 2005.* Available online at http://www.flip.org.co/informes/indice_informes.htm

Gaitán Pavía, Pilar, and Carlos Moreno Ospina. 1992. *Poder local: Realidad de la descentralización en Colombia.* Bogotá: Tercer Mundo Editores.

GAO (General Accounting Office, United States Congress). 2004. "Drug Control: U.S. Nonmilitary Assistance to Colombia Is Beginning to Show Intended Results, but Programs Are Not Readily Sustainable." Available online at http://www.gao.gov/new.items/d04726.pdf

García, Miguel, and Gary Hoskin. 2003. "Political Participation and War in Colombia: An Analysis of the 2002 Elections." Working Paper 38 from the Crisis States Programme Working Paper Series No. 1, Development Research Centre, London. Available online at http://www.crisisstates.com/download/wp/wp38.pdf

García-Peña, Daniel. 2000. "The National Liberation Army (ELN) Creates a Different Peace Process." *NACLA Report on the Americas* 34, 2 (September/October): 34–35.

———. 2007. "Colombia: In Search of a New Model for Conflict Resolution." In Christopher Welna and Gustavo Gallón, eds., *Peace, Democracy, and Human Rights in Colombia.* Notre Dame, Ind.: University of Notre Dame Press.

Ghilodes, Pierre. 1993. "Sistema de partidos y partidos políticos en Colombia." In *Modernidad, democracia y partidos políticos.* Santafé de Bogotá: FESCOL/FIDEC.

Gibson, William Marion. 1948. *The Constitutions of Colombia.* Durham, N.C.: Duke University Press.

Giraldo, Fernando. 2003. *Sistema de partidos políticos en Colombia: Estado del arte, 1991–2002.* Bogotá: Fundación Konrad Adenauer.

Giraldo, Javier. 1996. *Colombia: The Genocidal Democracy.* Monroe, Maine: Common Courage Press.

———. 1999. "Corrupted Justice and the Schizophrenic State in Colombia." *Social Justice* 26, 4 (Winter): 31.

González, Fernán. 1993. "Tradición y modernidad en la política colombiana." In *Modernidad, democracia y partidos políticos.* Santafé de Bogotá: FESCOL/FIDEC.

Grabe, Vera. 2000. *Razones de vida.* Santafé de Bogotá: Planeta Colombiana Editorial.

Grofman, Bernard, and Arend Lijphart, eds. 1986. *Electoral Laws and Their Political Consequences.* New York: Agathon Press.

Guerrero Barón, Javier. 1999. "Colombia, Vietnamización o proceso de Paz. Elementos críticos para la interpretación de la cris colombiana y su impacto en un contexto internacional." *Ensayos Históricos* 2, 11: 171–191.

Gutiérrez Roa, Élber. 2007. "23 de julio de 2001, el día que se firmó el pacto con el diablo." *Semana* (January 19). Available online at http://www.semana.com/ wf_InfoArticulo.aspx?idArt=100504

Gutiérrez Sanín, Francisco, and Richard Stoller. 2001. "The Courtroom and the Bivouac: Reflections on Law and Violence in Colombia." *Latin American Perspectives* 28, 1 (January): 56–72.

Gutkin, Steven. 1994. "DEA Agent Attacks Colombia as 'Narco-Democracy.'" *Washington Post* (September 30), A1.

Hagen, Jason. 2002. "New Colombian President Promises More War." *NACLA Report on the Americas* 36, 1 (July/August): 24–29.

Hanratty, Dennis M., and Sandra W. Meditz, eds. 1990. *Colombia: A Country Study.* Washington, D.C.: Library of Congress. Available online at http://lcweb2.loc.gov /frd/cs/cotoc.html

Hartlyn, Jonathan. 1988. *The Politics of Coalition Rule in Colombia.* London: Cambridge University Press.

Hartlyn, Jonathan, and John Dugas. 1999. "Colombia: The Politics of Violence and Democratic Transformation." In Larry Diamond, Jonathan Hartlyn, Juan J. Linz, and Seymour Martin Lipset, eds., *Democracy in Developing Countries: Latin America*, 2nd ed. Boulder, Colo.: Lynne Rienner Publishers.

Hartzell, Carolina, and Yolanda Marín. 1993. "Las reformas económicas en la constitución de 1991." In John Dugas, ed., *La constitucion de 1991: ¿Un pacto politico viable?* Bogotá: Departmento de Cienceia Política, Universidad de los Andes.

Hernández Becerra, Augusto. 2006. "Regulación jurídica de los partidos políticos en Colombia." In Daniel Zovatto, ed., *Regulación jurídica de los partidos políticos en América Latina.* Stockholm, Sweden: International IDEA. Available online at http://idea.int/publications/lrpp/index.cfm

Hoskin, Gary. 1980. "The Impact of the National Front on Congressional Behavior: The Attempted Restoration of El País Político." In Albert R. Berry, Ronald G. Hellman, and Mauricio Solaún, eds., *Politics of Compromise: Coalition Government in Colombia.* New Brunswick, N.J.: Transaction Books.

———. 1990. "Los partidos tradicionales: ¿Hasta donde son responsables de la crisis politica?" In Francisco Leal Buitrago and Leon Zamosc, eds., *Al dilo del caos: Crisis política en la Colombia de los años 80.* Bogotá: Tercer Mundo Editores.

———. 1993. "Sobre la ponencia 'Procesos y factores determinantes de la rucurrencia de la crisis gubernativa en Colombia.'" In Gabriel Murrilo C., ed., *Hacia la consolidación democrática andina.* Santafé de Bogotá: Tercer Mundo Editores.

———. 1994. "The Consequences of Constitutional Reform on the Colombian Party System." Paper presented at the 1994 meeting of the Latin American Studies Association, Atlanta, March 10–12.

———. 1995. "The State and Political Parties in Colombia." Paper presented at the 1995 meeting of the Latin American Studies Association, Washington, D.C., September 28–30.

Hoskin, Gary, Rodolfo Masías, and Miguel García, eds. 2003. *Colombia 2002. Elecciones, comportamiento electoral y democracia.* Santafé de Bogotá: Uniandes-Fundación Konrad Adenauer, Registraduría Nacional, Departamento Nacional de Planeación.

Hoskin, Gary, and Patricia Pinzón de Lewin. 1989. "Los partidos políticos colombianos y la crisis coyuntural." In Patricia Vásquez de Urrutia, comp., *Democracia en blanco y negro: Colombia en los años ochenta.* Bogotá: Fondo Editorial CEREC.

Hoskin, Gary, and Gerald Swanson. 1973. "Inter-Party Competition in Colombia: A Return to *La Violencia?" American Journal of Political Science* 17, 2 (May): 316–350.

Hoyos, Farid Abud, and Diego Fernando León Bonilla. 2005. "Un sistema implicado a fenómenos endógenos de crisis de racionalidad." In David Roll, *Partidos políticos y congreso: Elites políticas y mayorías parlamentarias en Colombia en la década de los neventa.* Santafé de Bogotá: Fundación Konrad Adenauer.

Hudson, Rex A. 1988. "Government and Politics." In Dennis M. Hanratty and Sandra W. Meditz., eds., *Colombia: A Country Study.* Washington, D.C.: Federal Research Division, Library of Congress. Available online at http://lcweb2.loc.gov/frd/cs/cotoc.html

———. 1995. "Colombia's Palace of Justice Tragedy Revisisted: A Critique of the Conspiracy Theory." *Terrorism and Political Violence* 7, 2 (Summer): 93–142.

Human Rights Watch. 1996. *Colombia's Killer Networks: The Military-Paramilitary Partnership and the United States.* New York: Human Rights Watch. Available online at http://www.hrw.org/reports/1996/killertoc.htm

———. 2000. *Colombia: The Ties That Bind; Colombia and Military-Paramilitary Links.* New York: Human Rights Watch. Available online at http://www.hrw.org/reports/2000/colombia

———. 2001. *The "Sixth Division": Military-Paramilitary Ties and U.S. Policy in Colombia.* New York: Human Rights Watch. Available online at http://www.hrw.org/reports/2001/colombia/6theng.pdf

———. 2002. "Colombia: FARC Kidnappings Documented." Available online at http://hrw.org/english/docs/2002/04/15/colomb3848.htm

———. 2005. *Smoke and Mirrors: Colombia's Demobilization of Paramilitary Groups.* New York: Human Rights Watch. Available online at http://hrw.org/reports/2005/colombia0805/colombia0805.pdf

Huntington, Samuel P. 1991. *The Third Wave: Democratization in the Late Twentieth Century.* Norman: University of Oklahoma Press.

Instituto Nacional de Medicina Legal y Ciencias Forenses. 2004. *Forenses 2004: Datos para la vida.* Bogotá: Centro de Referencia Nacional sobre Violencia.

Inter-American Commission on Human Rights. 1999. *Third Report on the Human Rights Situation in Colombia.* Organization of American States. Available online at http://*www.cidh.org/countryrep/Colom99en/table%20of%20contents.htm*

Jordan, David C. 1999. *Drug Politics: Dirty Money and Democracies.* Norman: University of Oklahoma Press.

Kalmanovitz, Salomon. 1990. "Los gremios industriales ante la crisis." In Francisco Leal Buitrago and Leon Zamosc, eds., *Al filo del caos: Crisis política en la Colombia de los años 80.* Bogotá: Tercer Mundo Editores.

Kirk, Robin. 2004. *More Terrible Than Death: Violence, Drugs, and America's War in Colombia.* New York: Public Affairs.

Kline, Harvey F. 1980. "The National Front: Historical Perspective and Overview." In Albert R. Berry, Ronald G. Hellman, and Mauricio Solaún, eds., *Politics of Compromise: Coalition Government in Colombia.* New Brunswick, N.J.: Transaction Books.

———. 1983. *Colombia: Portrait of Unity and Diversity.* Boulder, Colo.: Westview Press.

———. 1995. *Colombia: Democracy under Assault.* Boulder, Colo.: Westview Press.

———. 1999. *State Building and Conflict Resolution in Colombia, 1986–1994.* Tuscaloosa: University of Alabama Press.

Laakso, Markuu, and Rein Taagepera. 1979. "Effective Number of Parties: A Measure with Application to Western Europe." *Comparative Political Studies* 12:3–27.

Labrousse, Alain. 2005. "The FARC and the Taliban's Connection to Drugs." *Journal of Drug Issues* 35, 1 (Winter): 169–184.

Latorre, Mario. 1986. *Hechos y critica política.* Bogotá: Universidad Nacional de Colombia.

Leal Buitrago, Francisco. 1973. *Estudio del comportamiento legislativo en Colombia, tomo I: Análisis histórico del desarrollo político nacional, 1930–1970.* Bogotá: Tercer Mundo.

———. 1987. "La crisis política en Colombia: Alternativas y frustraciones." *Análisis Político* 1 (May–August).

———. 1989a. *Estado y política en Colombia.* 2nd ed. Bogotá: Siglo Veintiuno Editores.

———. 1989b. "Structural Crisis and the Current Situation in Colombia." *Canadian Journal of Latin American & Caribbean Studies* 14, 28: 31–9.

———. 1990. "Estructura y coyuntura de la crisis política." In Francisco Leal Buitrago and Leon Zamosc, *Al filo del caos: Crisis política en la Colombia de los años 80.* Bogotá: Tercer Mundo Editores.

———. 1996. *Tras las huellas de la crisis política.* Bogotá: Tercer Mundo Editores.

Leal Buitrago, Francisco, and Andrés Dávila. 1991. *Clientelismo: El sistema político colombiano y su expresión regional.* 2nd ed. Bogotá: Tercer Mundo Editores.

Leal Buitrago, Francisco, and Leon Zamosc. 1990. *Al filo del caos: Crisis política en la Colombia de los años 80.* Bogotá: Tercer Mundo Editores.

Lee, Rensselaer W. III, and Francisco E. Thoumi. 1999. "Colombia: The Political-Criminal Nexus in Colombia." *Trends in Organized Crime* (Winter): 59–84.

LeGrand, Catherine. 2003. "The Colombian Crisis in Historical Perspective." *Canadian Journal of Latin American and Cribbean Studies* 28, 55–56: 165–209.

Lijphart, Arend. 1977. *Democracy in Plural Societies.* New Haven, Conn.: Yale University Press.

———. 1990. "The Political Consequences of Electoral Laws, 1945–1985." *American Political Science Review* 84:481–496.

———. 1994. *Electoral Systems and Party Systems: A Study of Twenty-seven Democracies, 1945–1990.* New York: Oxford University Press.

Lijphart, Arend, and Bernard Grofman. 1984. *Choosing an Electoral System: Issues and Alternatives.* New York: Praeger.

Lijphart, Arend, Rafael Lopez Pintor, and Yasunori Sone. 1986. "The Limited Vote and the Single Nontransferable Vote: Lessons from the Japanese and Spanish Examples." In Bernard Grofman and Arend Lijphart, eds., *Electoral Laws and Their Political Consequences.* New York: Agathon Press.

Livingstone, Grace. 2004. *Inside Colombia: Drugs, Democracy and War.* New Brunswick, N.J.: Rutgers University Press.

Losada, Rodrigo. 1980. "Electoral Participation." In Albert R. Berry, Ronald G. Hellman, and Mauricio Solaún, eds., *Politics of Compromise: Coalition Government in Colombia.* New Brunswick, N.J.: Transaction Books.

Mainwaring, Scott. 1999. "The Surprising Resilience of Elected Governments." *Journal of Democracy* 10, 3 (July): 101–114.

Manwaring, Max G. 2002. "Nonstate Actors in Colombia: Threat and Response." Strategic Studies Institute Working Paper.

Martz, John D. 1992. "Contemporary Colombian Politics: The Struggle over Democratization." In Alvin Cohen and Frank R. Gunter, eds., *The Colombian Economy: Issues of Trade and Development.* Boulder, Colo.: Westvew Press.

Mazzuca, Sebastián, and James A. Robinson. 2006. *Political Conflict and Power-Sharing in the Origins of Modern Colombia.* Cambridge, Mass.: National Bureau of Economic Research Working Paper Series.

McDonald, Ronald H., and J. Mark Ruhl. 1989. *Party Politics and Elections in Latin America.* Boulder, Colo.: Westview Press.

McLean, Phillip. 2002. "Colombia: Failed, Failing or Just Weak?" *Washington Quarterly* 25, 3: 123–134.

Medellín Torres, Pedro. 1999. "Factores estructurales de la crisis colombiana." In Alfonso Monsalve Solérzano and Eduardo Domínguez Gómez, eds., *Colombia: Democracia y paz, tomo II*. Medellín: Universidad Pontificia Bolivariana.

Medina, Luis Fernando. 2004. "A Critique of 'Resource-Based' Theories of Colombia's Civil War." Paper presented at the 2004 conference of the Latin American Studies Association, Las Vegas, Nev., October 7–9.

Morales, Alberto. 1978. "Colombia: Elecciones y crisis política." *Nueva sociedad* 34 (January–February): 56–73. Available online at http://*www.nuso.org/upload/articulos/393_1.pdf*

Moreno, Erika, and Maria Escobar-Lemon. 2008. "Mejor Solo Que Mal Acompañado: Political Entrepreneurs in Colombia." In Peter M. Siavelis and Scott Morgenstern, eds., *Pathways to Power: Political Recruitment and Candidate Selection in Latin America*. University Park, Pa.: Penn State University Press.

Muñoz Yi, Patricia. 2003. "Renovación en el congreso colombiano elegido en 2002: Los partidos políticos tradicionales entre el estancamiento y el retroceso." *Alceu: Revista de comunicação, cultura epPolítica* 3, 6 (January/June): 215–228.

Murillo Castaño, Gabriel. 1999. "Representación, ciudadanía y nueva Constitución en Colombia." *Nueva Sociedad* 160:47–55.

Murillo Castaño, Gabriel, and Rubén Sánchez David. 1993. "Procesos y factores determinantes de la recurrencia de la crisis gubernativa en Colombia." In Gabriel Murrilo C., ed., *Hacia la consolidación democrática andina*. Santafé de Bogotá: Tercer Mundo Editores.

Murillo, Gabriel, and Javier Torres. 1991. "Elección y partidos politicos en la transición de los países andinos: Retos par alas superación de la crisis en la década de los noventa." In Rubén Sánchez David, ed., *Los nuevos retos electorales: Colombia 1990, antesala del cambio*. Bogotá: CEREC.

Murillo, Gabriel Castaño, Elisabeth Ungar Bleier, María Victoria Fajarado, and Paula Peña. 1993. "Hacia la construcción de una agenda de gobernabilidad: La reforma política y la superación de los obstáculos al fortalecimiento democrático." In Elisabeth Ungar, ed., *Gobernabilidad en Colombia: Retos y desafíos*. Santafé de Bogotá: Tercer Mundo.

Nielson, Daniel L., and Matthew Søberg Shugart. 1999. "Constitutional Change in Colombia: Policy Adjustment through Institutional Reform." *Comparative Political Studies* 32, 3 (May): 313–341.

O'Donnell, Guillermo. 1994. "Delegative Democracy?" *Journal of Democracy* 15, 1 (January): 55–69.

Orjuela E., Luis Javier. 1993. "Decentralización y gobernabilidad en Colombia." In Elisabeth Ungar, ed., *Gobernabilidad en Colombia: Retos y desafios*. Santafé de Bogotá: Tercer Mundo.

Partido Conservador Colombiano. 2006. *Historia.* Available online at http://*partido conservador.org/index.php?section=5*

Partido Liberal Colombiano. 2006. *Nuestra historia.* Available online at http://*www.partidoliberal.org.co/root/index.php?option=com_content&task=view&id =146&Itemid=6*

Payne, James L. 1968. *Patterns of Conflict in Colombia.* New Haven, Conn.: Yale University Press.

Payne, Mark, and Mercedes Mateo Díaz. 2006. "Tendencias de participación electoral." In J. Mark Payne, Daniel Zovatto G., and Mercedes Mateo Díaz, eds., *La política importa: Democracia y desarrollo en América Latina.* Washington, D.C.: Inter-American Development Bank. Available online at http://*www .idea.int/publications/dem_dev/upload/La_pol%EDtica_importa_2006_ content-2.pdf*

Pécaut, Daniel. 1989. *Crónica de dos décadas de política colombiana, 1968–1988.* 2nd ed. Bogotá: Siglo Veintiuno editores.

Peeler, John A. 1976. "Colombian Parties and Political Development: A Reassessment." *Journal of Interamerican Studies and World Affairs* 18, 2 (May): 203–223.

Pinzón de Lewin, Patricia, ed. 1987. *Los partidos politicos colombianos: Estatutos, reglamentos, programas.* Bogotá: FESCOL.

———. 1991. "Las elecciones de 1990." In Rubén Sánchez David, ed., *Los nuevos retos electorales: Colombia 1990, antesala del cambio.* Bogotá: CEREC.

———. 1994. *El ejercito y las elecciones: Ensayo historico.* Bogotá: Cerec.

Pinzón de Lewin, Patricia, and Dora Rothlisberger. 1991. "La participación electoral en 1990: Un nuevo tipo de votante." In Rubén Sánchez David, ed., *Los nuevos retos electorales: Colombia 1990, antesala del cambio.* Bogotá: CEREC.

Pizarro, Eduaro. 1992. "Revolutionary Guerrilla Groups." In Charles Bergquist, Ricardo Peñaranda, and Gonzalo Sánchez, eds., *Violence in Colombia: The Contemporary Crisis in Historical Perspective.* Wilmington, Del.: Scholarly Resources.

Pizarro Leongómez, Eduardo. 1996. "La crisis de los partidos y los partidos en la crisis." In Francisco Leal Buitrago, ed., *Tras las huellas de la crisis política.* Santafé de Bogotá: Tercer Mundo Editores.

Polo Democrático Aleternativo (PDA). 2007. *Polo Democrático Alternativo estatutos e ideario de unidad.* Available online at http://*www.polodemocratico.net/ IMG/doc/Cartilla2.pdf*

Posada-Carbó, Eduardo. 2004. "Colombia's Resilient Democracy." *Current History* 103, 670 (February): 68–73.

Presidencia de la República. 1969. *História de la reforma constitucional de 1968.* Bogotá: Imprenta Nacional.

Programa Democracia. 1990. *Una constituyente para la Colombia del futuro.* 2nd ed. Bogotá: FESCOL.

Rae, Douglas. 1971. *The Political Consequences of Electoral Laws*. Amplified ed. New Haven, Conn.: Yale University Press.

Ramírez Lemus, María Clemencia, Kimberly Stanton, and John Walsh. 2005. "Colombia: A Vicious Cycle of Drugs and War." In Coletta Youngers and Eileen Rosin, eds., *Drugs and Democracy in Latin America: The Impact of U.S. Policy*. Boulder, Colo.: Lynne Rienner Publishers.

Rangel Suárez, Alfredo. 1989. "Colombia: Una democracia sin partidos." *Revista foro* 10 (September): 72–78.

Registraduría Nacional del Estado Civil. 1958. *3,000,000 de Colombianos cedulados: Informe del Registraduría del Estado Civil*. Bogotá: La República de Colombia.

———. 2006. *Boletin de Prensa No. 010*. Available online at http://www.registraduria .gov.co/elec2006/congreso/congreso_2006.doc

———. Various years. *Estadisticas electorales*. Santafé de Bogotá: La República de Colombia.

Remmer, Karen. 1986. "Exclusionary Democracy." *Studies in Comparative International Development* 20 (Winter): 64–85.

Restrepo, Luís Alberto. 1992. "The Crisis of the Current Political Regime and Its Possible Outcomes." In Charles Bergquist, Ricardo Peñaranda, and Gonzalo Sánchez, eds., *Violence in Colombia: The Contemporary Crisis in Historical Perspective*. Wilmington, Del.: Scholarly Resources.

Richani, Nazih. 2000. "The Paramilitary Connection." *NACLA Report on the Americas* 34, 2 (September/October): 38–41.

———. 2002. *Systems of Violence: The Political Economy of War and Peace in Colombia*. Albany: State University of New York Press.

Riding, Alan. 1984. "Rebel Accord: Personal Coup by Colombian." *New York Times* (August 26). Available online at http://select.nytimes.com/search/restricted/article ?res=F30D17F7385C0C758EDDA10894DC484D81

Riker, William H. 1986. "Duverger's Law Revisted." In Bernard Grofman and Arend Lijphart, eds., *Electoral Laws and Their Consequences*. New York: Agathon Press.

Robles, Frances. 2003. "Colombian State of Emergency Invalidated." *San Diego Union-Tribune* (May 2), A14.

Rodríguez Raga, Juan Carlos, and Miguel García Sánchez. 2001. "Crisis política en un año electoral." *Síntesis 2001* (pp. 53–62). Santafé de Bogotá: IEPRI.

Rojas, Cristina, and Judy Meltzer, eds. 2005. *Elusive Peace: International, National and Local Dimensions of Conflict in Colombia*. New York: Palgrave Macmillan.

Roldán, Mary. 2002. *Blood and Fire: La Violencia in Antioquia, Colombia, 1946–1953*. Durham, N.C.: Duke University Press.

Roll, David. 2002. *Rojo azul y difuso pálido: Los partidos tradicionales en Colombia; Entre el debilitamiento y la persistencia*. Bogotá: Universidad Nacional de Colombia Facultad de Derecho, Ciencias Políticas y Sociales.

Ruhl, J. Mark. 1978. "Party System in Crisis? An Analysis of Colombia's 1978 Elections." *Inter-American Economic Affairs* 32:29–45.

————. 1981. "Civil-Military Relations in Colombia: A Societal Explanation." *Journal of Interamerican Studies and World Affairs* 23, 2 (May): 123–146.

Safford, Frank, and Marco Palacios. 2002. *Colombia: Fragmented Land, Divided Society*. New York: Oxford University Press.

Sánchez, Gonzalo, and Donny Meertens. 2001. *Bandits, Peasants and Politics: The Case of "La Violencia" in Colombia*. Alan Hynds, trans. Austin: University of Texas Press.

Sánchez David, Rubén. 1993. "Democrácia y política en Colombia." In *Modernidad, democracia y partidos políticos*. Santafé de Bogotá. FESCOL/FIDEC.

Sánchez Torres. 1993. "Participación ciudadana y democratización del estado." In *Modernidad, democracia y partidos políticos*. Santafé de Bogotá: FESCOL/FIDEC.

Santana, Julio. N.d. "Reseña sobre la Union Patriótica." Document from the Patriot Union's Office of the Press.

Scarpetta, Olga. 1991. "Political Traditions and the Limits of Democracy in Colombia." *International Journal of Politics, Culture, and Society* 5, 2: 143–166.

Schemo, Diana Jean. 1997. "Colombia's Death-Strewn Democracy." *New York Times* (July 24). Available online at http://select.nytimes.com/search/restricted/article?res=FA0E11FF355F0C778EDDAE0894DF494D81

Semana. 1995. "Aquel 19." *Semana* (January 31): 22–28.

————. 2007. "Un gobernador en la mira." *Semana* (February 15). Available online at http://semana.com/wf_InfoArticulo.aspx?IdArt=101020

————. 2008. "Tirofijo está muerto." *Semana* (May 25). Available online at http://www.semana.com/wf_InfoArticulo.aspx?idArt=112103

Seres, Philippe. 2000. "The FARC and Democracy in Colombia in the 1990s." *Democratization* 7, 4 (Winter): 191–218.

Sharpless, Richard E. 1978. *Gaitán of Colombia*. Pittsburgh: University of Pittsburgh Press.

Shugart, Matthew Søberg. 2000. "Towards a Representation Revolution: Constitutional Reform, Electoral Systems, and the Challenges to Democracy in Latin America." Prepared for delivery at the "Challenges to Democracy in the Americas" conference, Carter Center, Atlanta (October 16–18). Available online at http://www.cartercenter.org/documents/nondatabase/Shugart.pdf

Shugart, Matthew Søberg, Erika Moreno, and Luis E. Fajardo. 2007. "Deepening Democracy by Renovating Political Practices: The Struggle for Electoral Reform in Colombia." In Christopher Welna and Gustavo Gallón, eds., *Peace, Democracy, and Human Rights in Colombia*. Notre Dame, Ind.: University of Notre Dame Press.

Solaún, Mauricio. 1980. "Colombian Politics: Historical Characteristics and Problems." In Albert R. Berry, Ronald G. Hellman, and Mauricio Solaún, eds., *Politics of Compromise: Coalition Government in Colombia*. New Brunswick, N.J.: Transaction Books.

Strøm, Kare. 1990. "A Behavioral Theory of Competitive Political Parties." *American Journal of Political Science* 34, 2: 565–98.

Taagepera, Rein, and Matthew Søberg Shugart. 1989. *Seats and Votes: The Effects and Determinants of Electoral Systems*. New Haven, Conn.: Yale University Press.

Taylor, Steven L. 1995. "Third Party Activity in Colombia." Paper presented at the 1995 meeting of the Latin American Studies Association, Washington, D.C., September 28–30.

———. 1996. "Rules, Incentives, and Political Parties: Electoral Reform in Post-1991 Colombia." Ph.D. dissertation, University of Texas at Austin.

———. 1997. "Electoral Reform and Political Effects in the Post-1991 Colombian Senate." Paper presented at the 1997 meeting of the Latin American Studies Association, Guadalajara, Mexico, April 17–19.

———. 2002. "Personal List-PR and a Single National District: The Political Effects of the 1991 Constitutional Reform on Senate Elections in Colombia." Paper presented at the 2002 meeting of the Public Choice Society, San Diego, Calif., March 22–24.

———. 2003. "Electoral Reform and Party Adaptation: The Case of the Colombian Senate." Paper presented at the 24th conference of the Latin American Studies Association, Dallas, March 27–29.

———. 2005a. "Colombia: Democracy under Duress." In William Crotty, ed., *Democratic Development and Political Terrorism: The Global Perspective*. Boston: Northeastern University Press.

———. 2005b. "When Wars Collide: The War on Drugs and the Global War on Terror." *Strategic Insights* 4, 6 (June). Available online at http://www.ccc.nps.navy.mil/si/2005/Jun/taylorJun05.pdf

Taylor, Steven L., Felipe Botero, and Brian F. Crisp. 2008. "Precandidates, Candidates, and Presidents: Paths to the Colombian Presidency." In Peter M. Siavelis and Scott Morgenstern, eds., *Pathways to Power: Political Recruitment and Candidate Selection in Latin America*. University Park, Pa.: Penn State University Press.

Thoumi, Francisco E. 2002. "Illegal Drugs in Colombia: From Illegal Economic Boom to Social Crisis." *Annals of the American Academy* 582 (July): 102–116.

Tickner, Arlene B. 1998. "Colombia: Chronicle of a Crisis Foretold." *Current History* 97, 616 (February): 61–65.

———. 2003. "Colombia and the United States: From Counternarcotics to Counterterrorism." *Current History* 102, 661: 77–85.

Transparencia. 2005. "América Latina: Voto obligatorio o voto voluntario." *Datos electorale* (November 16). Available online at http://www.transparencia.org.pe/documentos/datos_electorales_no.01.pdf

Ungar Bleier, Elizabeth. 2003. "Qué pasó en el Senado de la República?" In Gary Hoskin et al., *Colombia 2002: Elecciones, comportamiento electoral y democracia.* Bogotá: Ediciones Uniandes.

United Nations Office on Drugs and Crime (UNODC). 2004. *The Seventh United Nations Survey on Crime Trends and the Operations of Criminal Justice Systems (1998–2000).* Available online at http://www.unodc.org/unodc/en/crime_cicp_survey_seventh.html

———. 2005. *World Drug Report 2005, Volume I: Analysis.* New York: United Nations Publications. Available online at http://www.unodc.org/unodc/en/world_drug_report_2005.html

———. 2007a. *Coca Cultivation in the Andean Region: A Survey of Bolivia, Colombia, Ecuador and Peru.* New York: United Nations Publications. Available online at http://www.unodc.org/pdf/andean/Andean_report_2007.pdf

———. 2007b. *World Drug Report 2007, Volume I: Analysis.* New York: United Nations Publications. Available online at http://www.unodc.org/unodc/en/world_drug_report.html

Uribe González, Carlos. 1986. *Constitución política de Colombia.* Bogotá: Ediciones Tercer Mundo.

Valencia, León. 2003. *Miserias de la guerra, esperanzas de la paz.* Santafé de Bogotá: Intermedio.

Valencia Villa, Hernando. 1978. "Una Atenas sin Sócrates: Sufragio analfabetismo en Colombia." *Nuevo sociedad* 38 (September–October): 111–120. Available online at http://www.nuso.org/upload/articulos/473_1.pdf

———. 1987. *Cartas de batalla: Una crítica del constitucionalismo colombiano.* Bogotá: Cerec.

Van Dongen, Rachel. 2003. "For Colombia's Mayors, It's a Year of Living Dangerously." *Christian Science Monitor* (July 1). Available online at http://www.csmonitor.com/2003/0701/p07s02-woam.html

Watson, Cynthia. 2005. "Civil Military Relations in Colombia: Solving or Delaying Problems?" *Journal of Political and Military Sociology* 33, 1: 97–106.

Weeks, Gregory. 2006. "Fighting Terrorism While Promoting Democracy: Competing Priorities in U.S. Defense Policy Towards Latin America" *Journal of Third World Studies* 23, 2 (Fall): 59–77.

Welna, Christopher, and Gustavo Gallón, eds. 2007. *Peace, Democracy, and Human Rights in Colombia.* Notre Dame, Ind.: University of Notre Dame Press.

Wilde, Alexander W. 1978. "Conversations among Gentlemen: Oligarchical Democracy in Colombia." In Juan J. Linz and Alfred Stepan, eds., *The Breakdown of Democratic Regimes: Latin America.* Baltimore: Johns Hopkins University Press.

———. 1982. *Conversaciones de caballeros: La quiebra de la democracia en Colombia.* Bogotá: Ediciones Tercer Mundo.

Wilson, James. 2002. "Colombia Court Deals Blow to Uribe's Security Crackdown." *Financial Times* USA ed. (November 28): 4.

INDEX

abstentionism, 63, 66–67, 74, 80
AD/M19. *See* Democratic Alliance/Movement of the 19th of April
Afghanistan, 5, 6, 145
alternates. See *suplentes*
Alternative Democratic Pole (PDA), 109, 126, 135, 158, 159, 161, 167, 172; origins of, 169
ANAPO. *See* National Popular Alliance
Army of Popular Liberation, 138, 140
Asamblea Nacional Constituyente. See National Constituent Assembly
AUC. *See* United Self-Defense Forces of Colombia
auxilios, 65, 76
Avispa strategy. See *Operación Avispa*

balloon effect, 145
ballots: and clientelism, 66, 100, 106; *papeletas,* 66, 179–183; *Séptima Papeleta,* 54, 183, 184 fig. A.4; split ticket versus straight-ticket voting, 100–101; *tarjetones,* 66, 106, 179, 183–188
Barco Vargas, Virgilio, 53, 54, 86
Betancourt, Ingrid, 122, 156, 175, 176
Betancur Cuartas, Belasario, 22, 140, 153
bipartidismo, 57, 69, 81, 92; defined, 60
Bogotazo, 139
Botero Zea, Fernando, 147
Bush, George W., 141

Cambio Radical. See Radical Change
campaign finance, 53
Cano Isaza, Guillermo, 147
Castaño, Carlos, 150–151
Castaño, Fidel, 150–151
civil-military relations, 22, 166
civil war, 1, 69; applicability of term to Colombia, 137–138; in 19th century, 40 table 3.1
clientelism, 63, 65–66, 67, 75–76, 80, 100, 163, 172
coca cultivation, 145, 146 fig. 7.1, 210n15
cocaine, 1, 5, 145

Cold War, 138–140, 142, 144
Communist Party, 48, 78, 141
Conservative Party: factions within, 30, 48, 199n13; fragmentation of, 97, 102–103, 120, 124, 133; and the National Constituent Assembly, 55–57, 103, 117, 124; and the National Front, 44, 46, 49; origins, 61–62; post-1991 Senate elections, 124–125; support for third term for Uribe, 176; usage of Social Conservative Party label, 55, 103, 117, 124, 199n25, 204n21. *See also* political parties
Constitution: article 120 of 1886, 52, 86; list of nineteenth-century versions, 41; of 1886, 23, 44, 53, 54; of 1886 v. 1991, 57 table 3.7, 104; of 1991, 16, 23, 24, 53, 57, 103, 166; and electoral rules, 114, 117. *See also* National Constituent Assembly
constitutional reform: pre-1953, 45 table 3.3; in 1957, 54; in 1968, 52, 65; in 1986, 53; in 2003, 90, 134, 167; process leading to 1991, 54–55
consociational democracy, 62–63

D'Hondt. *See* electoral rules
Death to Kidnappers (MAS), 150–151, 152, 154
demilitarized zone, 22
democracy: with adjectives, 15–16; Colombia as compared to the region, 3, 9, 14; defined, 15–18; Diamond's criteria for liberal, 20–21, 35 table 2.8; stages of Colombian, 19; types of, 18
Democratic Alliance/Movement of the 19th of April: list strategies, 125–126; and the National Constituent Assembly, 55–57, 103; in Senate elections, 120, 123, 125–126
Democratic Colombia, 107, 205–206n32
displacement, 2, 32 table 2.7
district magnitude, 116, 118, 121, 207n13
drug cartels: Cali, 147, 156, 157; *cartelitos,* 147; Colombian, in general, 144; Mexican, 5; Medellín, 146, 147, 150, 156, 157
drug traffickers, 31, 139, 143–148
Duverger's hypothesis, 206n2